DISABILITY DISCRIMINATION CLAIMS

AN ADVISER'S HANDBOOK

DISABILITY DISCRIMINATION CLAIMS

AN ADVISER'S HANDBOOK

Catherine Casserley LLB, LLM, Barrister at Law
Bela Gor BA(Hons)(Oxon), Solicitor

JORDANS
2001

Published by
Jordan Publishing Limited
21 St Thomas Street
Bristol BS1 6JS

British Library Cataloguing-in-Publication Data
A catalogue record for this book is available from the British Library.

ISBN 0 85308 642 7

Typeset by Mendip Communications Ltd, Frome, Somerset
Printed by MPG Books Ltd, Bodmin, Cornwall

PREFACE

In the 4½ years since the employment provisions of the Disability Discrimination Act 1995 (DDA 1995) came into effect, it has become increasingly apparent that this piece of legislation and its operation in the tribunals is very different from the race and sex discrimination legislation. This is something which we have learnt in taking some of the first cases from employment tribunals through to, in the case of *Abbey Life Assurance Co Ltd v Tansell* [2000] IRLR 387, the Court of Appeal. In particular, there is a need to bear in mind our own responsibility as advisers, as well as the courts' and tribunals' responsibilities, under Part III of the DDA 1995, to ensure that disabled clients and applicants can effectively use the legal system.

One of the major flaws of the DDA 1995 was that there was no statutory enforcement agency such as the Commission for Racial Equality and the Equal Opportunities Commission. There were relatively few advisers taking DDA cases and little opportunity to exchange information with those who were. This resulted in the establishment of the DDA Advisers Group in 1997 which was initially a small group of advisers who met on a regular basis to exchange information about cases they were taking and to provide support to each other. This is now a thriving forum with members who take forward the leading DDA cases. The contribution of members of the DDA Advisers Group has been invaluable in writing this book. Indeed, it was because we learnt so much from our own experience of taking cases and the experience of other members of the group that we decided to write what we hope will be both useful and practical guidance for those taking DDA cases.

In order to illustrate the practical issues which arise in running disability discrimination cases, we have included case studies which, we hope, will help the readers' understanding. Needless to say, those case studies are entirely fictional and any resemblance in them to actual events or real persons is entirely coincidental.

There is of course now a statutory enforcement body, the Disability Rights Commission, which came into existence during the writing of this book. The Commission should enable a greater number of disabled people to utilise the legislation and ensure that the DDA 1995 is as effective as possible in tackling the widespread discrimination experienced by disabled people.

We would like in particular to thank: Samantha Fothergill; Caroline Gooding; Elizabeth West; Employers' Forum on Disability; Royal National Institute for the Blind; Disability Law Service; Vishnu and Kanta Gor; Howard Phillis; Pip Jones; the late Nancy Casserley; and all the members of the DDA Advisers Group, as well as our clients. Finally, we would also like to thank Martin West and Gary Hill at Jordans for their faith and patience.

DEDICATION

In memory of Nancy Casserley

CONTENTS

TABLE OF CASES

References are to paragraph numbers, case studies (CS) and Appendices.

TABLE OF STATUTES

References are to paragraph numbers, case studies (CS) and Appendices.

TABLE OF STATUTORY INSTRUMENTS, CODES AND GUIDANCE

References are to paragraph numbers, case studies (CS) and Appendices.

TABLE OF EUROPEAN LEGISLATION

References are to paragraph numbers.

TABLE OF ABBREVIATIONS

ACAS	Advisory Conciliation and Arbitration Service
the Code of Practice	Code of Practice for the elimination of discrimination in the field of employment against disabled persons or persons who have had a disability
DDA 1995	Disability Discrimination Act 1995
DD(E)R 1996	Disability Discrimination (Employment) Regulations 1996, SI 1996/1456
DEA	disability employment adviser
DfEE	Department for Education and Employment
DP(E)A 1944	Disabled Persons (Employment) Act 1944
DSS	Department for Social Security
EAT	Employment Appeal Tribunal
ERA 1996	Employment Rights Act 1996
ETA 1996	Employment Tribunals Act 1996
the Guidance	Guidance on matters to be taken into account in determining questions relating to the definition of disability
HRA 1998	Human Rights Act 1998
RNIB	Royal National Institute for the Blind
RNID	Royal National Institute for the Deaf
RRA 1976	Race Relations Act 1976
SDA 1975	Sex Discrimination Act 1975
WHO	World Health Organisation

The regulations referred to in this book are applicable to England and Wales only. However, there are broadly equivalent provisions in both Scotland and Northern Ireland.

Chapter 1

INTRODUCTION

1.1 The Disability Discrimination Act 1995 (DDA 1995) marked a major milestone in the fight for equal rights for disabled people. While it was not the legislation that many wanted to see, as it was felt that it has a number of fundamental flaws (such as the exclusion of small employers),[1] it nevertheless provides rights and remedies for disabled people where previously there were none.

1.2 The Labour Government recognised the weaknesses of the Act and established a Task Force to carry out a review of civil rights legislation for disabled people. The Task Force consisted of 24 members drawn from the disability field, business, trades union and local authorities. It was chaired by Margaret Hodge, Minister for Disabled People, for the majority of its life (having been chaired initially by the previous Minister for Disabled People, Alan Howarth). In December 1999 the Task Force produced a report[2] which, among other things, recommended a number of changes to the DDA 1995. In March 2001 the Government produced its response[3] in which it committed itself to a number of changes to the Act. There is no data as yet for most of these changes.

COMPARISON WITH OTHER ANTI-DISCRIMINATION LAW

1.3 While the Sex Discrimination Act 1975 (SDA 1975) and the Race Relations Act 1976 (RRA 1976) can provide useful case-law for interpretation of issues under the DDA 1995, there are fundamental differences between these legislative regimes: there is no concept of 'indirect discrimination' in the DDA 1995, as there is in the SDA 1975 and RRA 1976; the concept of 'reasonable adjustments' (with the

---

1   See the discussion on small employer exemption at **1.23**.
2   *From Exclusion to Inclusion – the report of the Disability Rights Task Force on Civil Rights for Disabled People* (DfEE, London, 1999).
3   *Towards Inclusion – Civil Rights for Disabled People* (DfEE).

employer having to do something positive to ensure employment of disabled people) is completely new; and the justification of direct discrimination is something unique to the DDA 1995.

1.4   The Court of Appeal, in the case of *Clark v Novacold*,[1] emphasised the difference between this legislation and that relating to race and sex discrimination:

> 'Contrary to what might be reasonably assumed, the exercise of interpretation is not facilitated by familiarity with the pre-existing legislation prohibiting discrimination in the field of employment (and elsewhere) on the grounds of sex ... and race ...'

Indeed, it may be positively misleading to approach the DDA 1995 with assumptions and concepts familiar from experience of the workings of the SDA 1975 and the RRA 1976. Thus advisers must beware of making assumptions about certain DDA 1995 issues based on experience in race and sex cases – they are not always analogous.

RELEVANT PROVISIONS OF THE DDA 1995

1.5   The rest of this chapter constitutes an outline of the relevant provisions of the DDA 1995.

When dealing with a case which falls within the remit of the Act, it will be essential to have a copy of the Act and Regulations as well as the Codes of Guidance and Practice to hand.

The legislation and Official Guidance

1.6   The materials which advisers will need are as follows:

–   DDA 1995, as amended;
–   Disability Discrimination (Meaning of Disability) Regulations 1996, SI 1996/1455;
–   Disability Discrimination (Employment) Regulations 1996 (DD (E)R 1996), SI 1996/1456;
–   Guidance on matters to be taken into account in determining questions relating to the definition of disability (the Guidance);
–   Code of Practice for the elimination of discrimination in the field of employment against disabled persons or persons who have had a disability (the Code of Practice).

As well as the usual sources for case-law (*Industrial Relations Law Reports*, *Equal Opportunities Review*, etc), advisers can obtain

---

1   [1999] IRLR 318.

Employment Appeal Tribunal decisions from the EAT website at www.employmentappeals.gov.uk

Definition of 'disability'

1.7 The definition of 'disability' is contained in s 1 of the DDA 1995:

> 'a person has a disability ... if he has a physical or mental impairment which has a substantial and long-term adverse effect on his ability to carry out normal day-to-day activities.'

This apparently simple definition is supplemented by Sch 1 to the DDA 1995, the DD(E)R 1996 and the Guidance, so that, for example, 'mental impairment' includes an impairment resulting from or consisting of a mental illness only if the illness is a clinically well-recognised illness. By Sch 1, para 2(1) to the DDA 1995, the effect of an impairment is a long-term effect if:

> '(a) it has lasted for at least 12 months;
> (b) the period for which it lasts is likely to be at least 12 months; or
> (c) it is likely to last for the rest of the life of the person affected.'

1.8 The term 'likely' is said by the Guidance (para B7) to mean 'more probable than not'. With regard to normal day-to-day activities, Sch 1, para 4(1) to the DDA 1995 states that:

> 'An impairment is to be taken to affect the ability of the person concerned to carry out normal day-to-day activities only if it affects one of the following:
>
> (a) mobility;
> (b) manual dexterity;
> (c) physical co-ordination;
> (d) continence;
> (e) ability to lift, carry or otherwise move everyday objects;
> (f) speech, hearing or eyesight;
> (g) memory or ability to concentrate, learn or understand; or
> (h) perception of the risk of physical danger.'

1.9 The Guidance gives specific examples of what would or would not be reasonable to regard as amounting to substantial adverse effect.

Specific conditions

1.10 A number of situations which would not otherwise appear to fit within the definition of disability are specifically mentioned in order to ensure that they are covered by the DDA 1995. These are:

– past disabilities (s 2 and Sch 2);
– recurring conditions (s 2 and Sch 2);

- progressive conditions (Sch 1, para 8). These must have some effect (although it need not be substantial) such that it is likely that they will have a substantial effect in the future (eg HIV, cancer, MS);[1]
- severe disfigurements (Sch 1, para 3);
- controlled impairments (Sch 1, para 6). Impairments are to be assessed without the effects of any controlling medication/aids/ diet etc. The only exception to this requirement is impaired eyesight where its effects on the individual are to be evaluated when he is wearing glasses;
- those persons who were registered as disabled between January 1995 and December 1996 were deemed to be disabled persons for the purposes of the Act until December 1999. While this is no longer conclusive as to the person's current status, past registration may provide useful evidence indicating disability.

1.11 Under the Disability Discrimination (Meaning of Disability) Regulations 1996, SI 1996/1455, there are some conditions which might otherwise fall within the definition but are specifically excluded. These are:

- tendency to set fires;
- tendency to steal;
- tendency to physical or sexual abuse of others;
- exhibitionism;
- voyeurism;
- seasonal allergic rhinitis;
- addiction to alcohol, nicotine or another substance (unless the addiction was originally the result of administration of medically prescribed drugs or other treatment).

Cases on definition of disability

1.12 The question as to whether or not a person is disabled for the purposes of the DDA 1995 has given rise to the majority of appeals so far brought before the Employment Appeal Tribunal (EAT). The key decisions are as follows.

---

1   The Government response to the Task Force recommendations proposes that HIV should count as a disability from diagnosis and that those with cancer should count as disabled from when the cancer is diagnosed as being likely to require substantial treatment (*Towards Inclusion – Civil Rights for Disabled People*

Goodwin v the Patent Office[1]

1.13   The EAT set out guidance to employment tribunals on the proper approach to adopt when determining whether or not a person has a disability for the purposes of the DDA 1995.

1.14   Mr Goodwin, a paranoid schizophrenic, was dismissed from his employment at the Patent Office as a patent examiner following complaints from work colleagues about his odd behaviour. He complained to the employment tribunal that his employers had discriminated against him by dismissing him for a reason connected with his disability. The tribunal heard evidence from a doctor that Mr Goodwin had a mental illness. He experienced 'thought broadcasting', auditory hallucinations and paranoia. His ability to sustain concentration for any period of time was impaired due to these symptoms.

1.15   The tribunal held that whilst he had a mental impairment, and the impairment adversely affected his ability to concentrate, the effect upon him was not substantial because he could care for himself at home without assistance and he could get to work and carry out that work to a satisfactory standard. There was therefore no disability. Mr Goodwin appealed.

1.16   The EAT held that the evidence should have led the tribunal inevitably to the conclusion that Mr Goodwin was unable to carry on a normal day-to-day conversation with his colleagues and that he had a disability within the meaning of the DDA 1995. The appeal was allowed and the case remitted to a differently constituted tribunal to determine justification.

1.17   The EAT also laid down guidance for tribunals when faced with an issue relating to disability. It set out the four conditions which must be fulfilled in order to satisfy the definition of disability in s 1(1) with the following observations.

(1)   The applicant must have a physical or mental impairment. In an alleged mental illness case, the EAT stated that, if there is doubt as to whether there is a mental impairment, then whether or not the illness referred to is described in the International Classification of Diseases is likely to be determinative of whether the person has a mental illness that constitutes a mental impairment.

(DfEE)). It also proposes that people who have been certified, or registered under local authority schemes, as blind or partially sighted should be automatically counted as disabled for the purposes of the DDA 1995.

1   [1999] IRLR 4, EAT.

(2) There must be an adverse effect upon the ability to carry out normal day-to-day activities. The EAT believed this to be the most difficult issue to judge. The DDA 1995 is directed towards an impairment of a person's ability to carry out activities. The fact that the person can carry out an activity is not determinative of the issue. Where a person can carry out an activity, but only with great difficulty, that person's ability has been impaired. The abilities listed in para 4(1) of Sch 1 to the DDA 1995 are the sort of capabilities which a person requires to a greater or lesser extent to carry out normal day-to-day activities both at home and at work. The EAT cautioned against accepting applicants' assertions that they can cope with normal daily activities when in fact they may simply have developed avoidance or coping strategies, such as 'playing down' the effect of their disability. The EAT stated that there is no need to specify what constitutes a day-to-day activity. If a person has organised their home in such a way as to accommodate a disability, the fact that that person is able to manage at home is not determinative of the issue; if the person is unable to perform any normal daily activity, that person has an impairment. In order for the DDA 1995 to apply, it is necessary only for one capability to be affected. A person may, however, have a condition which does not have an effect on that particular capability but which has an adverse effect on a different capability. The example given is that of a person with exceptionally acute hearing. That person's ability to hear is obviously not affected but it may give rise to difficulties in coping with conversation in a group or may affect a person's ability to concentrate, or the ability to go into a busy shop, all of which are normal day-to-day activities.

(3) The impairment must be substantial. The EAT stressed that where a particular impairment is being treated or corrected, either with medication or other aids, such as a prosthesis, tribunals must assess the effect that the impairment would have on a person's abilities without the medication or other aid (apart from spectacles and contact lenses). This means that where a condition such as manic depression or diabetes is controlled by medication, whether the person has an impairment must be considered by reference to what effect that condition would have on that person's abilities without the treatment.

(4) The effect must be long term. This is clearly defined in para 2 of Sch 1 to the DDA 1995 and para B of the Guidance.

1.18 The EAT also stated that the Code of Practice 'gives practical guidance and a breach of the relevant provision of the Code must be taken into account when determining any issue of disability discrimination'.

Vicary v British Telecommunications plc[1]

1.19 Mrs Vicary was dismissed from her employment as a clerical officer. She had an upper arm condition, and sought to complain that she had been discriminated against contrary to the DDA 1995. An employment tribunal held that her impairment did not have a substantial effect on her ability to carry out normal day-to-day activities so as to fall within the Act's definition of 'disability'. The employment tribunal noted the opinion of the employers' regional medical officer that Mrs Vicary's impairment was not substantial.

1.20 The EAT held that the tribunal's decision was perverse and involved errors of law. The tribunal misdirected itself in law as to the meaning of 'substantial' and therefore misdirected itself as to the way in which the Guidance on the definition of disability is to be used. Having found that the ability of the applicant to do a number of activities was impaired, the tribunal should have concluded that she had a disability within the meaning of the DDA 1995. There was no need for the tribunal to refer to the Guidance once they had properly understood that 'substantial' as set out in the Code of Practice means more than a 'minor or trivial effect'.

1.21 The EAT also held that the employment tribunal misdirected itself as to the relevance of the medical evidence which they received from the employer's occupational health adviser. It is not for a doctor to express an opinion as to what is a normal day-to-day activity. Nor is it for the medical expert to tell the tribunal whether the impairments which had been found proved were or were not substantial. Those are matters for the employment tribunal.[2]

The definition of disability is discussed in more detail in Chapter 3.

Excluded employers

1.22 The employment provisions of the DDA 1995 do not apply to employers with fewer than 15 employees (s 7, as amended). It is clear from the cases so far brought to the EAT (eg *Hardie v CD Northern Ltd*,[3] *Colt Group Ltd v Couchman*[4]) that associated companies cannot be

---

1   [1999] IRLR 680, EAT.
2   See also: *Kapadia v Lambeth London Borough Council* [2000] IRLR 14, EAT; *Greenwood v British Airways* [1999] IRLR 600, EAT.
3   [2000] IRLR 87.
4   [2000] ICR 327.

counted together for the purposes of determining number of employees.

1.23   The DDA 1995 also excludes the following:

–   prison officers (with the exception of a custody officer or prison custody officer) (s 64(5)(b));
–   a fire-fighting member of the fire brigade (s 64(5)(c) and (6));
–   service in the naval military or air forces of the Crown (s 64(7));
–   members of the Ministry of Defence Police, the British Transport Police, the Royal Parks Constabulary and the United Kingdom Atomic Energy Authority Constabulary (s 68(1));
–   a statutory office holder (such as a police officer);
–   employees who work wholly or mainly outside Great Britain (s 68(2));
–   employees who work on board ships, aircraft or hovercraft (s 68(3)).

1.24   The small employer exemption is being challenged as being in conflict with the European Convention on Human Rights in *Whittaker v P&D Watson.*[1] The employment tribunal has stayed proceedings pending an appeal to the EAT to determine the issue.

In addition, the Government's Response to the Disability Rights Task Force report proposes repealing the small employer threshold in 2004. It also proposes to bring within the scope of the DDA 1995: partners and partnerships of any size; police officers; prison officers; fire-fighters; barristers in chambers and barristers' and advocate pupils; and employees on board a ship, aeroplane or hovercraft registered in Great Britain. There is also a proposal to cover members of county councils, district councils and London Borough Councils and to bring voluntary workers into coverage if necessary.[2]

The nature of employment

1.25   The DDA 1995 applies to employment under a contract of service or of apprenticeship or a contract personally to do any work (s 68). The Act also applies to contract workers, in that it is unlawful for a principal in relation to contract work to discriminate against a disabled person in respect of the terms on which he allows him to do that work; by not allowing him to do it or to continue to do it; in the way he affords him access to any benefits or by refusing or deliberately omitting to afford

1   7 December 2000; Case No 1805354/00.
2   See *Murray v Newham CAB* EAT No 1096/99 for a case where a 'volunteer' was held to be an employee under the DDA 1995.

him access to them; or by subjecting him to any other detriment (see s 12 for full details of the provisions). The issue of who is the principal in a contract worker situation has given rise to much confusion, and the EAT and subsequently the Court of Appeal have considered the point in the following case.

Abbey Life Assurance Co Ltd v Tansell [1]

1.26   Mr Tansell offered computer skills and services through Intelligents Ltd, a company in which he was sole shareholder and one of four directors. MHC is an employment agency specialising in placing computer personnel with third parties, and with whom Mr Tansell placed his name. MHC entered into an agreement to supply personnel to Abbey Life Assurance Co Ltd, and Mr Tansell was interviewed by them, following which a contract was entered into between MHC and Intelligents to supply Mr Tansell's services to Abbey Life. This contract had the effect of putting him under the control of Abbey Life, with fees paid to MHC, who in turn paid Intelligents. Mr Tansell was paid a salary by Intelligents, but funds were also retained within the company. Mr Tansell was withdrawn from the work site by MHC because Abbey Life rejected his services, due Mr Tansell said, to his disability. He made a claim of disability discrimination. An employment tribunal held a preliminary hearing on whether he was a contract worker within the meaning of s 12 of the DDA 1995. The tribunal took the view that s 12 requires a direct contractual relationship between the employer and the principal. On that basis, the applicant was not a contract worker for Abbey Life. However, the tribunal found that he was a contract worker for MHC and that he was an employee of his own company, Intelligents Ltd.

MHC appealed, and Mr Tansell cross-appealed against the tribunal's finding that he had no claim against Abbey Life.

1.27   The EAT allowed the appeal and the cross-appeal. It held that the employment tribunal erred in holding that the end-user was not a 'principal' for the purpose of s 12(6) because that requires a direct contractual relationship between the employer and the principal. Where there is an unbroken chain of contracts between an individual and the end-user, the end-user is the principal within the meaning of s 12(6). Such a construction gives effect to the general principle that the statute should be construed purposively and with a bias towards conferring statutory protection rather than excluding it. The Court of Appeal upheld the decision.

---

1   [2000] IRLR 387, CA; [1999] IRLR 677, EAT.

Unlawful actions by an employer

1.28   Under s 4 of the DDA 1995, it is unlawful to discriminate against a job applicant:

–   in the arrangements made for determining to whom a job should be offered;
–   in the terms on which employment is offered; or
–   by refusing to offer, or deliberately not offering, the disabled person employment.

In addition, it is unlawful to discriminate against a disabled employee:

–   in the terms of employment afforded to the employee;
–   in the opportunities afforded for promotion, transfer, training or receiving any other benefit;
–   by dismissing the disabled person or subjecting him or her to any other detriment.

Meaning of 'discrimination'

1.29   By s 5(1) of the DDA 1995, an employer discriminates against a disabled person if, for a reason relating to the person's disability, the employer treats that person less favourably than he treats or would treat others to whom the reason does not apply and the employer cannot show that the treatment is justified.

1.30   An employer also discriminates against a disabled person by failing to comply with a duty to make reasonable adjustments imposed on the employer by s 6 in relation to the disabled person, and the employer cannot show that this failure was justified (s 5(2)).

Reason relating to disability and less favourable treatment

1.31   The leading case relating to this issue is the Court of Appeal decision in *Clark v Novacold Ltd.*[1] The employment tribunal and, subsequently, the EAT held that the comparator for the purposes of less favourable treatment, in an ill-health dismissal case, would be someone with the same amount of time off but who did not have a disability. The Court of Appeal overturned the decision of the EAT, holding that the correct comparator is someone to whom the 'reason' for less favourable treatment does not apply. If a disabled employee is dismissed because of being unable to do a particular job, the treatment should be compared with treatment afforded to a person who does not have the disability and therefore can do the job, rather than a person who cannot do the job

---

1   [1999] IRLR 318, CA; [1998] IRLR 420, EAT.

but does not have a disability. The Court drew on examples from the Code of Practice relating to the provision of goods and services to illustrate the point.

Knowledge of employee's disability

1.32   Section 5(1) of the DDA 1995 does not specify that an employer must know that an individual is disabled in order for the employer to have discriminated against them. In the case of *O'Neill v Symm and Co Ltd*,[1] the EAT held that knowledge of disability was an essential ingredient for a claim of discrimination under s 5(1) to have been made out. This decision has not been followed, however, in the case of *Heinz and Co Ltd v Kenrick*,[2] where it was held that there was no requirement for the employer to have knowledge of disability for a s 5(1) claim. This decision was approved in the subsequent case of *London Borough of Hammersmith and Fulham v Farnsworth*.[3] Whether or not the employer had actual knowledge of the disability may, however, still be relevant when considering the issue of justification.

Duty to make reasonable adjustments

1.33   Section 6(1) of the DDA 1995 states that:

'Where –

(a)   any arrangements made by or on behalf of an employer, or
(b)   any physical feature of premises occupied by the employer,[[4]]

place the disabled person concerned at a substantial disadvantage in comparison with persons who are not disabled, it is the duty of the employer to take such steps as are reasonable, in all the circumstances of the case, for him to have to take in order to prevent the arrangements or feature having that effect.'

---

1   [1998] IRLR 233, EAT.
2   [2000] IRLR 144, EAT.
3   [2000] IRLR 691, EAT.
4   If any question arises as to whether the occupier has failed to comply with the s 6 duty, by failing to make a particular alteration to the premises, any constraint attributable to the fact that he occupies the premises under a lease is to be ignored unless he has applied in writing to the lessor for consent to the making of the alteration (DDA 1995, Sch 4, Part I, para 1). The lease for premises occupied by the employer is re-written so as to permit the occupier to make the alteration with the consent of the lessor and for the lessor not to unreasonably withhold such consent (DDA 1995, s 16). In addition, the Disability Discrimination (Employment) Regulations 1996, SI 1996/1456, provide that it is never reasonable for an employer to have to take steps which would involve altering a physical characteristic adopted with a view to meeting relevant building standards with regard to access for disabled people (reg 8).

1.34 Under s 6(2) of the DDA 1995, the duty applies to arrangements for determining to whom employment should be offered and to any term, condition or arrangement on which employment, promotion, transfer, training or any other benefit is offered or afforded. Subsection (3) gives examples of steps which an employer may have to take in relation to this duty such as making adjustments to premises or allocating some of the disabled person's duties to another person.

1.35 The leading case on the approach to be taken in a case alleging a failure to make reasonable adjustments is *Morse v Wiltshire County Council*.[1] In this case, the EAT sets out the steps which a tribunal should go through in order to determine whether or not the duty has been breached. These are as follows.

(1) Did or do any arrangements made by the employer or any physical features of premises occupied by the employer place the disabled person at a substantial disadvantage in comparison with non-disabled people?
(2) If so, the tribunal must then decide whether or not the employer had taken such steps as were reasonable to prevent the substantial disadvantage including the steps set out in DDA 1995, s 6(3)(a)–(l).
(3) In deciding whether the steps were reasonable, consideration must be given to the factors set out in DDA 1995, s 6(4)(a)–(e).
(4) Only after the tribunal has followed steps (2) to (3) above, and concluded that the employer has failed to comply with a s 6 duty, should the tribunal go on to decide whether or not that failure was justified.[2]

1.36 In the case of *Kenny v Hampshire Constabulary*,[3] the EAT considered the extent to which an employer must go in order to comply with the duty. It was held that the employer's duty does not extend to providing a personal carer to help a worker to go to the toilet. While the employer would have to consider adjustments to the physical premises to provide disabled access to toilets or to allow a personal carer provided by the worker to be present, it was not necessary actually to provide the carer.

1.37 An employer has no duty to take the above steps unless the employer knows, or could reasonably be expected to know, that in the

---

1   [1998] IRLR 352, EAT.
2   The Government's response to the Task Force recommendations proposes to remove the provision which allows employers to be able to justify failure to make reasonable adjustments as this is already covered in the concept of reasonableness.
3   [1999] IRLR 76, EAT.

case of an applicant, the disabled person concerned is, or may be, an applicant for the employment; or in any case, that that person has a disability and is likely to be affected in the way described in s 6(1).[1]

1.38 In the case of *Ridout v TC Group*,[2] the appellant had photosensitive epilepsy, of which she informed the respondents in advance of her interview with them. She was not contacted about interview arrangements, and when she arrived at the interview, she found that the room had bright fluorescent lighting without diffusers or baffles. Ms Ridout was wearing sunglasses around her neck. When she entered the room, she made some comments to the effect that she might be disadvantaged by the lighting. However, the employers considered that this was an explanation relating to her sunglasses. In the event, Ms Ridout never used the sunglasses and did not tell the employers that she was in any way unwell or felt disadvantaged.

1.39 The employment tribunal dismissed a complaint that the employers were in breach of s 6 of the DDA 1995 (duty to make reasonable adjustments). On appeal, the EAT held that the tribunal had not erred in law in finding that there had not been unlawful discrimination. It stated that the duty to make a reasonable adjustment under s 6 is to be construed in the light of s 6(6)(b), which provides that 'nothing in this section imposes any duty on an employer in relation to a disabled person if the employer does not know and could not reasonably be expected to know ... that that person has a disability' and is likely to be placed at a substantial disadvantage in comparison with persons who are not disabled. This requires a tribunal to measure the extent of the duty, if any, against the actual or assumed knowledge of the employer both as to the disability and its likelihood of causing the individual a substantial disadvantage in comparison with persons who are not disabled.[3]

1.40 The EAT stated that employment tribunals should be careful not to impose upon disabled people a duty to give a long, detailed explanation as to the effects of their disability merely to cause the employer to make adjustments which should probably have been made in the first place. On the other hand, it is equally undesirable that employers should be required to ask a number of questions as to

---

1   DDA 1995, s 6(6).
2   [1998] IRLR 628, EAT.
3   This is in contrast to the approach to knowledge and less favourable treatment (see **1.32**). Section 5(1) of the DDA 1995 does not specify that an employer must know about the individual's disability in order to be able to treat him less favourably for a reason relating to that disability. It is an objective test – *Heinz (HJ) and Co Ltd v Kenrick* [2000] IRLR 144.

whether a person with a disability feels disadvantaged merely to protect themselves from liability.[1]

Justification

1.41   Under the DDA 1995, discrimination under s 5(1) or s 5(2) can be justified only if it is both 'material to the circumstances of the case and substantial' (s 5(3)). Less favourable treatment cannot be justified where the employer is under a duty to make a reasonable adjustment but fails (without justification) to do so, *unless* the treatment would have been justified even after the adjustment (s 5(5)).

1.42   In the case of *Baynton v Saurus General Engineers Ltd,*[2] the EAT looked at the statutory test for establishing justification in a 'less favourable treatment' (ie s 5(1)) claim of disability discrimination. Their approach can be summarised as follows:

(1)   the disabled person shows less favourable treatment from the respondent, eg dismissal;
(2)   the respondent shows that the treatment, eg the dismissal, is justified if:

    (i)   the reason for the dismissal is both material to the circum-stances of the particular case and substantial; unless
    (ii) the employer is under a s 6 duty to make reasonable adjust-ments but fails without justification to comply with the duty;

subject to the less favourable treatment being justified even if the respondent had complied with the s 6 duty.

1.43   The EAT also held that in order to apply the test of justification, the interests of the disabled person and the interests of the employer must be weighed in the balance. All the circumstances of the case must be considered (including those of both the disabled person and the employer), not simply the justification reason offered by the employer.

1.44   However, in the case of *Heinz and Co Ltd v Kenrick,*[3] the EAT, although approving the 'balance' test referred to in *Baynton*, held that the specific wording in the statute meant that the threshold for justification was, in fact, 'very low'.

---

1   See also *Hughes v The London Borough of Hillingdon* Case No 6001328/98 EOR DCLD No 44 Summer 2000; *Gailey v Haes Systems Ltd* Case No 6002720/99 EOR DCLD No 43 Spring 2000 and *Murphy v Sheffield Hallam University* Case No 2800489/98, EOR DCLD No 40 Summer 1999.
2   [1999] IRLR 604, EAT.
3   [2000] IRLR 144.

1.45 The issue of the threshold for justification was considered again more recently in the Court of Appeal case of *Jones v The Post Office.*[1] Mr Jones had diabetes and was, following the obtaining of risk assessments, restricted to driving for two hours per day. He brought a s 5(1) claim under the DDA 1995, in respect of this and some other matters. The employment tribunal held that the driving restriction was not justified under s 5(3) of the Act, as they closely examined the medical evidence and held that the risk from the applicant was 'negligible' and that therefore the claim succeeded. This decision was appealed to the EAT which reversed the decision and remitted it to another employment tribunal.

1.46 On appeal, the Court of Appeal held that the employment tribunal is confined to considering whether the reason given for the less favourable treatment can properly be described as both material to the circumstances of the particular case and substantial. In order to rely on s 5(3), it is not enough for the employer to assert that his conduct was reasonable in a general way; he has to establish that the reason given satisfies the statutory criteria. Where a properly conducted risk assessment provides a reason which is on its face both material and substantial, and is not irrational, the employment tribunal cannot substitute its own appraisal. The employment tribunal must consider whether the reason meets the statutory criteria; it does not have the more general power to make its own appraisal of the medical evidence and conclude that the evidence from admittedly competent medical witnesses was incorrect or make its own risk assessment. Arden LJ stated that, when faced with a claim of justification, employment tribunals might find it helpful to ask the following questions.

– What was the employee's disability?

– What was the discrimination by the employer in respect of the employee's disability?

– What was the employer's reason for treating the employee in this way?

– Is there a sufficient connection between the employer's reason for discrimination and the circumstances of the particular case (including those of the employer)?

– Is that reason on examination a substantial reason?

---

1 Case No A1/2000/0294 EATRF [2001] EWCA Civ 558, CA.

Knowledge of disability, justification and the employers' duties under section 6

1.47   The issue of justification was considered again in *Quinn v Schwarzkopf Ltd.*[1] The EAT held that the employer could not justify an act which was subsequently held to be discriminatory but which it did not at the time consider to be so because it did not know that the applicant was disabled. This means that an employer cannot argue that it was justified in dismissing an employee if at the time of the dismissal it did not know that the employee was disabled and so that the act of dismissal was a potentially discriminatory act in need of justification. This is so even if the employer is trying to show that even if it had known about the disability there was nothing that could reasonably have been done to prevent the dismissal.

1.48   This case can be contrasted with the EAT's approach to the issue of knowledge of disability and the duty to make reasonable adjustments in *British Gas Services Ltd v McCaull.*[2] In this case the employment tribunal had found that since the employers had taken no action to comply with their duties under s 6 of the DDA 1995 to make reasonable adjustments (because they did not know that the employee was disabled) they could not argue before the tribunal that even if they had considered reasonable adjustments, there were none that they could have made. The EAT, however, held that the tribunal had erred in finding the employers must have failed to comply with their s 6 duties because they had not considered what steps might reasonably be taken. There is no automatic breach of the s 6 duty because an employer is unaware of that duty. The question is what steps did the employer take or not take? It is possible that an employer might take all reasonable steps as contemplated by s 6 whilst remaining entirely ignorant of their duties under s 6 either at all or because they were unaware that the employee was disabled for the purposes of the DDA 1995.

This case is currently the subject of an appeal.

1.49   The above two cases were both considered by the EAT in the most recent case of *Bradley v Greater Manchester Fire and Civil Defence Authority.*[3] Mrs Bradley had arthritis of the spine and wrists and could not sit for normal periods. Her manual dexterity was also affected. She was dismissed (and recommended for ill-health retirement) following a period of sickness absence. There had been a failure in communication between the occupational health physician and Mrs Bradley's manager

---

1   [2001] IRLR 67, EAT.
2   [2001] IRLR 60, EAT.
3   Eat No 253/00.

and, although adjustments had initially been considered by the employer, they were, as a result of the miscommunication, not considered immediately prior to dismissal. The tribunal held that there had been discrimination but that it was justified; they held that there would not have been any reasonable adjustments which could practicably have been made and so the employer was justified in its dismissal.

Mrs Bradley appealed, citing the main ground of appeal as being that the employer could not justify discrimination by means of failure to make reasonable adjustments when it had not applied its mind to these adjustments prior to the dismissal.

The EAT dismissed the appeal. It stated:

'(1) Where the dismissal is found to be for a reason relating to the Applicant's disability, as here, it is open to the employer to show that the reason is both material and substantial (section 5(3)). He is not precluded from raising that defence simply because he did not, up until the time of dismissal, consider that the employee was disabled or what should be done to accommodate the employee's disability.

...

(3) ... We agree with the EAT in *McCaull* that the first question here is whether, assuming there is a duty to make reasonable adjustments under section 6, the employer has failed so to do. We further agree that the test as to whether the employer has complied with his section 6 duty is an objective one. See *Morse v Wiltshire County Council* [1998] IRLR 352, paragraphs 46–47, (Bell J). It follows, in our view, that it is open to an employer to show, after the event, that he has taken all reasonable steps to comply with his section 6 duty or, put the other way, there are no further steps which he could reasonably have taken to remove the disadvantage to the employee envisaged by section 6(1). To that extent *ex post facto* evidence, for example as to the outcome of any consultation with the employee, or a search for alternative employment, is material and admissible. However, failure to consider what steps ought to have been taken at the time may cause evidential difficulties to the employer in establishing that defence.

(4) In any event, this is not a case, on its facts, where the Respondent failed to consider what steps could be taken during the currency of the employment to accommodate the Appellant's disablement. On the contrary, they took all reasonable steps, on the Tribunal's findings to make adjustments up until the final misunderstanding between Dr Almond and Mr Haslam. It is at this point that we prefer to follow the EAT approach in *McCaull* to that suggested in *Quinn*. In our view it was open to the Respondent to prove, after the event, that consultation with the Appellant would not have led to any further adjustments, nor would a search for alternative employment have assisted the Appellant to remain in the employment. They were not

thereby debarred from relying on the justification defence by the provisions of section 5(5).'

1.50   The DD(E)R 1996, SI 1996/1456, make special provisions for justification in relation to performance-related pay and occupational pension schemes.[1]

Victimisation (section 55)

1.51   As with the RRA 1976 and the SDA 1975, under the DDA 1995 a person can also bring a claim for discrimination if she has been victimised by another person in connection with the exercise of any rights contained in the Act. A claim for victimisation can be brought by a disabled person or a person who does not have a disability. The person making the claim needs to show that she has been subjected to any of the unlawful acts detailed in s 4(1) and (2) and that she has been treated less favourably because:

–   she has brought proceedings against the victimiser or any other person under the Act; or
–   she has given evidence or information in connection with proceedings brought by another person against the victimiser or any other person under the Act; or
–   she has otherwise done anything under the Act in relation to the victimiser or any other person; or
–   the victimiser believes that she has or intends to do any of the above.

The actions of the person claiming victimisation must have been done in good faith for her to be able to bring a claim. If the person bringing the claim is or was disabled, her disability is to be disregarded when considering whether she has been treated less favourably than any other person whether real or hypothetical.

1.52   Currently, a claim for victimisation can only be brought under the DDA 1995 by a person who is still employed. There are a number of DDA cases in which former employees have failed in their attempt to bring claims for discrimination in the employment tribunal because they were no longer employed.[2]

---

1   See *O'Neill v HSBC Bank plc* 20 December 2000 Case No 2202292/2000; EOR DCLD No 47 Spring 2000.
2   *Angel v New Possibilities NHS Trust* Case No 1500437/00. An EAT decision on this issue is awaited.

1.53 The position with regard to post-employment acts of discrimination or victimisation in race and disability discrimination cases can be distinguished from those in sex discrimination cases because of EC law and the Equal Treatment Directive.[1] However, the Government's response to the Task Force recommendations proposes that employment tribunals will be able to hear former employee's claims of discrimination taking place within 6 months of the end of employment when the discrimination has arisen directly out of that employment. It also proposes that tribunals would be able to consider claims about discrimination after this period if it was just and equitable.

Remedies

1.54 Under s 8 of the DDA 1995, following a successful complaint of disability discrimination, a tribunal can:

– award damages;
– make a declaration as to the rights of the complainant and the respondent in relation to the matters to which the complaint relates;
– order the respondent to pay compensation;
– recommend that the respondent takes action appearing to the tribunal to be reasonable for the purpose of obviating or reducing the adverse effect on the complainant of any matter to which the complaint relates.[2]

The Government's response to the Task Force recommendations proposes to allow tribunals to order reinstatement or re-engagement in DDA (and RRA and SDA) cases.

INTERACTION WITH OTHER LEGISLATION

1.55 As well as having claims under the DDA 1995, for s 5(1) or (2) discrimination, a client may also have a claim for unfair or constructive dismissal, including unfair selection for redundancy. Alternatively, in, for example, a capability dismissal there may be no way of succeeding in a claim for unfair dismissal, because of the test of 'reasonableness' in the Employment Rights Act 1996 being different from that of justification under the DDA 1995, but there may still be a DDA 1995 claim. However,

---

1 See *Adekeye v Post Office (No 2)* [1997] IRLR 105 and *Coote v Granada Hospitality Ltd (No 2)* [1999] IRLR 452, EAT. See also *Rathbone v Dudley College of Technology* (2 February 1999) Case No 1301325/98, EOR DCLD No 40 Summer 1999 – *DDA case re victimisation.*
2 See Chapter 9 for further details.

as it is difficult to be absolutely certain (sometimes not until the evidence has been heard), it is best to claim everything possible on behalf of the client.

1.56   The Human Rights Act 1998 (HRA 1998) may also have a part to play in the client's claim. If the client is employed by a public authority, she may have a direct claim under, for example, the right to respect for private and family life.[1] Alternatively, reference to the principles in the HRA 1998 may be made when considering, for example, the question of 'reasonableness' and whether or not an adjustment would be reasonable, or the question of justification. In addition, whilst employment tribunals are themselves subject to the provisions of Part III of the DDA 1995 (goods, facilities and services provisions) and so will have to make reasonable adjustments for the client under these provisions, the Right to a Fair Trial, under the HRA 1998, Sch 1, Art 6, may also be cited when inadequate provision is made for a disabled client to participate fully in the hearing.

DDA 1995 AND PERSONAL INJURY

1.57   In the case of *Sheriff v Klyne Tugs (Lowestoft) Ltd*,[2] the Court of Appeal has confirmed that the employment tribunal has jurisdiction to award compensation by way of damages for personal injury, including both physical and psychiatric injury caused by the statutory tort of unlawful discrimination. It upheld the decision of a county court judge to strike out as an abuse of process the appellant's claim for damages for personal injury caused by alleged racial harassment and abuse which he received during the course of his employment from the master of the ship on which he was employed, in circumstances in which the appellant had brought, and compromised, a claim of race discrimination in almost identical terms in an employment tribunal.

1.58   Personal injury matters are particularly likely to arise in DDA 1995 claims; not only for psychiatric injury such as depression (and in the case of disability, this may be quite severe) but also, for example, for a pre-existing disability which has been aggravated by a failure to make reasonable adjustments. Advisers must therefore ensure that any personal injury element of a claim is dealt with properly.[3] It may be necessary to obtain a medical report at an early stage of the proceedings to ensure that the correct route is followed (ie employment or negligence claim).

---

1   HRA 1998, Sch 1, Art 8.
2   [1999] IRLR 481.
3   See Chapter 2 for further details.

Chapter 2

ATTENDING THE CLIENT AND TAKING INITIAL INSTRUCTIONS

DUTIES AS SERVICE PROVIDERS

2.1 All solicitors, law centres and advice agencies, as providers of services to the public, are subject to the goods, facilities and services provisions of the DDA 1995; see ss 19–21. This means that not only must they not discriminate by refusing service or offering service on different terms or in a different manner, but they must also comply with duties imposed under s 21(1), part of s 21(2) and s 21(4) of the DDA 1995. (The bulk of s 21(2), which deals with alterations to physical features, is not due to be brought into force until 2004.)

2.2 Section 21 of the DDA 1995 provides:

'(1) Where a provider of services has a practice, policy or procedure which makes it impossible or unreasonably difficult for disabled persons to make use of a service which he provides or is prepared to provide to other members of the public, it is his duty to take such steps as it is reasonable, in all the circumstances of the case, for him to have to take in order to change that practice, policy or procedure so that it no longer has that effect.

(2) Where a physical feature (for example, one arising from the design or construction of a building or the approach or access to premises) makes it impossible or unreasonably difficult for disabled persons to make use of such a service, it is the duty of the provider of that service to take such steps as it is reasonable, in all the circumstances of the case, for him to have to take in order to –
(a) remove the feature;[1]
(b) alter it so that it no longer has that effect;[2]
(c) provide a reasonable means of avoiding the feature;[3] or
(d) provide a reasonable alternative method of making the service in question available to disabled persons.[4]

---

1   To be implemented in 2004.
2   To be implemented in 2004.
3   To be implemented in 2004.
4   Section 21(2)(d) in force now.

...

(4) Where an auxiliary aid or service (for example, the provision of information on audio tape or of a sign language interpreter) would –
(a)   enable disabled persons to make use of a service which a provider of services provides, or is prepared to provide, to members of the public, or
(b)   facilitate the use by disabled persons of such a service,
it is the duty of the provider of that service to take such steps as it is reasonable, in all the circumstances of the case, for him to have to take in order to provide that auxiliary aid or service.'

2.3   Therefore, solicitors' firms and advice agencies must examine their policies and procedures to ensure that they do not create barriers for disabled people. For example, they might change their complaints procedure so that a complaint does not have to be made in writing where this is difficult for a disabled person. Firms and advice agencies will also need to consider making information available in alternative formats such as in braille, on tape or on disc. Auxiliary aids may also be necessary for their clients or potential clients (as service providers have an anticipatory duty), for example a sign language interpreter, a textphone or type talk facility or an induction loop for clients with hearing impairments. They will also need to consider making their services available by reasonable alternative means and this could mean providing home visits or arranging client meetings in venues which are accessible for that particular client.

2.4   It should be noted that it has to be 'impossible or unreasonably difficult' for a disabled person to make use of the service before a practice, policy or procedure has to be changed or a reasonable alternative means of providing the service found (or a physical feature removed or altered in 2004).

2.5   The Code of Practice, Rights of Access, Goods, Facilities, Services and Premises, issued in July 1999,[1] provides guidance on the duties under s 21 of the DDA 1995. This Code of Practice will be reissued in 2001 to provide guidance on the duties relating to physical features which will come into force in 2004.

2.6   Disability awareness training will also be crucial for all staff who will be dealing with members of the public.[2]

---

1   DfEE, July 1999.
2   See Appendices for disability etiquette, alternative formats, transcription services and interpreters.

TAKING INSTRUCTIONS FROM THE CLIENT

2.7 In a disability discrimination case, detailed instructions will need to be taken from the client and usually it will be necessary to have a meeting with the client to do this. It is always good practice to ask the client if there needs to be any adjustment for this meeting.[1]

2.8 The purpose of the first meeting with the client is to ascertain whether the client has a viable case. If there is a case, it should be possible, from the information obtained at this initial meeting, to produce the first draft of the client's witness statement which will be used at the hearing.

2.9 The following checklist details the information that should be sought from the client at the first meeting. Although not all the information will be available or appropriate in every case, it is a useful guide for advisers of what needs to be asked of the client.

2.10 It is worth noting that clients will often focus on the specific incident of discrimination, such as a dismissal, without mentioning other problems they may have had at work, for example, a visually impaired client who has been dismissed and fails to mention that minutes for staff meetings had never been made available in an accessible format throughout her employment, thus forming a separate claim. Advisers will need to question their clients about all aspects of their work and any problems which they experienced.

All cases

2.11 The following information should be requested in all cases.

1   Client details
    – The client's full name, address and contact details, including the preferred format for future communication (eg large print, disc, tape or braille). A note on the file sleeve recording the preferred format is helpful, especially if other advisers or caseworkers are likely to be dealing with the matter.
    – Details of any other reasonable adjustments that the client might need. For example, a client with mental health problems might be unable to make decisions quickly or during telephone conversations. A note should be made on the file to ensure that the caseworker always allows that client extra time when taking instructions. This may be particularly relevant

---

1   See **2.3** and Appendices regarding the use of auxiliary aids and provision of the service by reasonable alternative means.

when a settlement is being negotiated close to a hearing date and the respondent is putting the applicant under pressure to accept an offer quickly so as to save costs (see Chapter 9 on Remedies). Clients with learning difficulties may need all correspondence to be in simple language or advice to be given verbally either by telephone or in face-to-face meetings. (Note: if the client has severe learning difficulties or a severe mental health problem, the adviser will need to consider whether he has the mental capacity to give instructions. If not, a 'next friend' will be needed to give instructions on the client's behalf.)

–   The client's age, date of birth, gender, ethnic origin and nationality. It may be that there are other discrimination claims that should be pursued instead of or as well as the disability discrimination claim.

2   The nature of the disability

–   Does the client have a physical or mental impairment, which has a substantial, long-term adverse effect on her ability to carry out normal day-to-day activities?[1]

–   The name and address of the doctor or specialist treating the client (if any).

–   The date and place of any injury sustained. There may be a possible personal injury claim.

–   When and how was the disability disclosed to the employer?

–   The details of any disability benefits being claimed by the client such as Disability Living Allowance or Disabled Person's Tax Credit.

–   Does the client have a blue badge (formerly an orange badge) for disabled parking?[2]

–   Was the client registered disabled with the Employment Service and does the client still have a Green Card?[3]

–   Is the client registered as disabled with the local authority?

3   The nature of the discrimination

–   A chronological account of the events that led to the client seeking legal advice, including precise dates of the acts of discrimination. Is the claim in time?[4]

–   Has there been less favourable treatment for a reason relating to the client's disability?

---

1   See Chapter 3.
2   See Chapter 3.
3   See Chapter 3.
4   See Chapter 5.

- How have other people been treated in similar circumstances?
- Details of any arrangements or physical features of premises which placed the client at a substantial disadvantage with specific reference to how the disadvantage is substantial.
- Whether or not the employer leases the premises and, if so, has consent been sought from the landlord for alterations?[1]
- Has the client made a request for reasonable adjustments and, if so, what adjustments, on what date(s) and with what response from the employer?
- Are there any reasonable adjustments that would remove the substantial disadvantage?
- Details of any possible witnesses.

4 Employer's details
- The employer's name and address.
- Whether or not the employer has made a commitment to any disability friendly schemes such as the Employment Service's Positive about Disabled People Scheme (known as the 2 tick scheme). The employer may also be a member of an organisation such as the Employers' Forum on Disability, which provides advice and information for employers. This information can be useful in trying to settle the matter if the client so wishes. For example, the Forum may be able to provide contact details for someone within a member organisation who can discuss the case with a view to providing the adjustments the client needs. If the case does go to a hearing, an employer is less likely to be able to argue that it was not aware of the adjustments that can be made if it is a member of an organisation that provides advice on such issues.
- The number of employees the employer had in total at the date of the act of discrimination. This includes all staff, for example cleaning, security and catering staff, workers at other sites or branches, temporary, part-time and casual staff. (Note: the employer must employ 15 or more employees for the client to be able to bring a claim under the DDA 1995.)
- Whether the job was paid or voluntary.[2]

5 Third party involvement
- Has the client sought advice from another solicitor or legal adviser?

---

1   See Chapter 1.
2   See *Murray v Newham CAB* EAT No 1096/99. Following this EAT decision, it is not fatal to a claim of disability discrimination that the work done was not paid.

- Is the client a member of a trade union and, if so, what has the union's involvement been to date and is it willing to provide representation?
- Does the client have legal expenses insurance?
- Is the client eligible for legal help?[1]

Recruitment cases (including failure to make reasonable adjustments to the recruitment process)

2.12 The following information should be requested if the client believes that there was discrimination in failing to be short-listed for a position or failing to be appointed after an interview.

- How and where the client heard about the vacancy.
- A copy of the job advertisement.
- A copy of the job description and person specification.
- A copy of any medical questionnaire completed by the client.
- The salary and benefits on offer.
- Details of how the client meets the person specification and a copy of the client's curriculum vitae if appropriate.
- A copy of the completed job application or details of the information requested.
- The deadline for completed applications and whether or not the client complied with it.
- Copies of any additional literature supplied by the employer with the job application pack (eg a brochure, annual report or equal opportunities monitoring form).
- The names, position and status of members of the interview panel.
- Whether or not the employer asked applicants if they had any particular needs and whether or not the client asked for any reasonable adjustments regarding the application form or arrangements for interview.
- Whether or not the client asked for any reasonable adjustments to be made to enable her to do the job.
- Details of the manner in which the interview was conducted.
- Whether or not the client was asked about her disability at the interview and, if so, what questions were asked.

---

1   Legal help does not extend to representation. However, under s 6(8)(b) of the Access to Justice Act 1999, the Lord Chancellor has the power to fund representation in certain complex employment tribunal cases in England and Wales. In DDA cases, particularly where the client has significant difficulties in representing himself because of his disability, there may be good grounds for an application under this section. In Scotland, funding is available for tribunal representation under the Advice and Assistance (Assistance by Way of Representation) (Scotland) Amendment Regulations 2001, SI 2001/2.

- Whether or not the client was asked to undergo a medical examination by the employer's medical expert. If so, was the employer's medical expert a specialist in the client's particular disability? If not, did the expert ask the client to be examined by or obtain a report from an appropriate expert? Also details of questions asked by the medical adviser, in particular those relating to any serious illnesses or disability, any medication being taken and the number of days sick taken in the past.[1]
- A copy of the letter informing the client that her application has been unsuccessful or details of how the client was told if not by letter.
- Any feedback given about why the client's application was unsuccessful.
- Whether or not an offer would have been subject to satisfactory references and, if so, whether or not these were taken up.
- Copies of the references are also useful.
- Details of efforts to find other work.
- Details of the effect of the discrimination on the client's emotional, physical and family life.

Dismissal/termination of contract cases

2.13 The following information should be requested if the client's employment has been terminated.

- The client's position and duties.
- Salary details including payslips. If the position was voluntary, it will be necessary to look closely at any expenses which were paid. In the case of *Chaudri v The Migrant Advisory Service,*[2] the employment tribunal held that payment of £40 per week as 'volunteer expenses', including when the employee was sick and during holidays, was a salary. The applicant was, therefore, allowed to take proceedings under the ERA 1996 and the SDA 1975. More recently in the DDA case *Murray v Newham* (above), the EAT held that voluntary work could be employment for the purposes of s 68 of the DDA 1995 and entry to a voluntary training programme could be an arrangement for the purposes of determining to whom employment should be offered.

---

1   See *London Borough of Hammersmith and Fulham* [2001] IRLR 691; *Sandy v Hampshire Constabularly* (unreported) July 1997.
2   (Unreported).

- Details of any other benefits the employee received such as pension rights, private health insurance and bonuses which it may be possible to claim as part of the financial loss or which may give rise to a separate claim, eg breach of contract.
- The date on which employment started and ended. There may also be an unfair dismissal or wrongful dismissal claim to consider.
- A copy of the contract of employment, including any grievance and disciplinary procedures.
- Whether or not the client has ever used the grievance procedure or been disciplined whilst working for that employer.
- Copies of appraisals and supervisions and details of how often these were conducted and by whom.
- Has the client consulted a disability employment adviser (DEA) at the local job centre and, if so, has a workplace assessment been carried out?[1]
- Did the employer ask the client to be examined by the employer's medical adviser? If so, who was the employer's medical adviser and what information did that adviser request of the client and what recommendations were made? Was the medical adviser a specialist in the client's condition and, if not, did the adviser seek expert reports?
- What efforts the client has made to find alternative work to mitigate her losses and details of any unemployment benefits claimed.
- The effect of the dismissal on the client's emotional and physical health and family life.

Cases of failure to make reasonable adjustments

2.14   The following information should be sought where the client claims that her employer has failed to make reasonable adjustments for the client. This may be while the client is still employed or after the contract of employment has been terminated. For cases of failure to make reasonable adjustments to the recruitment process, see **2.12**.

- Has a DEA carried out a workplace assessment?
- What arrangements or physical features of premises put the client at a substantial disadvantage?
- Would reasonable adjustments to the working arrangements or physical features of the premises remove a substantial disadvantage the client is placed under because of her disability?

---

1   See Appendix 3.

- What is the cost of the necessary adjustments and has the employer investigated grants and assistance available from the Access to Work Scheme or other assistance schemes?[1]
- Information about the employer's annual turnover and profits – what is the size and wealth of the employer?
- Is there a health and safety issue and, if so, when was the last risk assessment carried out and by whom?
- If special equipment is needed, has the employer or client contacted organisations that adapt or provide specialist equipment, such as Ability Net or Remap?[2]
- If alterations to the physical features of premises are needed, is consent from a landlord required and, if so, has the employer requested it?
- If the client requires additional sick leave or time away from work for treatment, what effect does this have on the employer and is cover available?
- If the client wishes to reduce working hours or work from home, does the client know of any other part-time workers or job sharers or of anyone else within the organisation who works from home? What evidence is there that the employer has investigated flexible working schemes?
- Has the employer provided training to all staff on the DDA 1995 and on disability awareness?

CHECKLIST OF DOCUMENTS NEEDED FROM CLIENT

2.15   Wherever possible, the adviser should ask the client to bring to the first meeting as many of the following documents as may be relevant or that the client has in his possession. If these documents are not available, they may be sought later either via the questionnaire or the discovery process.[3]

All cases

2.16   The following documents should be brought in all cases.

- Letters or reports from the client's GP, consultant or other specialist about the nature of the disability and the effect it has on the client's day-to-day activities.
- Details of benefits being claimed by the client.

---

1   See Appendix 3.
2   See Appendix 4.
3   See Chapters 4 and 6.

- The blue disabled parking badge (formerly orange badge).
- Evidence of registration as a disabled person, for example with the local authority or (under the old Green Card system) with the Employment Service.
- Details of the client's salary and dates of any current employment (eg payslips or bank statements).
- Letters to and from the employer.
- The employer's annual reports and brochures.
- Job description.
- Employer's equal opportunities policy/disability policy.

Recruitment cases

2.17   The following documents should be brought in recruitment cases.

- The job advertisement.
- The job description and person specification.
- A copy of the job application.
- The literature accompanying the job pack.
- Any other information about the respondent (eg a copy of the employer's annual report).
- Details of the salary and benefits offered.
- Details of other jobs which the client has applied for or other evidence that the client has been seeking work if still unemployed.
- Details of benefits claimed whilst unemployed.

Dismissal/termination of contract cases

2.18   The following documents should be brought in dismissal/termination of contract cases.
- The contract of employment.
- Details of disciplinary and grievance procedures.
- Copies of the client's appraisals and supervisions.
- Minutes of the meetings at which the client's employment was discussed.
- Sickness absence procedures, where relevant.
- The redundancy procedures, where relevant.
- The client's recent payslips.
- The client's pension scheme documents.
- Details of contractual bonuses or commission earned by the client.
- The client's private health insurance documents.
- Letters from the Benefits Agency detailing benefits being claimed by the client.

- Details of any other benefits afforded to the employee (eg concessionary travel or corporate club membership).
- Details of other jobs which the client has applied for or other efforts to find work.

Cases of failure to make reasonable adjustments

2.19   The following documents should be brought in cases of failure to make reasonable adjustments.

- Copies of workplace assessments.
- Copies of risk assessments or health and safety reports.
- Redeployment policies.
- Sickness absence procedures, where relevant.
- Correspondence with disability employment advisers.
- Correspondence between the employer and its landlord regarding consent to make alterations.
- Correspondence with or information from other organisations or individuals about equipment or reasonable adjustments.
- Minutes or notes of meetings at which reasonable adjustments were discussed.

2.20   In practice, it may be simpler to ask the client to bring with him all documents in his possession which relate to his employment. The adviser can then extract those of the above documents which are relevant to the case.

ASSESSING THE STRENGTHS AND WEAKNESSES OF THE CASE

2.21   Once the above information has been obtained from the client, it should be possible for the adviser to assess the strength of the case. It may be that a case based on the DDA 1995 is weak, for example because the client is unlikely to meet the definition of disability, but it might still be possible to go ahead with the case based on unfair or constructive dismissal.

2.22   If the client has sustained an injury at work or if the disability has been caused by the actions of the employer, the adviser will need to consider whether or not a personal injury claim should be pursued instead of or as well as the claim based on the DDA 1995. If both claims are to be pursued simultaneously or consecutively, it is vital that the advisers dealing with the separate claims notify each other of precisely what is being claimed in each case.

2.23   Following the initial meeting and after assessing the strengths of the case, it is good practice to set out for the client:

–   what the strengths of the case are;
–   what the weaknesses of the case are;
–   what the likelihood of success is if the case is to proceed;
–   what the client is likely to achieve by pursuing the case (ie the likely level of compensation and a declaration of discrimination)[1] – this is particularly important as the client may have an unrealistic expectation about the level of compensation, especially if high awards have been reported in the press;
–   if there is likely to be a preliminary hearing, eg on whether the client meets the definition of disability;[2]
–   how long the case is likely to take to conclude;
–   what steps the adviser will take next and what the client is likely to have to do, including giving evidence at the hearing and being cross-examined;
–   the likelihood of the need for experts' reports and their estimated cost; and
–   the possibility that the costs may be awarded by the tribunal against the client.

2.24   All of the above should be confirmed to the client in writing or an appropriate alternative format together with a request for confirmation that the client wishes to pursue the case. If the client does wish to pursue the case, he should be advised to keep records of all jobs applied for and correspondence related to this where appropriate.

2.25   If the client does wish to proceed with the claim, the next step for the adviser is to prepare a draft witness statement from the information collected at the initial interview. The adviser also needs to consider the questionnaire and originating application as well as what expert evidence may be required.

---

1   See Chapter 9.
2   See Chapter 3.

CASE STUDIES

The case studies in this book are entirely fictional and any resemblance in them to actual events or real persons, living or dead, is purely coincidental.

DAVID JOSEPH AND READYMADE LTD

David Joseph has written the following letter asking if you will represent him in a case under the DDA 1995 at an employment tribunal. After reading his letter, you arrange an appointment to take further instructions from him. What information will you need from him to enable you to assess whether his case is viable?

Dear Sir/Madam,

Re: DDA

I am writing to request your help. I have been working as a pharmaceutical representative for several years and have spent the last 3 years with one employer. In December 1999 I saw an advertisement for a very similar post with Readymade Ltd and I decided to apply as the salary was higher. I went for an interview on 15 December 1999 which went well.

I was asked to see the company doctor on 19 December. I told the doctor that I thought I might have an inguinal hernia. The doctor, Dr Milne, examined me and confirmed that I did have a hernia. He agreed with me, however, that this would not affect my ability to do the job, as most of this was sitting down and driving. He passed me fit to work and I was formally offered the job by way of a letter dated 21 December. I was asked to sign a copy of the letter and return it to Readymade Ltd to indicate my acceptance and I did this on the same day. I wrote to Readymade at the same time to let them know that I may need time off work in the following year for a hernia repair operation.

On 23 December, I was telephoned on my mobile phone by Ms Rhodes, who I understand works in personnel, saying that the job offer had been withdrawn. She told me that I would need too much time off sick and she did not think that I would be up to the job of driving for several hours a day. I told her that my hernia would not affect my ability to drive, especially if I could have a car with power assisted steering. Ms Rhodes said that it was not possible to pick and choose and I would have to use the car allocated, but that in any event it was irrelevant as the job offer was withdrawn.

I gave up my old job because I thought that I had a job with Readymade. I have been unemployed for 2 months and have currently found temporary work.

I would be grateful if you would contact me to let me know whether or not you can help.

Yours faithfully,

David Joseph

Questions to ask Mr Joseph

(1) His full name, address and age.
(2) The full name and address of Readymade Ltd.
(3) How many employees does Readymade Ltd have and if fewer than 15:
  (a) does the company have more than one office and if so how many employees are there at each office?
  (b) are the separate offices branches of the same company or franchises or sister, subsidiary or parent companies?[1]
  (c) are there any contract staff working for the company? The law on whether or not these count as employees is currently unclear.
(4) Does Mr Joseph meet the definition of disability?
  (a) Is the condition long term?
  (b) Does the condition have a substantial adverse effect on his ability to carry out day-to-day activities and if so which activities (with examples)?
  (c) Is he receiving any treatment for the condition and if so what?
  (d) Is the condition progressive?
(5) Does Mr Joseph get any disability benefits (eg disability living allowance)?
(6) Is he a Blue Badge holder?
(7) Has he ever been registered disabled, either with the employment service, with the old Green Card or with his local authority?
(8) Did Readymade Ltd know about his condition?[2]

---

1   In *Hardie v CD Northern Ltd* [2000] IRLR 87, the EAT held that it could not pierce the corporate veil. See also *Colt Group Ltd v Couchman* [2000] ICR 327, EAT.

2   Mr Joseph states in his letter that he told EPC Ltd's doctor about his hernia. Paragraph 4.62 of the Code of Practice states that:

(9)   The names, position and status of the members of the interview panel.

(10) What questions were asked at interview?

(11) Was he ever asked either on the application form, the letter inviting him for interview or at the interview itself if he needed any reasonable adjustments because of a disability or any questions about disability at all?

(12) What exactly did Dr Milne ask him? What happened at the medical examination?

(13) Details of Dr Milne's qualifications (if known).

(14) Was Mr Joseph asked to complete a medical questionnaire?

(15) What were the contents of the letter offering him the job? Was it a firm offer or conditional, ie is this a dismissal case or a recruitment case?

(16) How many days sickness leave did he take in his previous employment?

(17) Why did he leave the previous job? He says for a higher salary, but were there any other reasons? How well did he meet the person specification for the job with Readymade Ltd?

(18) Did he meet targets etc in his last job? If not, was this because of his hernia?

(19) Did the car in his previous job have power assisted steering?

(20) Can he drive a car that does not have power assisted steering, ie would it put him at a substantial disadvantage not to have one?[1]

(21) What temporary work is he doing now and how much is he paid?

(22) How long was he unemployed?

(23) Did he claim benefit while unemployed? If so, what and how much?

(24) Does he think that his hernia is the only reason for the job offer being withdrawn, ie might he have other possible discrimination claims?

'If an employer's agent or employee (for example an occupational health officer, a personnel officer or line manager) knows in that capacity of an employee's disability, then the employer cannot claim that he does not know of that person's disability ... This will be the case even if the disabled person specifically asked for such information to be kept confidential. Employers will, therefore, need to ensure that where information about disabled people may come through different channels, there is a means, suitably confidential, for bringing the information together so that the employer's duties under the Act are fulfilled.'

See also *London Borough of Hammersmith and Fulham v Farnsworth* [2000] IRLR 691.

1   Consider what his claim is: s 5(1) only or are there s 5(2) and s 6 claims as well?

Documents Mr Joseph must supply

(1)   All correspondence with Readymade Ltd, including the letters inviting him for an interview, asking him to attend the medical examination and the letter offering him the position and the letter withdrawing the offer (if any).

(2)   Copies of any medical questionnaires he was asked to complete.

(3)   A copy of the completed application form.

(4)   All accompanying literature with the application pack, for example an equal opportunities monitoring form, a brochure about company and equal opportunities policy or statement.

(5)   A copy of the job advertisement and/or information about salary and benefits.

(6)   A copy of the job description and the person specification.

(7)   Letters/reports from doctors about his hernia.

(8)   Current payslips or bank statements showing his income.

(9)   Letters from the benefits agency about any benefits received.

(10)   Any Blue Badge documentation.

(11)   The disability registration documentation (if appropriate).

(12)   References from previous employer (if available).

Chapter 3

THE DEFINITION OF DISABILITY

3.1 In many cases under the DDA 1995 the first hurdle for the applicant to overcome is to prove that she meets the definition of disability contained in the Act. If the respondent disputes that the applicant is disabled, the tribunal is likely to order a preliminary hearing to decide this issue alone. If it does not, the issue will be dealt with at the beginning of the main liability hearing.

3.2 In the case of *Goodwin v The Patent Office*,[1] however, the EAT said that when the tribunal is faced with an issue as to whether the applicant has a disability within the meaning of the DDA 1995, it should look carefully at what the parties have said in their originating application and response.[2] The issue of disability should then be identified and 'it will be unsatisfactory for the disability issue to remain unclear and unspecific until the hearing itself'. In *Goodwin*, the EAT also stated that a directions hearing to identify the issues would usually be advisable in disability discrimination cases.

3.3 An adviser who believes that it would be tactically better to have a separate hearing on the definition of disability should cite this case as authority. It may be tactically better to have a separate hearing on disability if the cost and disruption of two separate hearings might induce the respondent to settle or if the issue of disability is the weakest aspect of the applicant's case. Success at a preliminary hearing on disability may result in an offer of settlement if the applicant has a strong case in other respects.

3.4 This means that the applicant will have to prove to the tribunal at the outset of the case that she cannot perform various normal day-to-day activities. Only if the applicant succeeds in doing this will she be able to proceed to the main liability hearing at which it will be necessary to prove that the applicant could do or could have done a particular job with the respondent.

---

1   [1999] IRLR 4, EAT.
2   See Chapters 4 and 5.

When advisers are preparing to argue the preliminary issue of whether or not their client meets the definition of disability, they should be aware of the case to be argued at the main liability hearing. Care should be taken to ensure that the evidence for this preliminary point does not contradict that which will be used to prove that the respondent discriminated against the applicant.

3.5   Nevertheless, if the applicant cannot show as a preliminary point that she meets the definition of disability, there will be no main liability hearing on whether or not discrimination took place.

THE LAW

The meaning of 'disability'

3.6   The definition of 'disability' and a 'disabled person' is contained in s 1 of the DDA 1995 and is supplemented by Schs 1 and 2 to the Disability Discrimination (Meaning of Disability) Regulations 1996.[1] Section 1 of the DDA 1995 states that a person has a disability if he has a physical or mental impairment that has 'a substantial and long-term adverse effect on his ability to carry out normal day-to-day activities'.

3.7   Schedule 1, para 1 to the DDA 1995 states that 'mental impairment' includes an impairment resulting from or consisting of a mental illness only if the illness is a clinically well-recognised illness.

3.8   'Long term' is defined by Sch 1, para 2 to the DDA 1995 as follows:

'(1)   The effect of an impairment is a long-term effect if –

(a)   it has lasted for at least 12 months;
(b)   the period for which it lasts is likely to be at least 12 months; or
(c)   it is likely to last for the rest of the life of the person affected.'

3.9   In determining whether an outcome is 'likely' or not it must be 'more probable than not'.[2]

3.10   According to Sch 1, para 4 to the DDA 1995:

'(1) An impairment is to be taken to affect the ability of the person concerned to carry out normal day-to-day activities only if it affects one of the following –

(a)   mobility;
(b)   manual dexterity;
(c)   physical co-ordination;

1   SI 1996/1455.
2   Guidance, para B7.

    (d) continence;
    (e) ability to lift, carry or otherwise move everyday objects;
    (f) speech, hearing or eyesight;
    (g) memory or ability to concentrate, learn or understand; or
    (h) perception of the risk of physical danger.'

3.11 The Guidance on matters to be taken into account in determining questions relating to the definition of disability (the Guidance) gives specific examples of what would or would not be reasonable to regard as amounting to a substantial adverse effect. However, these examples should not be followed too rigidly as they are only examples.

Special conditions

3.12 A number of situations which appear not to fit within the definition of disability are specifically stated to fall within the DDA 1995:

–   past disabilities (s 2 and Sch 2);
–   recurring conditions (s 2 and Sch 2);
–   progressive conditions (Sch 1, para 8) – these must have some effect, although it need not be substantial, and it must be likely that they will have a substantial effect in the future (eg HIV infection, cancer or MS);[1]
–   severe disfigurements (Sch 1, para 3); and
–   controlled impairments (Sch 1, para 6) – impairments are to be assessed without the effects of any controlling medication, aids, diet, etc (the only exception is the wearing of glasses or contact lenses where the effects are to be considered with glasses or contact lenses).

3.13 In addition, those persons registered as disabled between January 1995 and December 1996 were automatically included within the definition until December 1999.

Excluded conditions

3.14 The following conditions do not of themselves constitute 'disability' for the purposes of the DDA 1995, s 1:

–   a tendency to set fires;

---

1   The Government response to the Task Force recommendations proposes that HIV should be treated as a disability from diagnosis and that those with cancer should count as disabled from when the cancer is diagnosed as being likely to require substantial treatment (*Towards Inclusion – Civil Rights for Disabled People* (DfEE)).

-   a tendency to steal;
-   a tendency to physical or sexual abuse of others;
-   exhibitionism;
-   voyeurism;
-   seasonal allergic rhinitis (ie hayfever); and
-   addiction to alcohol, nicotine or another substance (unless the addiction was originally the result of administration of medically prescribed drugs or other treatment).

See the Disability Discrimination (Meaning of Disability) Regulations 1996.[1]

How to prove that the applicant meets the definition of disability

3.15   In order to prove that the applicant is a disabled person, it is vital for advisers to:

(1)   be clear about the law and the sections of the DDA 1995 which apply in the particular applicant's case, including any special conditions;
(2)   have evidence in the form of the applicant's own statement, medical evidence and other evidence[2] of the effect of the applicant's condition on her normal day-to-day activities; and
(3)   consider the Guidance and the examples given on what it would be reasonable to regard as having a substantial adverse effect with specific reference to the day-to-day activities listed in the Act.

3.16   The most important case to date on the definition of disability is *Goodwin v The Patent Office.*[3] Mr Goodwin, a paranoid schizophrenic, was dismissed from his job after complaints by other members of staff about his behaviour. Mr Goodwin experienced 'thought broadcasting', which meant that he believed that other people were accessing his thoughts and he misinterpreted the words and actions of colleagues in a paranoid fashion. He also experienced auditory hallucinations, which often affected his ability to concentrate for a sustained period, and caused him to leave the building. On one occasion he was found walking along a railway line. Mr Goodwin cared for himself at home and was able to do his own shopping and cooking and could attend to his personal hygiene.

3.17   The employment tribunal held that his condition did not have a 'substantial' adverse effect on his ability to carry out normal day-to-day activities.

---

1   SI 1996/1455.
2   See **3.20**.
3   [1999] IRLR 4.

3.18 The EAT overturned the employment tribunal's decision. In doing so, it gave general guidance for tribunals as to how to determine whether an applicant meets the definition of disability. Advisers should bear this guidance in mind when preparing their client's case and when formulating submissions to the tribunal at the end of the hearing.

3.19 In particular, the EAT said the following.

(1) Tribunals should adopt a 'purposive' approach to social legislation such as the DDA 1995. The language of the Act should be construed so as to give effect to the stated or presumed intention of Parliament. This means that tribunals should consider the situation as a whole bearing in mind the reason why the DDA 1995 was thought to be necessary rather than concentrating solely on technicalities.

(2) If there is any doubt as to whether the condition is a mental impairment, reference should be made to the World Health Organisation's International Classification of Diseases as this will be evidence as to whether or not it is 'clinically well-recognised'.

(3) When deciding the issue of disability, explicit reference should be made to the Guidance on the definition of disability. However, the Guidance should not be used as an extra hurdle for the applicant to overcome.

(4) Some disabled people are unable or unwilling to accept their disability. The DDA 1995 is concerned with the impairment of a person's *ability* to carry out activities. The fact that a person carries out such activities does not mean that her ability to carry them out has not been impaired as she may only be able to do them with difficulty. Therefore, tribunals should adopt an inquisitorial or interventionist role in disability cases and ask questions directly of the applicant.

(5) The Guidance on the definition of disability makes it clear that a 'substantial' effect means that the effect must only be 'more than minor or trivial' rather than 'very large'.

(6) A tribunal may take into account how the applicant appears to 'manage' before it, but it should be slow to regard a person's capabilities in the relatively strange adversarial environment as a reliable guide to how that person performs normal day-to-day activities.

(7) A tribunal should examine how an applicant's abilities have actually been affected whilst on medication and consider the 'deduced effects', ie the effects it thinks there would have been but for the medication. Then a tribunal should consider whether the

actual or the deduced effects on the applicant's ability to carry out normal day-to-day activities is 'more than minor or trivial'.

EVIDENCE

The applicant's witness statement

3.20   The applicant's own evidence about the effect of her disability on normal day-to-day activities is likely to be the most important evidence that the tribunal will hear. It is vital, therefore, for advisers to take detailed instructions from their clients and draft as full a statement for the applicant as possible. Statements should contain the following information.

All statements
3.21   The following list applies to all statements.

(1)   The date when the applicant first became aware of the symptoms of the disability. This will be important in assessing whether or not the disability is long term.

(2)   The date of diagnosis of disability, if any. However, it is not vital for the applicant to have a definite diagnosis, as the test is whether or not the symptoms have a long-term substantial adverse effect on normal day-to-day activities. In the case of *Howdon v Capital Copiers (Edinburgh) Ltd*,[1] Mr Howdon experienced a sharp, gripping, intense pain which forced him to lie down. He was admitted to hospital on several occasions, but no satisfactory cause was found for the pain. However, there was no suggestion that his condition was other than genuine. Mr Howdon took morphine and pethidine on a daily basis to control the pain and his medical practitioner saw no 'likelihood at least in the short term of this problem resolving'. The tribunal found that 'without effective pain control Mr Howdon was unable to walk, had to lie down, lost the use of his hands, was doubled up, suffered spasms, lack of co-ordination, speech impediment, blurred vision, loss of concentration and manual dexterity'. It accepted on this evidence that Mr Howdon was disabled even though there was no diagnosis of a specific disability. If the applicant does have a diagnosis this should be stated with reference to any medical evidence that is being submitted to the tribunal.

(3)   A description of the symptoms experienced by the applicant, including details of the effect of the symptoms on normal day-to-day activities and specific reference to the list of normal

---

1   (1997) IDS Brief 598/14.

day-to-day activities contained in the DDA 1995. For example, does the applicant have symptoms which make it particularly difficult to do basic housework such as ironing, washing up and chopping vegetables because lifting or manual dexterity is a problem? In the case of *Vicary v British Telecommunications plc*,[1] the employment tribunal was told that Mrs Vicary was unable to prepare vegetables, cut meat or roast potatoes, carry saucepans full of water, manually open jars, tins or packets, carry baskets of washing, read without resting the book on the arm of a chair, do heavy shopping, do any DIY tasks, file her nails, tong her hair, shake quilts, groom animals, polish furniture, knit, sew, cut with scissors, hold a briefcase, suitcase or handbag with hand-held handles, or carry a chair. However, the tribunal held that she did not meet the definition of disability because 'she can reasonably be expected to modify her behaviour to prevent or reduce the effects of the impairment'. In addition, the tribunal considered some of the activities not to be normal day-to-day activities as set out in the Guidance. In coming to its conclusion, the tribunal relied on the evidence of the employer's Regional Medical Officer who said that in her opinion there was no substantial adverse effect on Mrs Vicary's ability to carry out normal day-to-day activities.

The EAT, however, disagreed and pointed out that para C9 of the Guidance makes it plain that the lists of examples given 'are not exhaustive; they are only meant to be illustrative'. It stated:

> 'the fact that the Medical Advisor had been told on some disability discrimination course or seminar that something was or was not a normal day-to-day activity is not of relevance to the Tribunal's determination. It is not for a doctor to express an opinion as to what is a normal day-to-day activity . . . Equally, it was not for the expert to tell the Tribunal whether the impairments which had been found proved were or were not substantial.'

This case illustrates the importance of the applicant's own evidence about the effect of her impairment on normal day-to-day activities.

Do the symptoms mean that the applicant cannot climb stairs or run for a bus because of mobility problems? Is the applicant unable to drive or travel distances because continence is a problem and easy access to toilet facilities is necessary?

(4) Details of any drugs or treatment for the symptoms taken by the applicant and/or any coping strategies employed by the applicant.

---

1   [1999] IRLR 680, EAT.

(a) If the applicant is taking medication or drugs, the statement should state:
    (i)   the name of the drug or medication;
    (ii) who prescribed the medication;
    (iii) how often the medication has to be taken;
    (iv) what effect the medication has on the applicant (eg alleviates pain, lessens inflammation or alleviates depression); and
    (v)   what would happen if the applicant failed to take the medication (eg would the applicant experience greater pain, feel unable to leave the house or become hypoglycaemic and risk going into a coma).

(b) Details should be given of any treatment other than medication being received by the applicant. For example, counselling or psychotherapy which was held to be treatment by the EAT and the Court of Appeal in the case of *Kapadia v London Borough of Lambeth*.[1] The tribunal in *Poulton v H Walton*[2] held that diet to control diabetes constituted treatment. The applicant should give evidence about what would happen if she stopped taking this treatment. However, advisers should bear in mind that the client may not know or may be unwilling to address the issue of what would happen if she ceased to take medication or treatment. This may be particularly so with clients who have mental health problems or if the disability has been diagnosed only recently. In such instances, the information will have to be sought from the client's medical practitioners.

(c) Does the applicant have coping strategies to deal with the symptoms of the disability? Examples of coping strategies are:
    (i) avoiding situations where the disability may be more noticeable, for example those with poor hearing may avoid environments where there is a great deal of background noise and those with eyesight problems may avoid dimly lit environments and not go out after dark;
    (ii) carrying out normal day-to-day activities in an unusual manner, for example ironing whilst sitting down, arranging the living area to ensure that nothing is above or below a certain height or making several shopping trips rather than one to avoid carrying more than light weights;

---

1   [2000] IRLR 14, EAT.
2   (Unreported) Case No 1805515/97.

(iii) re-organising the day so that certain activities are carried out when the applicant experiences less pain (eg at the beginning of the day) or ensuring that more than a usual amount of time is spent sleeping in order to cope with extreme fatigue;[1] and

(iv) having assistance in carrying out activities, for example help dressing, shopping or reading and understanding correspondence.

All of the above should be discounted by the Tribunal when assessing whether or not the applicant's impairment has a substantial adverse effect on his or her normal day-to-day activities.[2]

Advisers should also ensure that the applicant gives detailed evidence if normal day-to-day activities are carried out with difficulty. For example, such activity might cause the applicant pain or result in extreme fatigue requiring more sleep or rest than a person without the condition would need.

If the applicant has avoided treatment (eg painkillers), the applicant should give the reasons for that in the witness statement. It may be that the drugs have unpleasant side effects or the applicant prefers alternative remedies or treatment. If such reasons are not given, the respondent may try to argue that the symptoms cannot be as severe as the applicant is claiming as she is taking no treatment for them.

Statements where the applicant's disability is progressive
3.22 The following information should be included in statements where the applicant's disability is progressive.

(1) The date when the condition started to have some effect on the applicant's normal day-to-day activities and what that effect was.

(2) Examples, if any, of deterioration in the condition with dates when the applicant experienced a further symptom or when an activity became more difficult to carry out.

(3) Any related conditions, for example the problems with eyesight that are commonly associated with MS.

(4) Any information the applicant has been given by doctors or specialists of the likely progress of the condition.

---

1   See the Guidance, paras A1 to A10 for factors to be taken into account when determining 'substantial' such as the time taken to carry out an activity and the effects of environment.

2   See also *Abadeh v British Telecommunications plc* [2001] IRLR 23, EAT and *Leonard v Southern Derbyshire Chamber of Commerce* [2001] IRLR 19, EAT.

(5) Any change or increase in medication or treatment with details of what might happen if this treatment were not taken (eg additional or stronger painkillers or more frequent appointments at hospital for treatment).

Statements where the applicant has a remitting or recurring condition

3.23 The following information should be included in statements where the applicant has a remitting or recurring condition.

(1) The number of times (with dates if possible) the condition has recurred (or is likely to have recurred but for medication).
(2) The details of each episode, including the effect on the applicant's normal day-to-day activities during that time.

Medical evidence

3.24 Medical evidence can be expensive. In some cases, the applicant's doctors may be willing to provide a report free of charge, but these instances are rare. Consequently, in the past acquiring adequate medical evidence was the greatest hurdle for the applicant in trying to prove that they met the definition of disability. However, the tribunal now has the power to pay for medical evidence. Since 1 February 1999, where the attendance of medical professionals or the production of medical reports is essential to a case, reasonable costs may be reimbursed by the Employment Tribunals Service subject to the provision of an invoice or other written documentation. There are no limits or fixed rates for reimbursement as the nature of the medical evidence can vary from case to case. However, when determining what is reasonable, the Employment Tribunals Service will be guided by the British Medical Association's Treasury Rates.[1]

Guidance on expert reports

3.25 Advisers will need to be aware that, in the case of *De Keyser Ltd v Miss L Wilson*,[2] the EAT laid down guidance for the use of expert reports. This guidance is, in summary, as follows.

– Careful thought needs to be given before any party embarks upon instructions for expert evidence. It does not follow that because a party wishes such evidence to be admitted, that it will be. Parties

---

1 Under s 5(3) of the Employment Tribunals Act 1996, the Secretary of State has discretion to determine what expenses in connection with a tribunal the Employment Tribunals Service can pay and in February 1999 this was extended to cover medical expenses.
2 EAT No 1438/00, 1 March 2001.

should explore with the employment tribunal at a directions hearing or in correspondence whether, in principle, expert evidence is likely to be acceptable.

– Save where one side or the other has already committed itself to the use of its own expert (which is to be avoided in the absence of special circumstances), the joint instruction of a single expert is the preferred course.

– If a joint expert is to be instructed, the terms which the parties will need to agree will include the expenses and fees of the expert.[1]

– If the means available to one side or another are such that it cannot agree to share or to risk exposure to fees, the other party can reasonably be expected to prefer to require their own expert but the weight to be attached to that evidence may be found to increase if the instructions are submitted to the other side for comment before being finalised and sent to the expert.

– If a joint expert is to be used, tribunals may fix a period within which the parties should agree the expert's identity and the joint letter of instruction and a date by which the report is to be available.

– Any letter of instruction should specify any particular questions for the expert and should avoid partisanship.

– The tribunal may specify that if a joint expert is not agreed by a particular date, the matter should be restored for the tribunal to assist the parties in settling the identity and instructions.

– The tribunal may give formal directions as to the issues to which an expert is or is not to address himself.

– Where there is no joint expert, the tribunal should, where the parties do not agree, specify a timetable for disclosure or exchange of experts' reports and where there are two or more experts, for meetings.

– Any timetable may provide for the raising of supplementary questions with the expert(s) and for the disclosure or exchange of the answers in good time before the hearing.

– Where separate experts are instructed, the tribunal should encourage arrangements for them to meet on a without prejudice basis with a view to their seeking to resolve any conflict between them and, where possible, to their producing and disclosing a schedule of agreed issues and of points of dispute between them.

– If a party fails without good reason to follow these guidelines and if in consequence another party suffers delay or is put to expense which performances of the guidelines would have been likely to avoid, then the tribunal may wish to consider whether there has

---

1   It should be noted that the EAT did not appear to be take account of the tribunal's power to reimburse witness expenses, as referred to in **8.62**.

been unreasonable conduct within the meaning of r 12(1) (as to costs).[1]

The applicant's GP

3.26   In many cases, the applicant's GP may be able to give the most useful evidence about the effect of the applicant's disability on normal day-to-day activities. This is because of all the medical professionals involved the GP is likely to have had the longest and most frequent contact with the applicant. If they have had a good relationship, the applicant is likely to have discussed with the GP the difficulties of carrying out certain normal day-to-day activities. It is also probable that the GP will have provided evidence for any disability benefits claim by the applicant.[2]

Specialists

3.27   The specialist most likely to be able to give useful evidence will be the consultant at the hospital to whom the applicant was referred by the GP. Specialists should be able to give detailed evidence of the type of condition the applicant has, the medication or treatment being taken to control it and the likely prognosis. Most medical experts, however, are reluctant to give prognoses. If this is the case, the specialist should be asked to include in the evidence the reasons for such reluctance. The specialist may be willing to list the range of possible progressions or outcomes in cases such as the applicant's without specifying which is the most likely in the applicant's case.

3.28   Occasionally the applicant's GP or specialist is unhelpful or unwilling to give evidence. If this is the case, there is no point in calling the GP or specialist to give evidence or forcing them to do so by witness summons. If they are unhelpful, the adviser should write to the local hospital to ask for a list of doctors who are specialists in the applicant's condition. Most hospitals will be willing to provide such a list, although some may charge for the information. An independent specialist can then be approached to examine the applicant. That specialist can provide a report or be called to give evidence. Charities specific to the applicant's condition may also be able to refer the adviser to appropriate specialists.

Occupational health physicians

3.29   The employer may have asked for the applicant to be examined by an occupational physician. Although it is possible for the applicant to

---

1   Employment Tribunals (Constitution and Rules of Procedure) Regulations 1993, Sch 1, para 12(1).

2   See **3.39–3.44**.

seek an independent occupational physician's report, in most cases this report will have been obtained by the employer for its own use. It may nevertheless be helpful to the applicant's case and may recommend adjustments.

Advisers should, however, be aware that occupational health physicians will not be specialists in a particular condition or disability. In addition, in a number of cases employers have been criticised for relying on their occupational health physicians.[1]

Occupational health physicians do not always have a good understanding of the DDA 1995 and the need to make reasonable adjustments. The Society of Occupational Medicine has, however, produced guidance on the DDA 1995 for its members.[2]

Physiotherapists

3.30   In certain cases, a statement or report from the applicant's physiotherapist can be very useful. The physiotherapist is more likely than other specialists to be able to give evidence of the effect of the applicant's disability on normal day-to-day activities. If the applicant is not seeing a physiotherapist or if the applicant's physiotherapist is reluctant to give evidence, an independent physiotherapist could be approached. Contact details of independent physiotherapists are available from the Chartered Society of Physiotherapy.[3]

Private or independent medical centres

3.31   Depending on the nature of the applicant's disability, there may be a privately run establishment that provides medical treatment. An example of this is the British Hernia Centre. Such organisations often produce brochures or booklets which may be useful as evidence.

Research papers

3.32   Information on medical research is available from medical journals such as *The Lancet* or from specific disability charities. The easiest way to find information about recent medical developments in the diagnosis and treatment of specific conditions is by carrying out an Internet search. This can provide useful information from trials and research carried out internationally (eg in the United States and

---

1   *Vicary v British Telecommunications plc* [1999] IRLR 680; *Abadeh v British Telecommunications plc* [2001] IRLR 23; *London Borough of Hammersmith and Fulham v Farnsworth* [2000] IRLR 691.

2   See Appendix 1 for address.

3   See Appendix 1 for address.

Australia). There is no reason why the results of such research should not be adduced as medical evidence if they support the applicant's case.

How to obtain a useful written report from a medical practitioner

3.33   An adviser who simply writes to the applicant's GP or specialist asking for a report on the applicant's condition is likely to get only a brief report or letter in return. In many cases, the report will state only how long the applicant has been the patient of that doctor, the name of the condition the applicant has and the treatment being given. This may be no more than a paragraph or two in length and will not be adequate for the tribunal.

3.34   When asking for the report, some advisers send the medical expert the relevant extract from the DDA 1995 or a copy of the Guidance on matters to be taken into account when determining questions relating to the definition of disability. However, a busy medical practitioner may be unlikely to read these and frame the report accordingly. Therefore, advisers need to word their request for a report more carefully. The most effective method is to provide a list of specific questions. An example of such a request for a medical report is set out at the end of this chapter.

3.35   If the medical expert does not answer all the questions or the answers are difficult to understand, the adviser should write back asking the questions again or asking for clarification. The adviser could also telephone the expert to discuss the nature of the case and the type of report needed. This is particularly pertinent if the medical expert is being paid for the report. When all the questions have been answered, the adviser should use the answers given to prepare the final report. The medical expert should then be asked to check, sign and date the report before returning it to the adviser for use at the hearing.

Medical experts as witnesses at the tribunal

3.36   Although oral evidence always carries more weight than written evidence at a tribunal, it is worth taking a few precautions before calling a medical expert as a witness at the hearing. Even though the tribunal will pay reasonable expenses for medical evidence, a medical expert can be an expensive witness. The adviser should try to do the following.

(1)   Check whether the medical expert has given evidence in a court or tribunal before. Some medical experts are frequently asked to do so and therefore are more familiar with the procedure.

(2)   Meet or at least speak to the medical expert to ascertain how well they are likely to perform at the hearing and especially under cross-examination.

(3) Ensure that any consultant is a specialist in the applicant's disability.

(4) Establish the level of seniority of any specialist to be called. The adviser should also try to discover the seniority of any medical expert being called by the respondent and try to match this level of expertise. The tribunal may suggest that the two medical experts meet to agree a single report. In such instances it is particularly important that the adviser feels sure that the applicant's expert will not be so overawed by the seniority or expertise of the respondent's expert as to backtrack from what has previously been said. It should be made clear to the expert that the report should specify in detail not only where the two experts agree but also those areas of disagreement. An agreed report does not have to be one in which both experts agree on everything – it can specify where they have agreed to disagree. If it is not possible to find an expert of the same level or seniority as that of the respondent or one who is not overawed by the respondent's expert, the adviser should try to resist the tribunal's suggestion for an agreed report.

Information from disability organisations

3.37 Some of the disability specific organisations and charities can provide information about particular conditions. It is worthwhile obtaining this information and adding it to the hearing bundle as a supplement to the medical expert's report as it is often in more accessible language.

The World Health Organisation's Classification of Diseases (ICD 10)
3.38 Where the respondent is maintaining that a particular condition is not a disability (as opposed to maintaining that a well-recognised condition does not have a substantial adverse effect on the applicant), advisers should always check to see whether it is recognised by the World Health Organisation (WHO).

Other useful evidence

Disability benefits
3.39 In many cases where the applicant is claiming a disability benefit, it will have been necessary to pass a medical test to show eligibility for that benefit. Although passing this test does not automatically mean that the applicant meets the definition of disability contained in the DDA 1995, it does mean that another tribunal or body has accepted the applicant's medical evidence regarding the disability. This may be persuasive evidence for the employment tribunal. Disability benefits

that an applicant in an employment case might be claiming include disability living allowance (DLA).

Disability living allowance – lower rate care component
3.40   To be eligible for the lower rate care component, a person must either:

–   require in connection with her bodily functions attention from another person for a significant portion of the day (whether during a single period or a number of periods); or
–   be unable to prepare a cooked main meal for herself if she had the ingredients.[1]

3.41   For the first requirement, bodily functions are considered to be breathing, hearing, seeing, eating, drinking, walking, sitting, sleeping, getting in or out of bed, dressing and undressing, going to the toilet, getting in or out of the bath, washing, shaving, communicating, speech practice and help with medication or treatment. Attention means active help from another person, for example someone with back or hand or arm problems might need assistance with such bodily functions.

3.42   The second requirement involves a hypothetical cooking test in which the person must show that she is unable to prepare a traditional, labour-intensive, edible main meal freshly cooked on a traditional cooker (ie not a microwave). To produce such a meal, the person needs to be able to carry out alone all of the physical and mental actions, tasks and stages involved in the process. A person with a severe mental disability which makes it difficult to plan ahead or complete complex tasks is likely to pass this test. A person with the lack of motivation to begin to prepare a meal or complete the preparations because of a mental disability may also pass this test.

3.43   The process of preparing a cooked main meal includes:

–   planning what ingredients to prepare (eg each type of food and seasoning) and the quantities required;
–   carrying out all the stages in the correct order and timings;
–   lifting, carrying, washing, peeling and chopping the ingredients as required;
–   using taps, saucepans, cutlery and utensils;
–   using a cooker (eg lighting the gas, adjusting the heat and opening and closing the oven door);
–   putting the ingredients into pans, stirring, tasting and checking that the food is properly cooked;

---

1   See, generally, Social Security Contributions and Benefits Act 1992.

– lifting and moving full or hot pans on and off the cooker or bending to lift dishes into or out of the oven;
– draining cooked ingredients (eg vegetables, rice, pasta) from hot pans; and
– serving the meal.

These activities are, of course, also normal day-to-day activities and so should be relevant for the purposes of the DDA 1995.

Disability living allowance – higher rate mobility component
3.44 To qualify for the higher rate the person must:

– be unable to walk or virtually unable to walk; or
– use such exertion to walk that it would constitute a danger to that person's life; or
– use such exertion that it would be likely to lead to a serious deterioration in that person's health; or
– be both deaf and blind or have no legs or feet.

These mobility problems may be caused by a physical or mental disability. The test requires that the person be unable to walk and to take unfamiliar routes without supervision. Therefore, a person with a mental health problem may meet this requirement.

The Blue Badge Scheme
3.45 The Blue Badge Scheme of parking concessions (previously known as the Orange Badge[1]) allows people with disabilities to park (subject to some restrictions) close to shops and public buildings without being wheel clamped or receiving parking tickets. To be eligible for a Blue Badge, the person must be aged 2 or over and:

– receive the higher rate mobility component of disability living allowance (see **3.41**); or
– be in receipt of the war pensioners' mobility supplement; or
– use a vehicle supplied by a government department or be in receipt of a grant towards the running of her own car; or
– be registered blind; or
– drive regularly and have such a severe disability in both arms that the person cannot turn a steering wheel by hand (even if the wheel is fitted with a turning knob); or

---

1   In April 2000, the Orange Badge was replaced by the new European Blue Badge. However, the new design did not change the parking concessions in Britain or the eligibility requirements.

– have 'a permanent and substantial disability which causes inability to walk or very considerable difficulty in walking' (obviously, this is the condition most likely to have been fulfilled by an applicant with a claim under the DDA 1995 where the disability is in dispute).

Registration – The Green Card

3.46 The DDA 1995 repealed large sections of the Disabled Persons (Employment) Act (DP(E)A) 1944, including the sections establishing a register for 'occupationally handicapped' persons. However, people who were registered under the DP(E)A 1944 were deemed by the DDA 1995 to have been disabled for a period of 3 years from 2 December 1996, which was when the employment provisions of the DDA 1995 came into force, provided that they had been on the register on 12 January 1995. As the 3-year period expired on 2 December 1999, however, registration under the DP(E)A 1944 will no longer mean that the applicant is deemed to be disabled for the purposes of the DDA 1995. The registration, however, may still be used as additional evidence of the applicant's disability.

3.47 Some local authorities still maintain a register of disabled people within their area. This may entitle the person so registered to some local benefits such as concessionary rates of travel on local transport. Once again, this may be used as evidence of the applicant's disability.

Evidence from the applicant's partner, spouse, relative or friend

3.48 Some applicants may be unwilling to accept the extent to which their disability affects normal day-to-day activities. It may be sensible in these instances to speak to someone who has close everyday contact with the applicant with a view to that person giving evidence at the hearing. Remember that such a witness may be able to give evidence both about the effect of the applicant's disability on normal day-to-day activities and, where appropriate, on the effect of the discriminatory acts on the applicant's emotional and home life which may be relevant for calculating compensation.

AN EXAMPLE OF A WITNESS STATEMENT FOR A PRELIMINARY HEARING ON DISABILITY

3.49   In The Employment Tribunal   Case Number: 5678/1999

Between

David Joseph   Applicant

and

Readymade Limited   Respondent

Statement of David Joseph

I David Joseph of 27 Pinkerton Avenue, Manchester make this statement which to the best of my belief and knowledge is true:

(1)   I have been diagnosed as having a bilateral direct inguinal hernia or a double groin hernia. A hernia is a rupture usually noticed as a lump in the groin or umbilical region. It appears when a portion of the tissue which lines the abdominal cavity breaks through a weakened area of the abdominal wall. I have been told that if the hernia enlarges, a piece of intestine may become trapped and the hernia will become strangulated.

(2)   In 1988, I was told during a BUPA health check that there were signs indicating the likely development of an inguinal hernia on the right-hand side. I then began to experience groin aches if I remained in a standing position for any length of time, lifted a heavy shopping bag or stretched on to tiptoes.

(3)   In September 1995, I applied for a job with Healthway Ltd, as a pharmaceutical sales representative. I had to have an examination prior to my employment being confirmed, and this examination was carried out by Dr Patel, a GP appointed by Healthway Ltd to examine me. He drew my attention to evidence of my hernia, in the form of a bulge. He advised me to urinate when necessary in a sitting position and to avoid straining. He passed me as fit to work and I worked for Healthway Ltd from September 1995 to December 1998, when I was offered the position with Readymade Ltd.

(4)   In the autumn of 1995 I experienced a particularly painful episode at work when I had to walk approximately 500 to 600 yards. I felt a crippling pain in the lower right abdomen that was so acute that initially I believed that I had appendicitis. There were no other symptoms of appendicitis but the bulge, which Dr Patel had drawn to my attention, had grown larger. The pain subsided after a day and so I did not see my doctor.

(5)   Since that episode I often experience pain but it is only occasionally acute, debilitating pain. This may be because I try to avoid any activity that is likely to bring on such acute pain such as stretching, bending or carrying heavy objects. I have, for example, stopped going to the gym where I used to exercise three to four times a week, because it is too painful. The usual pattern at present is for me to feel relatively little effect in the first half of the day but for the discomfort to grow to a dull but steady ache by the afternoon and evening.

(6)   I cannot stand or walk for more than an hour or carry or move objects heavier than a light shopping bag without experiencing pain. I also cannot stretch upwards, for example to a high shelf or cupboard, without pain. I try not to kneel or squat down or run. I often have to place my hand over the right-hand swelling to ease the pain and counter the feeling of outward pressure and I do this when climbing stairs or reaching upwards or carrying a shopping bag in my left hand. In one room in my flat I have full-length curtains which I cannot draw without experiencing pain. I have to draw them with one hand while 'holding' the bulge at my groin with the other hand. I also have a cylinder vacuum cleaner, which I can only use with one hand as the other has to be placed over the bulge to try to ease the pain. All these activities are more painful towards the end of the day and so I try to carry them out in the mornings when the pain is less acute.

(7)   I did not consult a doctor again about my hernia until December 1998 when I moved house to a new neighbourhood and had to register with a new GP. At the initial check-up with my new GP, Dr McLeod, I mentioned the increasing discomfort and persistent groin ache. Dr McLeod examined me and recommended that I be referred to a surgeon for hernia repair. Dr McLeod advised me that the hernia should be repaired before it developed to a point where a piece of intestine became trapped inside the hernia and it became what is known as strangulated. She indicated that my hernia would progress in this manner and if a repair were not carried out there was a likelihood that emergency surgery would be necessary when the hernia became strangulated.

(8)   On 29 March 1999 I had an appointment at the British Hernia Centre with a senior consultant surgeon, Mr Jonathan Davies. Mr Davies examined me and described the procedure that he recommends to repair hernias which is outlined in his letter of the same date. Mr Davies favours the method of prosthetic mesh repair, which involves a piece of fine polypropylene mesh being inserted inside the abdominal wall to reinforce it. The British

Hernia Centre maintains that there is less risk of the hernia recurring by using this method rather than the traditional method of stitching the abdominal wall. The prosthetic mesh repair procedure and the more traditional methods of repair are described in more detail in the booklet produced by the British Hernia Centre and in the paper by the National Ambulatory Hernia Institute. The British Hernia Centre is, however, a private clinic which specialises in hernia repair and I cannot afford to have my hernia repaired there by Mr Davies.

(9) On 13 May 1999 I had a hospital assessment appointment with the surgeon, Mr Crawshaw, to whom Dr McLeod had referred me. Mr Crawshaw confirmed that my hernia should be repaired because it was likely to get larger, as had already happened, and result in the obstruction or strangulation of the intestine which can be life threatening and would require a major surgical operation. Mr Crawshaw placed me on a waiting list, currently 18 months,[1] for in-patient surgery to effect a bilateral repair. He too favours using the prosthetic polypropylene mesh method, which may now be available on the National Health Service.

(10) My GP, Dr McLeod, and the two specialists I have seen, Mr Davies and Mr Crawshaw, have all indicated that the hernia I have is progressive in nature. I have experienced increasing discomfort and pain since 1995 when I first became aware of the hernia on the right-hand side to the point that some of my day-to-day activities, such as vacuuming, drawing curtains, reaching high shelves and walking up and down stairs, are now affected. I understand that if hernias are not treated they may become life-threatening conditions.

(11) The treatment recommended by Mr Davies and Mr Crawshaw and in papers I have found on the Internet such as that by AW Robbins and IM Rutkow at the Hernia Centre in New Jersey, USA, involve the use of what is described by them as a prosthetic mesh to reinforce the abdominal wall. I also understand, however, that this treatment may fail and that I may need a further operation at a later date to re-repair the hernia. The British Hernia Centre claim that the recurrence rate for hernias repaired by their surgeons is less than 1%, but that there are recurrence rates of 10% to 20% elsewhere. Their booklet states that where a hernia repair operation is unsuccessful, further repair operations are more

---

1   The NHS waiting list of 18 months is likely to mean that even if Mr Joseph's hernia had not had a substantial adverse effect for 12 months at the date of the act of discrimination, it is likely to do so for 12 months if it is not found to be progressive.

difficult and the chances of success will diminish with each successive attempt at repair. I have multiple hernias which means that the operation I need will be more complex. The British Hernia Centre booklet describes in detail complications that may arise in hernia repair and recurrence rates.

3.50   This example shows that applicants with conditions, such as a hernia, which may not appear at first to be a disability may nevertheless meet the definition of disability when questioned closely about the effect on normal day-to-day activities.

CASE STUDIES

SAMPLE CONSULTANT'S LETTER OF INSTRUCTION IN THE CASE OF DAVID JOSEPH

To Mr Crawshaw
Westland Hospital
Westland
Manchester

Dear Mr Crawshaw,

Re: Mr David Joseph, 27 Pinkerton Avenue, Manchester M9 8LD
Date of birth: 14/06/50

I am acting on behalf of the above-named client in respect of his claim of disability discrimination. He applied for employment and, although he was initially offered the job, it was subsequently withdrawn as a result of the employer discovering that he had a hernia. I understand that Mr Joseph has been under your care for treatment of his hernia. I have enclosed a signed authority by which Mr Joseph authorises you to communicate with me and to release any necessary documents to me.

In order to succeed in a claim under the Disability Discrimination Act 1995, Mr Joseph must first show that he is disabled for the purposes of the Act. The Act has a very specific – but potentially quite wide – definition of disability, and, essentially, I must show that Mr Joseph's hernia has a substantial adverse effect on his ability to carry out normal day-to-day activities.[1]

I would be most grateful if you would provide me with details of the following:

– what a hernia is;
– when Mr Joseph was first diagnosed with the hernia;
– whether or not the condition is progressive, and if so, how;
– the effect upon Mr Joseph of his hernia, if this is something of which you are aware;
– whether someone with a hernia might feel pain or discomfort when walking up and down stairs, drawing curtains, vacuuming or reaching high shelves;

---

1   Advisers may also wish to include the relevant points from the Guidance, eg concerning mobility. Where little is known about a client's condition, however, it is advisable not to provide narrow instructions for the consultant, so that they can give as much useful information as possible.

—   the treatment available for a hernia;
—   the length of time Mr Joseph is likely to have to wait for such treatment; and
—   the prognosis if Mr Joseph were not to have any treatment.

I appreciate that providing the above information may be time-consuming, but your assistance in this matter will be invaluable. If you wish to discuss any matter contained in this letter, please do not hesitate to call me on my direct line: 09765 43210.

I look forward to hearing from you, at your earliest convenience.

Yours sincerely,

S. Jones
Advice Worker

Chapter 4

THE QUESTIONNAIRE

SIGNIFICANCE OF THE QUESTIONNAIRE

4.1 The existence of the questionnaire for discrimination cases in general acknowledges the unique nature of such cases; they can be very difficult to win, irrespective of their merits and often require the extra information that questionnaires can elicit. Therefore, the questions procedure, or questionnaire as it is more commonly known, is a crucial part of any discrimination case.

4.2 The DDA 1995, like the SDA 1975 and RRA 1976, allows applicants to serve questions on a respondent or potential respondent, with the answers being admissible in evidence at any tribunal hearing. The questionnaire can provide extremely useful information not only to support a case but, in the very initial stages, to determine whether or not to bring a case at all. It can also identify where matters of fact are in dispute.

4.3 Although respondents do not have to answer the questionnaire, if they do not do so within a reasonable time, or if they provide evasive answers to the questions posed, the tribunal can draw appropriate inferences at the tribunal hearing. This could prove decisive where a case is finely balanced.[1]

4.4 In the case of *King v Great Britain China Centre*,[2] a case which advisers may be familiar with in relation to proof in discrimination cases, the Court of Appeal stated:

> '(2) It is important to bear in mind that it is unusual to find direct evidence of racial discrimination. Few employers will be prepared to admit such discrimination, even to themselves. In some cases, the discrimination will

---

1   The Government's response to the Task Force recommendations propose to extend the time-limit from 3 weeks to 4 weeks within which a disabled person may issue a questionnaire following a complaint being made to a tribunal. It also proposes to limit the period for the alleged discriminator to respond to such a questionnaire to 8 weeks and tribunals will be required to draw inferences about failure to reply to a questionnaire.

2   [1991] IRLR 513, [1992] ICR 516, CA.

not be ill intentioned but merely based on an assumption "he or she would not have fitted in".

(3) The outcome of the case will therefore usually depend on what inferences it is proper to draw from the primary facts found by the tribunal. These inferences can include, in appropriate cases, any inferences that it is just and equitable to draw in accordance with s 65(2)(b) of the 1976 Act from an evasive or equivocal reply to a questionnaire.'

4.5   The case of *Virdee v ECC Quarries Ltd*[1] concerned a claim for racial discrimination following the applicant's two unsuccessful applications for a position. The industrial tribunal (as it was then called) held that the respondent's failure to answer all but one of nine questions put to it by the applicant under s 65(1) of the RRA 1976 constituted an 'evasive' reply within the meaning of s 65(2)(b). As the respondent's manager had read and understood s 65 before replying, the tribunal concluded that the evasion must have been deliberate and that it would be just and equitable to draw the inference that the respondent had unlawfully discriminated against the applicant in its selection arrangements.

4.6   In addition, any discrepancies between responses in the questionnaire, the Notice of Appearance,[2] and the witness evidence can be used to undermine the respondent's case.[3]

THE RELEVANT LAW

4.7   Section 56 of the DDA 1995 introduces the concept of the questions procedure, and provides for it to be admissible as evidence:

'(1) For the purposes of this section –

(a)   a person who considers that he may have been discriminated against, in contravention of any provision of Part II, is referred to as "the complainant"; and

(b)   a person against whom the complainant may decide to make, or has made, a complaint under Part II is referred to as "the respondent".

(2) The Secretary of State shall, with a view to helping the complainant to decide whether to make a complaint against the respondent and, if he

---

1   [1978] IRLR 295.
2   Often known as an IT3 or, since the change of name from Industrial Tribunal to Employment Tribunal, ET3.
3   See also *Berry v Bethlem and Maudsley NHS Trust* 21 November 1996, EAT No 478/95 and *Hinks v Riva Systems and Lumsden* 22 November 1996, EAT No 501/96, both EOR DCLD No 31 Spring 1997.

does so, to formulate and present his case in the most effective manner, by order prescribe –

(a) forms by which the complainant may question the respondent on his reasons for doing any relevant act, or on any other matter which is or may be relevant; and

(b) forms by which the respondent may if he so wishes reply to any questions.

(3) Where the complainant questions the respondent in accordance with forms prescribed by an order under subsection (2) –

(a) the question, and any reply by the respondent (whether in accordance with such an order or not), shall be admissible as evidence in any proceedings under Part II;

(b) if it appears to the tribunal in any such proceedings –

(i) that the respondent deliberately, and without reasonable excuse, omitted to reply within a reasonable period, or

(ii) that the respondent's reply is evasive or equivocal,

it may draw any inference which it considers it just and reasonable to draw, including an inference that the respondent has contravened a provision of Part II.

(4) The Secretary of State may by order prescribe –

(a) the period within which such questions must be duly served in order to be admissible under subsection (3)(a); and

(b) the manner in which a question, and any reply by the respondent, may be duly served.

(5) This section is without prejudice to any other enactment or rule of law regulating interlocutory and preliminary matters in proceedings before an industrial tribunal, and has effect subject to any enactment or rule of law regulating the admissibility of evidence in such proceedings.'

WHEN TO SERVE THE QUESTIONNAIRE

4.8 Section 56 of the DDA 1995 was supplemented by the Disability Discrimination (Questions and Replies) Order 1996,[1] which provides for the questions procedure to be implemented and specifies the requirements to be met for the procedure to be valid and so admissible as evidence in the tribunal proceedings. In order for the questions to be admissible, the questionnaire has to be served on the respondent:

– where a complaint has not yet been made to the tribunal, within 3 months of the alleged act of discrimination; or

– where an application has already been submitted to the tribunal, within 21 days of the application being received by the tribunal; or

---

1   SI 1996/2793.

–   where it has been served with leave of the tribunal, within the period specified by that tribunal.[1]

4.9   It is preferable to serve the questionnaire prior to issuing the tribunal proceedings, in order to gather as much information as possible, so as to fully inform the claim. In addition, the questions and replies can be submitted to the tribunal along with the originating application. It may be tactically advantageous for an applicant to put his name to a questionnaire, rather than the adviser. By doing so, it is possible that the questions will be dealt with by the respondent itself and not its legal advisers, who may be less forthcoming with responses. Whether or not to do this will depend on the size of the company and whether or not it has, in any event, an in-house legal team to deal with such matters.

4.10   However, it will not always be possible to serve the questionnaire in advance of the tribunal application, as the client may have only reached an adviser at a comparatively late stage. In this case, it should be sent to the respondent at the same time as the originating application is submitted.

WHAT IF THE QUESTIONNAIRE IS OUT OF TIME?

4.11   There may be cases where a client approaches an adviser at a comparatively late stage in the proceedings, and after the 21-day time-limit has expired.

4.12   Where a complaint has been made to a tribunal and the time-limit has expired, the applicant can ask the tribunal for leave to serve a questionnaire. In such a case, the adviser will need to send a written application for leave to the secretary of the tribunal. This should state the name of the applicant and the name of the respondent and set out the grounds for the application. It may be persuasive to argue that the questions procedure is likely to expedite the case and save time, as tribunals are particularly concerned with effective case management. It is also vital to include the proposed questions to be sent to the respondent.

4.13   In *Williams v Greater London Citizens Advice Bureau,*[2] a case under the RRA 1976, at a directions hearing the applicant had requested leave to serve an RRA 1976 questionnaire out of time. Leave was refused on the ground that no satisfactory explanation had been given for the

1   Disabilty Discrimination (Questions and Replies) Order 1996, art 3.
2   [1989] ICR 545.

failure to serve the questionnaire within the prescribed period when leave would not have been required. The EAT held that having regard to the fact that no explanation had been given to the industrial tribunal for the late application, and no copy of the proposed questionnaire had been placed before it, the industrial tribunal was entitled to exercise its discretion and refuse leave; and that, in the circumstances, the tribunal's decision would be upheld.

4.14   If the tribunal gives leave to serve a questionnaire, it will specify the time within which the questionnaire should be served.

THE QUESTIONNAIRE ITSELF

Format

4.15   The Department for Education and Employment (DfEE) has produced a questionnaire[1] which is similar to those provided for sex and racial discrimination cases. The use of this form is not compulsory – so long as the main provisions specified in the Disability Discrimination (Questions and Replies) Order 1996 are met, a letter will suffice. The Order specifies that the questions may be served on the respondent by:

– delivering it to him or by sending it by post to him at his usual or last known residence or place of business; or
– where the person to be served is acting by a solicitor, by delivering it at or by sending it by post to the solicitor's address for service; or
– where the person to be served is a body corporate or is a trade union or employers' association within the meaning of the Trade Union and Labour Relations (Consolidation) Act 1992, by delivering it to the secretary or clerk of the body, union or association at its registered or principal office or by sending it by post to the secretary or clerk at that office.

Alternative formats

4.16   Whilst the questions procedure booklet is available in alternative formats (tape and Braille), the guidance contained in the booklet points out that applicants would be advised to serve the standard printed questionnaire on the respondent because:

– the tribunal is likely to insist on submission in a standard format (although it may well be open to challenge under s 19(1)(b) of the DDA 1995 if it does so); and

---

1   This form is set out in Schs 1 and 2 to the Disability Discrimination (Questions and Replies) Order 1996, art 2.

–   perhaps more importantly, the respondent may have a reasonable excuse for not responding to the questionnaire if it is served in a format it cannot access. This may not apply if the applicant generally communicates with the respondent in another format, but it may still be wise to send an additional copy in a written format.

4.17   However, it is usually easier to use the questionnaires provided by the DfEE, with additional pages inserted for questions which will overrun the space provided. This chapter considers the questionnaire as provided by the DfEE.

COMPLETING THE QUESTIONNAIRE

The respondent

4.18   The first thing to be completed is the name and address of the respondent. If the respondent is a limited company or other corporate body, the documents should be sent or delivered to the secretary or clerk at the registered or principal office of the organisation. If this address is unknown, it can be found in a variety of ways:

–   the local library may have details of the registered or principal office;
–   Companies House will be able to provide the details of the registered office of a limited company; or
–   the address of the registered or head office will often be found on the bottom of headed notepaper.

4.19   If the registered office cannot be found, advisers will have to send the documents to the place where they think it is most likely that they will reach the secretary or clerk (eg care of the company's local office). If advisers know that the respondent is acting through a solicitor, the documents can be sent directly to the solicitor.

Question 2

4.20   Having completed the applicant's details, paragraph 2 requires a description of the factual details of the complaint, including the dates when the relevant incidents occurred. As advisers should already have a detailed statement from the client, it would be advisable to put either the full or an abridged version of what it is proposed be submitted as paragraph 11 of the originating application to the tribunal.[1] This

---

1   Often known as an IT1 or, since the change of name from industrial tribunal to employment tribunal, ET1. See Chapter 5 for details of this.

ensures both that there is consistency on the part of the applicant and that the respondent's response covers the issues that are likely to arise in the tribunal hearing.

Question 3

4.21 Paragraph 3 of the questionnaire states: 'I consider this treatment or failure on your part may have been unlawful because . . .'. The guidance accompanying the questionnaire suggests that this paragraph gives the applicant an opportunity to identify any legal issues between the applicant and the respondent. However, this phrase does not have to be completed, and the general view is that, rather than tying oneself to a particular legal argument before having seen the respondent's reply, it is advisable merely to delete 'because' and to leave this section blank.

Questions 4 and 5

4.22 Paragraphs 4 and 5 contain standard questions asking for the respondent's view of the information contained in paragraph 2 and for any justification under the DDA 1995 for any discriminatory treatment. These can be left unchanged.

Question 6

4.23 Paragraph 6 is perhaps the most important section in the questionnaire. It allows the applicant to ask any question that may help to obtain relevant information for the discrimination case. There are a number of fairly standard questions which can usefully be asked in disability discrimination cases, as well as specific questions based on the applicant's circumstances and the treatment that the applicant was subjected to. These are detailed below. They are not in any way compulsory and are intended only as guidance. Applicants can ask any questions provided they are relevant; if they are not, the respondent is unlikely to answer them and it may undermine the rest of the questions asked.

Standard questions and requests for paragraph 6 in all cases
- How many employees does the respondent have?
- How many of these employees are disabled?
- What positions do those with disabilities hold?
- How many of these employees have [*insert specific disability of client*]?

–   What positions do these disabled employees hold?
–   Does the respondent have an equal opportunities policy? If so, please provide a copy.
–   Does the respondent have a specific disability policy? If so, please provide a copy.
–   What steps has the respondent taken to ensure that the DDA 1995 has been complied with? Please provide details and provide copies of any relevant documentation.[1]
–   What training has been given to staff on the provisions of the DDA 1995? What did the training consist of and when did it take place? Please provide copies of any training materials used.
–   What training did those involved in the management/recruitment of the applicant[2] [*specify names if possible*] have in the provisions of the DDA 1995? What did this training consist of and when did it take place? Please provide copies of any of the materials used.
–   What statement is made in the annual report about the employment of disabled employees? Please provide a copy of the statement.[3]
–   Has the respondent been the subject of any claims of disability discrimination before an employment tribunal? If so, please detail how many, when and what the outcome was.

Standard questions and requests in a recruitment case (including adjustments to the recruitment process)
–   Where was the post advertised?
–   Please provide a copy of the job description, person specification and all materials provided to applicants for the post.

---

1   Some sectors, such as the NHS, will have issued guidance as to how to implement the DDA 1995, both in relation to employment and goods, facilities and services. If the respondent belongs to such a sector, the adviser can request a copy of any such guidance issued, and, if they do not have it, try to obtain it from other sources, as it may be useful in cross-examination.
2   Or complainant if the tribunal application has not yet been issued.
3   This will be relevant where there are more than 250 employees. The Companies Act 1985, Sch 7, para 9 provides that where the average number of persons employed by the company in each week during the financial year exceeded 250, the directors' report must contain a statement describing such policy as the company has applied during the financial year for giving full and fair consideration to applications for employment by the company made by disabled persons; for continuing the employment of and for arranging appropriate training for, employees of the company who have become disabled persons during the period when they were employed by the company; and otherwise for the training, career development and promotion of disabled persons employed by the company.

–   In what alternative formats was this information available to the applicant?
–   What reasonable adjustments to the recruitment process were considered for the applicant?
–   How many applications were received?
–   How many of those applications were from disabled people?
–   Does the respondent monitor disability? If so, how?
–   How many of the applicants had [*insert specific disability*]?
–   How many people were shortlisted?
–   How many of those shortlisted were disabled?
–   How many of those shortlisted had [*insert specific disability*]?
–   Please provide copies of all application forms (with personal details such as name and address blanked out if necessary) used by those shortlisting.
–   What were the qualifications and experience of those shortlisted? Please indicate which are the application forms of those shortlisted.
–   Who was involved in the shortlisting process?
–   Please provide notes made in the course of shortlisting.
–   Did those involved in the shortlisting process have training in the DDA 1995 and its application?
–   If so, please state when each person had such training, what the training consisted of, and please provide copies of the training materials used. Please also provide the same information in relation to any equal opportunities training provided.
–   Who was involved in the interview process? If not the same people as involved in the shortlisting, did they have training in the DDA 1995 and its application? If so, please state when each person had such training, what the training consisted of and provide copies of training materials used. Please also provide the same information in relation to any equal opportunities training provided.
–   What system was used to determine the successful candidate? Please provide copies of notes made during the interview process.
–   Who was appointed to the post and what qualifications and experience did that person have?
–   Did any reasonable adjustments have to be made for the person appointed to the post?
–   Was the decision to appoint unanimous? If not, who dissented and why?
–   In what way did the applicant not meet the required elements for the job?
–   What reasonable adjustments were considered for the applicant to enable him to carry out the duties of the job?

Standard questions and requests in a case involving failure to make reasonable adjustments[1]

- What was the organisation's income or company's profits for the last financial year? Please provide a copy of the annual accounts.[2]
- Which outside organisations were contacted in relation to making reasonable adjustments? When was this contact made, with whom and what was the outcome?
- Was any contact made with [*insert name of disability specific charity*]? If so, when and with what staff member? What was the outcome of the contact?
- Was any contact made with the Disability Employment Adviser or Disability Services Team?
- What other posts were considered for the applicant?
- Was consideration given to transferring [*insert details of the parts of the job the applicant cannot do*] to another worker?

Standard questions and requests where health and safety is alleged to be an issue

- What risk assessments were carried out in relation to the applicant? When were they carried out and by whom? Please provide a copy of the assessments.
- Were any outside bodies, such as [*insert disability specific organisation*], contacted to look at the particular risks in light of the applicant's specific disability? If not, why not?
- What reasonable adjustments were considered to deal with any issues raised in the risk assessment?
- What health and safety policies does the respondent have? Please provide copies of these.
- Was the Health & Safety Executive contacted in relation to the applicant?

Standard questions and requests in a (non-redundancy) termination of contract case (including ill health retirement)

- How many days off sick did the applicant take in [*state relevant period*]?
- How many days off sick did other members of the department in which the applicant worked take in [*same period*]?
- What is the average level of sickness absence for all employees?

---

1   Advisers may wish to insert questions about specific adjustments requested (eg adjustments to a piece of equipment).

2   Advisers may also wish to ask for details of profits throughout the applicant's time with the respondent.

– How is sickness absence recorded and is disability related absence recorded separately?
– Is there a sickness absence policy? If so, please provide a copy.
– Is sick leave paid for all employees and, if so, at what rate and for what period?
– Is there a disability leave policy? If so, please provide a copy.
– Was the applicant referred to an occupational health physician? If so, please provide details and a copy of any subsequent report.
– Were medical reports sought from the applicant's GP/consultant? If so, please provide copies.
– Was a Disability Employment Adviser contacted in connection with the applicant?
– Were any outside organisations contacted in respect of the applicant and, if so, which ones and when; and what was the outcome of this contact?
– Is there a redeployment policy? If so, please provide a copy.
– Was the applicant considered for any alternative vacancies?
– How many vacancies were there within the organisation within [*state relevant period*]?
– How was the applicant notified of these vacancies and by whom?
– What reasonable adjustments were considered for the applicant to enable him to meet the criteria for appointment to these vacancies?
– Who recommended the applicant for ill health retirement, when and on what basis was this recommendation made? Please provide a copy of the ill health retirement policy/scheme.[1]

Standard questions and requests in a redundancy case
– What consultation took place on the proposed redundancy with employees and/or their representatives?
– Who was involved in drawing up the redundancy procedure applied in this case?
– Please specify details of the equal opportunities training received by those involved in drawing up the procedure including training on the DDA 1995 and provide copies of materials used.
– What criteria were applied?
– In what way did the applicant not meet the criteria for being retained in employment?
– Who was involved in the decision to terminate by reason of redundancy? Please provide notes of meetings regarding the decision to make the applicant redundant.

---

1 Advisers should ask questions regarding any specific reasonable adjustments which may have been appropriate or required by the particular applicant, for example working from home or part-time working.

- What consideration was given to alternative employment?
- Who else was made redundant? Please provide details of why those people were made redundant.
- Were any of those made redundant disabled? If so, how many were disabled and what were their disabilities?
- Were any of the others selected for redundancy redeployed?

Standard questions and requests in a harassment case
- What policy does the respondent have to deal with disability harassment? If there is no such policy, why not?
- How was this policy implemented in relation to the applicant?
- How many allegations of harassment have been made against the respondent in the last 5 years?
- How many of these allegations involved (a) race, (b) sex, and (c) disability?
- How were these allegations dealt with and what was the outcome of the investigatory procedure in each case?

SERVING THE QUESTIONNAIRE

4.24   The questionnaire should be sent to the respondent, at its registered office (see **4.18**) as soon as possible after the client has contacted the adviser. It should be either delivered by hand or posted (using special delivery), to ensure that there is proof of the respondent having received it.

4.25   While it is desirable to have a response prior to submitting the ET1, this is not always possible. However, it is always worth submitting a questionnaire whatever the stage of the process (see **4.11–4.14**).

4.26   Respondents will need to be given a 'reasonable' time in which to respond.[1] The Disability Discrimination (Questions and Replies) Order 1996 does not state what is considered as 'reasonable', but the general practice is to allow between 14 and 21 days, depending on how much information is requested. Advisers should send the questionnaire with a covering letter, drawing the respondent's attention to s 56 of the DDA 1995 and reminding them that the tribunal can draw adverse inferences from either their failure to answer the questionnaire within the reasonable time allowed or any evasive answers. If the respondent requires additional time, it should write to the applicant's representative to indicate that it will not be possible to respond by the date requested, but that a response will be forthcoming within a specified

---

1   See **4.3** at footnote 1.

number of days. Advisers should diarise dates for reply and send reminder letters. These can be used at the tribunal hearing as evidence of the respondent's unwillingness to reply and the tribunal can be requested to draw an adverse inference from this.

THE RESPONDENT'S RESPONSE

4.27   Once a response has been received from the respondent, advisers will need to study this carefully and take their client's instructions on it. If there are any evasive or equivocal answers, or questions which have not been answered at all, advisers can either:

–   write to the respondent to advise that if it does not provide answers/clear answers, its lack of response/evasive response will be drawn to the attention of the tribunal, and that the tribunal will be invited to draw an adverse inference from this; or
–   if proceedings have not been issued or if the applicant is still within 21 days of having issued the ET1, serve a supplemental question-naire (there is nothing to prevent any number of questionnaires being served upon the respondent, provided that they are served within the time-limit).

4.28   Finally, although respondents cannot be compelled to respond to the questionnaire, if they do not respond, some of the questions asked may be asked again under the questions procedure provided for the Tribunal rules.[1]

---

1   Employment Tribunals (Constitution and Rules of Procedure) Regulations 1993, Sch 1, para 4(3)). See Chapter 6 for further details.

CASE STUDIES

CONTENTS OF THE QUESTIONNAIRE

Rajesh Mistry sends you the following statement. He would like your advice on what he should put in his questionnaire at Question 6.

Statement of Rajesh Mistry

(1) I am Rajesh Mistry of 79 Astor Close, Ealing, London. I am 55 years old. I have had a visual impairment since birth and am registered blind, although I can see shadows. I prefer to read in Braille. I am fully mobile, walking with the aid of a long cane.

(2) I have a degree in music and a certificate in Education. I have been a fully qualified teacher for 21 years and have taught in a variety of primary schools in and around Liverpool. For the last 6½ years I was a music teacher at a school in Liverpool.

(3) At the beginning of this year, the school made a number of cuts in various teaching budgets and I was made redundant. I looked for similar employment in a variety of locations. The post of music co-ordinator for which I applied was advertised in the *Times Educational Supplement* in February. I get this and other newspapers on tape. I requested an application form which I received together with a job description and a person specification. The job was paying £30,000 per year. I believed that I had all the qualifications and experience requested for the post and so I completed the application form on my word processor. However, I deleted the part of the form which asked if I had any disabilities. I did not believe it to be necessary to answer this question because I did not need any adjustments to be made for me at the interview.

(4) I was shortlisted for the post and was invited for interview on 12 March. I travelled to the interview alone. I was shown into the interview room and to a chair by the receptionist. The head teacher of the school, Andrew Holden, who was chairing the interview, greeted me but he did not introduce me to any of the other panel members. I was aware that there were other people in the room so I asked Mr Holden politely if I could know who else was in the room. Mr Holden started to give me the names of the other three panel members, so I asked if they would introduce themselves to me so that I could get a better impression of who they were and where they were sitting. Mr Holden agreed to my request, but I thought from the tone of his voice that he was irritated.

(5) During the interview the panel members acknowledged that I was extremely well qualified for the post. One of the panel members, Mrs Alison Martin, asked how I would deal with the level of paperwork involved with the post of music co-ordinator. She remarked that unlike a music teacher, as the music co-ordinator my job would involve planning the music curriculum for the whole year and preparing and checking lesson plans. I would also be expected to prepare reports about the provision of music teaching within the school on a regular basis. I started to explain that I used a personal computer with specialist software for music and a Braille embosser as well as a personal assistant/reader, but Mr Holden interrupted me by saying that the school's resources would not stretch to the cost of such equipment. I went on to explain that I personally owned some of the necessary equipment and that the Access To Work Scheme part funds the rest and the personal assistant/reader.

(6) At the end of the interview, Mr Holden told me that they would be writing to all the candidates being interviewed within the next 2 weeks. I asked if I could be informed by telephone or tape. I was not telephoned, but 2 weeks later received a letter from Mr Holden informing me that I had been unsuccessful for the post. I telephoned the school and was put through to Mr Holden's secretary. She was a little impatient with me and said that Mr Holden was a difficult man to get hold of and then she said he was just a difficult man generally. I left a message asking him to call me but when he did not do so I wrote to ask him why I had been unsuccessful. I received a letter from his secretary a week later saying that Mr Holden would be out of the country during the Easter break.

(7) I believe that the reasons why I was unsuccessful for the post were all related to my disability. I believe that the panel members were surprised when they realised that I had a visual impairment and that the Chair of the interview panel, Mr Holden, was irritated by my request that the other panel members introduce themselves to me. This influenced the way in which he conducted the interview. I also believe that Mr Holden thought that I would be a financial burden on the school and would not be able to deal with all the paperwork involved with the job.

Question 6 of the questionnaire in the case of *Raj Mistry v Whitemoor Primary School and Andrew Holden*

(1) Why was the complainant not successful in his application for the post of music co-ordinator?

(2) Please provide copies of the job description and person specification for the post of music co-ordinator for which the complainant applied.

(3) Who was appointed to this post?

(4) Please give details of the qualifications and experience of the successful candidate.

(5) How many people were shortlisted for this post?

(6) Please provide details of the qualifications and experience of each candidate shortlisted.

(7) How many people shortlisted for the post had a disability?

(8) What was the nature of their disability?

(9) Please provide a copy of the application forms for each shortlisted candidate which each interviewer had.

(10) Please give the name, position and status of each person on the interview panel.

(11) Was the panel decision to appoint the successful candidate unanimous? If not, please specify who dissented and why?

(12) Whose decision was it to appoint the successful candidate and what is his or her position and status?

(13) What criteria were used to judge candidates for the post?

(14) Did each panel member make notes about each candidate? If so, please supply copies of these notes.

(15) Why was the complainant notified that he had not been successful for the post in writing?

(16) Please give details of the equal opportunities training received by each member of the interview panel.

(17) Please specify which aspects of the Disability Discrimination Act 1995 were covered in the equal opportunities training. Please also supply copies of the training materials.

(18) What steps have been taken to implement the provisions of the Disability Discrimination Act 1995 and when were these taken?

(19) How many people with disabilities are employed by the school and what are their positions and status?

(20) How many people with a visual impairment are employed by the school and what are their positions and status?

(21) What steps does the school take to ascertain how many of its employees have a disability?

(22) Does the school have an equal opportunities policy? If so, please supply a copy.

(23) Does the school have a recruitment and selection policy? If so, was this policy followed? If not, why not? Please provide a copy of the policy.

(24) Does the school have a disability policy? If so, please provide a copy.

Chapter 5

THE ORIGINATING APPLICATION

TIME-LIMITS

5.1 A complaint of disability discrimination under Part II of the DDA 1995 must be presented to the employment tribunal within 3 months[1] of the date of the act complained of. However, a tribunal may consider a complaint of disability discrimination which is out of time, if in all the circumstances of the case it considers that it is just and equitable to do so.

5.2 In *Harvey v Port of Tilbury (London) Ltd*[2] the EAT held that an amendment adding a claim that is, or is analogous to, a fresh cause of action is a new claim being 'presented' to the tribunal and so must be presented within the 3-month time-limit. The fact that there are existing proceedings, however, may be a consideration for the tribunal when deciding whether it would be just and equitable to extend the time-limit. In this case, Mr Harvey had lodged his originating application[3] with the tribunal on 7 February 1997 claiming unfair dismissal on the basis that he had been unfairly selected for redundancy. Port of Tilbury (London) Ltd in its Notice of Appearance, which Mr Harvey saw for the first time on 16 April 1997, gave as one of the reasons for selecting him for redundancy the fact that he had back problems which prevented him from performing all of his duties. On 17 September 1997, Mr Harvey applied to amend his originating application to add a complaint of discrimination contrary to the DDA 1995. The tribunal refused the application on the grounds that the proposed amendment was a new cause of action pursuant to s 8 of the DDA 1995 which had not been made within the 3-month period stipulated by para 3(1) of Sch 3 to the DDA 1995. The tribunal also held that it was not just and equitable to extend time to allow the new complaint.

---

1 Schedule 3, para 3(1).
2 [1999] IRLR 693.
3 Often known as an IT1 or since the change of name from industrial tribunal to employment tribunal, ET1.

5.3   Mr Harvey appealed to the EAT. The EAT stated that there was a fundamental difference between an unfair dismissal case that has within it a complaint of unlawful disability discrimination, but where no relief is sought under the DDA 1995, and a complaint invoking the jurisdiction of the DDA 1995 and asking for relief under it. The latter would attract the time bar in Sch 3 to the Act, whereas the former would only attract the time bar appropriate to complaints of unfair dismissal. The EAT said that the amendment sought by Mr Harvey was raising a complaint under the DDA 1995 and, as such, it raised an new cause of action. As this was out of time and the tribunal had decided that it would not extend time, the amendment could not be admitted.

5.4   The EAT went on to emphasise that when an amendment is sought, the applicant should set out clearly and verbatim the terms of the amendment sought and its intended effect. In reality, however, it is unlikely that an applicant will wish to make a complaint about unlawful disability discrimination and not wish to invoke the jurisdiction of the DDA 1995.

5.5   Schedule 3, para 3(3) of the DDA 1995 lists specific rules for determining the date from which the 3-month period will run:

'(a)   where an unlawful act of discrimination is attributable to a term in a contract, that act is to be treated as extending throughout the duration of the contract;

(b)   any act extending over a period shall be treated as done at the end of that period; and

(c)   a deliberate omission shall be treated as done when the person in question decided upon it.'[1]

5.6   Schedule 3, para 3(4) states that unless there is evidence to the contrary, a person is taken to have decided upon an omission either:

'(a)   when he does an act inconsistent with doing the omitted act; or

(b)   if he has done no such inconsistent act, when the period expires within which he might reasonably have been expected to do the omitted act if it was to be done.'

Presenting the complaint in time

5.7   It is important that the claim is presented to the tribunal 'before the end of the period of 3 months beginning when the act complained of was done' (Sch 3, para 3(1)). The day of the act of discrimination is the first day from which to start counting. In practical terms, the way to

---

1   That is where a claim is based on the employer's deliberate omission to carry out an act, that omission is treated as taking place when the person in question decided upon it.

calculate the time-limit is to count on 3 calendar months from the date of the act of discrimination and deduct one day to arrive at the last date on which the application can be made. Thus, for example, if the discriminatory act occurred on 25 March, the last day on which the complaint could be presented to the tribunal would be 24 June.

5.8   The application may be presented to the tribunal by fax. The Originating Application form expressly discourages following up the faxed application with a hard copy, but it may still be wise to do so in case there is a fault with the transmission. In any event, if faxed, the adviser should telephone the tribunal to check that all the pages of the complaint have been received. An attendance note of this telephone call should be kept on file, noting the name of the person who confirmed receipt and the date and time of the call. Keeping on file the fax transmission record may also be useful in case a dispute arises later as to whether or not the complaint was presented in time. It is currently not possible to submit a complaint by e-mail.

The act of discrimination
5.9   The act of discrimination may not always be easy to identify. It could be:

- the date when the decision not to promote or appoint the applicant was made as this is an omission to appoint;[1]
- the date when a warning is given;
- the date when a request for a reasonable adjustment was refused;
- the date of an incident of harassment;
- the date when a decision to employ the applicant on less favourable terms or conditions was made;
- the date of dismissal; however, the date from which time starts to run is not the date when any notice of dismissal is given but the date when, by reason of the notice, the employment is terminated;[2]
- the date of a failure to grant a pay rise or put the applicant forward for promotion or training; as this is an omission, time will run from the date when the omission was decided upon. In the absence of evidence to the contrary this is the date when the respondent does an act inconsistent with doing the omitted act, ie granting the applicant the pay rise, promotion or training. This could be when

---

1   Obviously the client will only know the date that the decision was communicated to her and not the date that it was made. If a dispute arises as to whether the claim has been made in time because of this, the applicant can ask the tribunal to exercise its discretion to hear the late claim as she could have had no knowledge of when the decision was actually made by the respondent.
2   *Lupetti v Wrens Old House Ltd* [1984] ICR 348, EAT.

the period expires within which the respondent might reasonably have been expected to do the omitted act if it was to be done. Where the act of discrimination complained of is the refusal to grant promotion, it is open to the tribunal to find that the time-limit starts to run from either the actual date of the refusal or the date when someone else is granted promotion.[1]

Internal appeals

5.10 It is a common trap for applicants and advisers to believe that time starts to run from the end of any appeal or grievance procedure against the alleged act of discrimination. It does not – it runs from the date of the discriminatory act. If, however, the appeal or grievance was dismissed on grounds that are themselves discriminatory, then that is a further act of discrimination about which a claim can be made within a further 3-month period.

5.11 In *Dean v London Borough of Islington*,[2] the EAT upheld a tribunal's decision that an internal appeal against dismissal was a separate 'act complained of' under the RRA 1976. The facts of the case were that Ms Dean, who is Asian, was suspended by the London Borough of Islington for events which occurred in 1993. She was off sick from work and was called to appear before a disciplinary hearing on 17 March 1995. After this hearing, she was given a final written warning and demoted. She appealed against this decision and this was heard by a panel of councillors on 13 July 1995. They upheld the penalty previously imposed on her and so she made a complaint of racial discrimination to the tribunal. The tribunal found that the only act complained of within the 3-month time-limit was the appeal hearing and that this was a one-off act. The tribunal also declined to exercise its discretion to extend the time-limit so as to bring in the whole disciplinary process. It did not accept that the outcome of appeal was part of a continuing act of discrimination (see **5.13**). Ms Dean appealed to the EAT which held that the tribunal had been correct to conclude that the appeal hearing was a separate act of discrimination complained of.

5.12 Particular care should be taken where the applicant has appealed against dismissal and wishes to claim that the dismissal of the appeal is a discriminatory act in itself. The operative date from which time starts to run will depend on whether or not the applicant can show that the employment contract continued pending the outcome of the appeal. If the employment does not continue, then the applicant will not fall

---

1   *Clarke v Hampshire Electro-Plating Co Ltd* [1991] IRLR 490.
2   (Unreported) EAT No 594/97.

within the definition of 'a disabled person whom he [the employer] employs' under s 4(2) of the DDA 1995 and so will not be able to bring the claim at all. In such a case, if the dismissal occurred more than 3 months before the conclusion of the appeal process, the applicant may be left with no remedy at all.[1]

Continuing discrimination

5.13 There may be cases where the discrimination continues over a period of time. In these cases, the time within which to lodge the application with the tribunal runs from the end of the period of time during which the discrimination lasted. Continuing discrimination is, however, a difficult concept and advisers should be wary of relying on it for time-limit purposes. The tribunal may decide that there has not been continuing discrimination but a single act of discrimination with continuing effects. For example, a failure to promote resulting in continued employment at a lower grade and salary is a single act of discrimination rather than continuing discrimination.[2] In these circumstances, the worker will have to apply once again for promotion and if the application is unsuccessful again, time will start to run from the date the decision was made again not to promote. If, however, the employer has a policy or rule of not promoting or appointing to certain posts persons with a disability (or a particular type of disability), that would be continuing discrimination.

5.14 In *Akhatar v Family Services Unit*,[3] it was held that the fact that there are a number of steps in a disciplinary process carried out by an employer does *not* mean:

(1) that the process must or should be treated as a continuing act; or
(2) that the process as a whole must or should be treated as the complaint or the 'act complained of'.

The decision in *Akhatar* also emphasises the need for the act complained of to be identified clearly and precisely.

5.15 Continuing discrimination, therefore, occurs where an employer has a discriminatory regime, rule, practice or policy, which has a clear and adverse effect on the complainant. For example, in the sex

---

1   *Adekeye v Post Office (No 2)* [1997] IRLR 105, [1997] ICR 110, CA. See also *Relaxion Group plc v Rhys-Harper* (2000) EOR DCLD No 45 Autumn 2000, EAT No 727/99; *D'Souza v London Borough of Lambeth* 27 June 2000, EAT No 360/96; *Coote v Granada Hospitality Ltd (No 2)* [1999] IRLR 452, EAT; *Robinson v The Post Office* [2000] IRLR 804 at **5.19**.
2   *Amies v ILEA* [1977] 2 All ER 100, (1976) 121 SJ 11, [1977] ICR 308, EAT.
3   (1996) 30 EOR DCLD 18 June 1996, EAT No 1285/95.

discrimination case of *Calder v James Finlay Corporation Ltd*[1] there was a continuing mortgage subsidy scheme for male employees only. In the case of *Barclays Bank plc v Kapur*,[2] the employer continued to have a pension scheme containing a provision that discriminated racially against employees whose previous service was in Africa. In each of these cases, the schemes in question continued throughout the applicant's employment. In *Littlewoods Organisation plc v Traynor*,[3] the employer failed to implement remedial measures which it had promised to take in response to an employee's complaint of racial abuse. The employee was able to found a claim against that failure which constituted continuing discrimination.

5.16   A case which graphically illustrates the difference between a single act of discrimination with continuing effects and a continuing discriminatory policy is *Owusu v London Fire and Civil Defence Authority*.[4] The applicant, who was employed as a fire safety case worker, made a claim for racial discrimination on the basis that:

(a)   his employer had failed to promote or shortlist him on seven occasions between 1986 and 1990; and
(b)   his employer had repeatedly failed to upgrade him or allow him to act up at a higher grade when the opportunity arose.

The tribunal held that he was out of time on both counts, but the EAT disagreed. It held that as far as the first category was concerned the failure to promote or shortlist him were specific one-off acts and so he was out of time to make a claim as regards them. The persistent failure to upgrade him or allow him to act up, however, could amount to a case of a continuing act of discrimination (whether it was or not would depend on the evidence) and, therefore, it was in time. The distinction between a continuing act and a single act with continuing effects is therefore a fine one and in most cases it will only be decided on the evidence.

5.17   In *Cast v Croydon College*,[5] the Court of Appeal held that, provided the subsequent refusal(s) resulted from a further consideration of the matter and did not merely refer back to the earlier decision, then each refusal could amount to a new act of discrimination even if it was based on the same facts as before. Repeated refusals by an employer to a request may, however, give rise to both an act which continues over time

---

1   [1989] IRLR 55, [1989] ICR 157n, EAT.
2   [1989] IRLR 387, [1989] ICR 753, CA; *affirmed* [1991] IRLR 136, [1991] ICR 208, HL.
3   [1993] IRLR 154, EAT.
4   [1995] IRLR 574.
5   [1998] IRLR 318, [1998] ICR 500.

or a policy that lasts until the end of the employment depending on the facts.

Requests for reasonable adjustments

5.18 Note, however, that in cases under the DDA 1995 an employer's duty to make reasonable adjustments is statutory. If an employer fails to make such adjustments, the discrimination will, in the authors' view, have continued throughout the period that the substantial disadvantage persisted. This may be so even if the employer has explicitly refused to make the adjustment and the claim is submitted more than 3 months from the date of the refusal. It is arguable that the act of discrimination is not the refusal but the failure to comply with the statutory duty to make reasonable adjustments. In these circumstances, time will start to run only from the date the adjustments were made. There is no EAT case, so far as the authors are aware, on this issue.

When is it just and equitable for the tribunal to hear a complaint that is presented out of time?

5.19 The discretion allowed to the tribunal to hear a claim for disability (and sex and race) discrimination is wider than that for unfair dismissal claims and so such claims are more commonly allowed out of time. It has been held that being able to do what it thinks is just and equitable in the circumstances entitles the tribunal to take into account anything which it judges to be relevant.[1] However, in *Robinson v The Post Office*,[2] the EAT ruled that an unexhausted internal appeals procedure is not necessarily an acceptable reason for presenting a discrimination complaint to a tribunal outside the statutory time-limit. The employment tribunal in this case had decided that it would not be just and equitable to extend the time-limit in order to allow Mr Robinson to present his claim. This decision was appealed by Mr Robinson to the EAT on the basis that the tribunal should have followed the decision in *Aniagwu v London Borough of Hackney*[3] and found that it was just and equitable to hear his complaint because his appeal against dismissal was still in progress at the time of his disability discrimination application. The EAT, however, held that 'parliament has quite deliberately not provided that invariably the running of time against an employee should be delayed until the end of the domestic processes'. The tribunal in this case had taken into account that the applicant knew of the time-limit and had ignored his union advice about it, and that he was

---

1   *Hutchinson v Westward Television Ltd* [1977] IRLR 69, [1977] ICR 279, EAT.
2   [2000] IRLR 804.
3   [1999] IRLR 303.

able to look after his own affairs and had done so in respect of the internal appeal.

5.20   Unfair dismissal claims may be admitted late only if the tribunal is satisfied that it was *not reasonably practicable* to present the claim in time. In these circumstances, it must also be shown that the claim was presented within a period of time that the tribunal considers reasonable, after it became reasonably practicable for the applicant to present the claim. Thus, there are two tests. The first test is to show that there was good reason why the claim could not be presented in time and the second that the claim was presented as soon as it became possible to do so. The latter more rigorous test means in practice that late unfair dismissal claims are rarely allowed.

5.21   It is not uncommon for an applicant representing herself to have stated on the originating application that the claim is for 'unfair dismissal because of disability'. If the claim has been made out of time, it is important to separate the two claims and to be aware of the different tests the tribunal will apply when deciding whether or not to exercise its discretion to hear the late claims.

Test applied to a claim for unfair dismissal because of disability

5.22   *Shultz v Esso Petroleum Ltd*[1] was an unfair dismissal case in which the applicant had been dismissed for long-term absence due to depression. During the early stages of the period within which the claim had to be made, the applicant had tried to appeal internally against his dismissal. However, whilst he had been physically capable of giving instructions to his solicitor for the first 7 weeks of the 3-month period, he was too ill to do so for the last 6 weeks. The tribunal and the EAT both held that it was reasonably practicable for the applicant to have presented his claim within the 3-month period, but the Court of Appeal disagreed and overturned the decision. The Court of Appeal said that it was necessary to consider whether or not a particular step was reasonably practicable 'against a background of the surrounding circumstances and the aim to be achieved'. Potter LJ said:

> 'In a case of this kind, the surrounding circumstances will always include whether or not, as here, the claimant was hoping to avoid litigation by pursuing alternative remedies. In that context, the end to be achieved is not so much the immediate issue of proceedings as issue of proceedings with some time to spare before the end of the limitation period.'

---

1   [1999] 3 All ER 338, [1999] IRLR 488.

5.23 Therefore, the Court of Appeal held that the tribunal and the EAT had erred by giving a period of disabling illness similar weight irrespective of the part of the 3-month period in which it fell. If the disabling illness had occurred in the first part of the 3-month period and the applicant had recovered sufficiently before the end of the 3 months to be able to give instructions to his solicitor, it is likely that he would not have been allowed to present his claim late. In this case, however, in the early part of the 3-month period, when he was capable of dealing with the matter, the applicant was trying to resolve the situation by using an internal appeal. By the time he needed to give instructions to his solicitor to make the claim because the internal appeal had not resolved the situation in time, his illness had made it impossible for him to do so.

Test applied to a claim for disability discrimination
5.24 The tribunal may take the following factors into consideration when deciding on whether or not to allow a late claim for disability discrimination.

–   The applicant's illness or hospitalisation during the relevant period.[1]
–   The nature of the applicant's disability if it made it impossible or unreasonably difficult for the applicant to seek advice and/or make the application in time. This may be particularly relevant where the applicant has:
    (a) a mental health problem that makes it particularly difficult to make decisions or meet the pressure of deadlines,
    (b) a condition which causes chronic fatigue and concentration problems,
    (c) learning difficulties which may mean that she has difficulty in understanding her rights and the importance of time-limits, or
    (d) a hearing or visual impairment or mobility problem which make it difficult to access the usual sources of information and advice (eg libraries and free local advice agencies). It should be noted, however, that Part III of the DDA 1995 requires all service providers to make their services accessible to disabled

---

1   See *Etherington v ATS Midlands Limited* Case No 2602204/97, where a visually impaired applicant called expert evidence from a local Association for the Blind to the effect that the experiences which he went through in relation to his visual impairment were 'so traumatic and shattering that he was not able to cope with the ordinary stress of life, such as the need to seek legal advice in the way that a sighted person would be able to'. The claim was allowed, although the act of discrimination had taken place on 22 April 1997 and the claim was submitted on 17 October 1997 – some 3 months outside the time-limit.

people. This may make this a more difficult argument to run in future.

– A newly diagnosed disability, which the applicant has had difficulty coming to terms with. In the period immediately after diagnosis, some applicants are unable to accept the effects and nature of their disability or to deal effectively with surrounding circumstances. In such situations, evidence from an appropriate disability organisation (eg the RNIB or MS Society) may be useful on the range of normal reactions to a diagnosis.

5.25   The tribunal will also consider the following factors.

– The length of the delay in presenting the claim.
– The promptness with which the applicant acted once she knew of the act of discrimination.
– The apparent strength of the case and the extent to which the cogency of the evidence is likely to be affected by the delay.
– Whether or not the employer was already aware of the allegation and so is not caught by surprise.
– Whether or not any harm is done to the employer or the chances of a fair hearing by the late claim.
– The extent to which the employer had co-operated with any requests for information (eg the questionnaire).
– Whether or not the applicant utilised an internal grievance procedure prior to starting proceedings.[1] The tribunal may also consider the extent to which the employer contributed to the delay by, for example, unreasonably drawing out a grievance or appeal procedure.
– The steps taken by the applicant to obtain appropriate professional advice once the applicant knew of the possibility of taking action. Where the claim is late because the applicant has received negligent advice, the tribunal may be persuaded to allow the claim on the basis that financial compensation from suing the adviser is not an adequate substitute for having lost the opportunity of the tribunal making a declaration of discrimination. Although whether or not the applicant could have any other remedy if the claim is not allowed is also a factor that the tribunal will consider.
– In practice, where there is likely to be a dispute about whether or not a claim has been brought in time, advisers can argue their case in the alternative, for example that it is within time because there was a continuing act of discrimination or in the alternative, if it is

---

1   See *Aniagwu v London Borough of Hackney; Aniagwu v Owens* [1999] IRLR 303, EAT and also *Dean v London Borough of Islington* (unreported) EAT No 594/97.

not a continuing act of discrimination, it would be just and equitable for the tribunal to allow the claim out of time.

THE ORIGINATING APPLICATION

5.26 The originating application (ET1 form) is the document on which the applicant makes her claim to the tribunal to start the proceedings. All that is required to present a claim to the tribunal is for the complaint to be made in writing and contain the following details.

– The applicant's name and address and, if different, an address within the United Kingdom to which notices and other documents relating to the claim can be sent.
– The names and addresses of the person or persons against whom the claim is made.
– The grounds (ie facts in some detail) and the reasons why it is alleged that discrimination has occurred.[1]

5.27 The application can therefore be on a home-made form or even by letter.[2] The easiest way to make the application, however, is to use the ET1 form supplied by the Central Office of Employment Tribunals. ET1 forms are available from any local office of the Employment Service, including jobseekers' allowance offices and job centres, and from most advice centres. An explanatory booklet (ETL1) is also available from the same sources. In Scotland the ET1 is known as the 'ET1 (Scot)' and in Northern Ireland it is the 'ET1(NI)'. In Northern Ireland, forms and booklets are available from any local training and employment agency.

5.28 The ET1 form indicates to which tribunal office the originating application should be sent. This is determined by the postcode of the employer. In certain circumstances, the applicant may later ask for the case to be transferred to another more convenient tribunal.[3]

---

1   However, tribunals are fairly flexible where claims do not meet these requirements. For example, it is not vital that application contains particulars of the grounds because under Sch 1, para 4(1)(a) to the Employment Tribunals (Constitution and Rules of Procedure) Regulations 1993 the tribunal can order further particulars of a complaint to be provided if necessary. The reason why the tribunal is so flexible is because the originating application is not a formal 'pleading' such as the statement of case in the county court.
2   *Smith v Automobile Pty Ltd* [1973] ICR 306, NIRC; Employment Tribunals (Constitution and Rules of Procedure) Regulations 1993, Sch 1.
3   See Chapter 7.

Completing the originating application

5.29   The originating application is the first stage in formally starting proceedings in the employment tribunal. As this is the first document that the tribunal members will read, it is in the applicant's interest to complete the ET1 form with care and to set out the case to the best advantage.

Box 1 – type of complaint
5.30   In this box, the applicant should state the type of complaint being made. Care should be taken to ensure that everything that can be claimed is claimed in this box. For example, in addition to the disability discrimination claim, can an unfair or constructive dismissal claim also be made? Advisers should question the applicant carefully about the possibility of there being a claim for victimisation. If the applicant has made a complaint about disability discrimination in the past and there is evidence to suggest that subsequent actions on the part of the employer are the result of this, then victimisation should be claimed. Advisers should also take care not to overlook possible wrongful dismissal or breach of contract claims. The adviser should already have obtained a copy of the applicant's contract of employment. If the employer's equal opportunities policy forms part of the contract of employment and the applicant has been dismissed for a discriminatory reason, it may be possible to claim breach of contract in the employment tribunal.[1] If the applicant has not been dismissed, then breach of contract may be claimed only in the county court or the High Court. The applicant may also have a breach of contract claim in the county court or the High Court if he was not permitted to claim on a private health insurance scheme. Such claims can be extremely valuable and should not be overlooked.

5.31   However, whilst applicants and their advisers should consider casting their net widely to ensure that all the applicant's causes of action are claimed, it is generally unwise to plead weak cases. This is particularly true where the different claims might contradict each other or weaken other claims. Obviously, the strongest claims will be those with the most supporting evidence.

Box 2 – the applicant's details
5.32   As much information as possible should be given here and, in particular, accurate information about the address to which future documents should be sent.

---

1   *Taylor v Secretary of State for Scotland* [2000] IRLR 502, HL.

Box 3 – details of the applicant's representative

5.33 If an address is given for the applicant's representative, the tribunal will send all notices and other correspondence to that address. Any adviser whose details are given in this box (and so is 'on the record') must keep the client informed about the progress of the case and dates and times of any hearings. The tribunal should be notified of any changes to the representative or the contact details.

5.34 Applicants do not have to be represented to bring claims in the employment tribunal and so it is not necessary to complete this box when making the application. If an applicant acting in person makes the claim himself and subsequently finds a representative, the tribunal can be notified at that stage of the representative's details.

Box 4 – dates of employment

5.35 The start date should be the date when the applicant's continuous employment started – this may have been with a previous employer who was taken over by the current employer or under a different contract of employment. The date of termination is the date when notice given to or by the applicant expired or, where no notice was given or the applicant received payment in lieu of notice, the date on which the applicant left employment. The dates given here are important, as the tribunal will consider them to assess whether or not it has the jurisdiction to hear all the applicant's complaints.

Box 5 – details of the respondent

5.36 The applicant's adviser should ensure that the correct respondent is named here and that sufficient detail is given to be able to identify the respondent and enable the tribunal to communicate with them. More than one respondent can be named. In discrimination cases, the applicant may wish to name both the employer organisation and an individual if there has been an element of harassment in the discrimination. Naming an individual has the following advantages.

– It ensures that the person named will attend the hearing. It may be important to the applicant that a particular individual attends to give evidence. The applicant cannot force the respondent to call a particular witness and so naming the individual as a respondent is the only way to ensure that that person attends the hearing to give evidence. If the person is not named, the best way to make him attend is by obtaining a witness order from the tribunal forcing attendance. In these circumstances, however, that person is a witness for the applicant (albeit a hostile one) and not for the respondent.

– It ensures that the applicant still has a case with which to proceed if the employer is able to establish that it has done everything reasonably possible to prevent the discrimination, including disciplining another employee.[1] In these circumstances, the applicant's only remaining case will be against the individual. If the individual has not been named as a respondent in this box at the outset, the tribunal may not allow him or her to be added at a later stage.[2]

5.37   Proceedings can only be brought against a legal 'person' or body whether that 'person' is an individual, a collection of individuals or a company. A claim cannot be brought against an unincorporated association, as this is not a legal 'person'. If the employer is an unincorporated association, the correct respondent is the individual or individuals with effective day-to-day control of the association – this is often the chairman or members of the management or executive committee. In *Sivanandan v London Borough of Enfield and Others*,[3] the tribunal dismissed an unincorporated association named by the applicant as a respondent because it did not exist as a legal entity. However, the tribunal also rejected Ms Sivanandan's subsequent application to join as respondents the relevant members of the executive committee of the unincorporated association who she claimed had knowingly aided her employer to commit an act of unlawful race discrimination. Ms Sivanandan appealed to the EAT, which held that the tribunal had made an error of law in refusing her application which had been made to cure a technical defect, especially as the applicant had sued the association at the outset.

5.38   If the employer is a company in administration, tribunal proceedings may only be started or continued against it with leave of the High Court or the administrator.[4] Failure to obtain leave of the court is not, however, fatal to the claim as the tribunal should stay the proceedings while leave of the court is obtained. If the administrator adopts the employee's contracts of employment, the administrator will be liable to be sued personally and so leave of the court is not required.

5.39   If one of the parties is bankrupt, the trustee in bankruptcy will have an interest in the outcome and so will be entitled to apply to be joined as a party.[5]

---

1   See, however, *Canniffe v East Riding of Yorkshire Council* [2000] IRLR 555.
2   See Chapter 7.
3   2 February 1999, EAT 450, 628 and Case No 1351/98.
4   Insolvency Act 1986, s 11(3); *Carr v British International Helicopters Ltd (In Administration)* [1994] ICR 18, EAT(S).
5   See Chapter 7.

5.40   If the applicant or the adviser is unsure against whom the case should be brought, ie who the applicant's employer was or who had discriminated against the applicant or whether there was more than one employer, all the parties should be named here as respondents. This may be the case if:

– the applicant was employed by an employment agency and placed with a principal;
– the applicant was in supported employment where part of the applicant's salary was paid by the supporting agency via the employer;
– the applicant's employer was taken over by another undertaking and the transfer of undertakings regulations apply;[1] or
– the applicant is or was employed by an agency funded by another organisation such as the local authority (eg schools or voluntary organisations).[2]

5.41   The tribunal will generally allow the applicant to withdraw her case against a specific respondent, but it will be more reluctant to allow new respondents to be added at a later date. This is especially so as the applicant is likely to be out of time to bring the claim against that respondent by that time.

Box 6 – connection with the respondent

5.42   In most cases, the applicant's job title should be given in this box. In recruitment cases, the job the applicant applied for should be given. If the complaint being made is of harassment by a co-worker who is named as the respondent, the applicant's connection with that worker should be stated in this box.

---

1   Transfer of Undertakings (Protection of Employment) Regulations 1981, SI 1981/1974, as amended.
2   When bringing proceedings against a school, where there is a delegated budget in a maintained school, the governing body of the school (and not the local education authority) will be the primary respondent. This is so even if the employee is or was employed by the local education authority (Arts 3, 4 and 6(1) and (2) of the Education (Modification of Enactments Relating to Employment) Order 1999, SI 1999/2256). Therefore, where a local education authority dismisses an employee following notification from the governing body that the person should cease to work at the school, this is a dismissal by the governing body for sex, race and disability discrimination and unfair dismissal claims. However, any award of the tribunal (except for an order of re-instatement or re-engagement) of the person has effect against the local authority. The governing body must notify the local education authority within 14 days for receiving notification of tribunal proceedings and the authority is entitled to be made a party to the proceedings by writing to the tribunal.

Box 7 – normal basic hours

5.43 The applicant's normal basic hours are usually the contractual minimum hours the applicant is required to work. This may include overtime where the applicant is contractually obliged to work overtime.

Box 8 – details of earnings

5.44 This information may be used to calculate the compensation the applicant would be entitled to if successful. The 'basic wage/salary' is the applicant's gross wage or salary. The 'average take home pay' is the applicant's net wage or salary (ie after deduction of tax and National Insurance). If the applicant's wage varied from week to week, the average amount calculated over the preceding 12 calendar weeks should be given. It is important to remember to include any additional employment 'perks' such as pension entitlement, private health insurance, concessionary travel and bonuses under 'other bonuses/ benefits', as the loss of these should be claimed in the compensation award.[1] In recruitment cases, the salary plus benefits that the applicant would have received had they been appointed to the post should be given.

Box 9 – date of action complained of other than dismissal

5.45 The date of the act of discrimination should be specified here. The tribunal will check this to see if the claim is in time. If it is difficult to give an exact date, if for example continuing discrimination is being claimed, this can be clarified in the further particulars of the claim and the word 'continuing' can be inserted in this box.

Box 10 – remedy sought (unfair dismissal)

5.46 If in addition to the discrimination claim the applicant is claiming unfair dismissal, this box should be completed. Advisers should note that in discrimination cases the tribunal does not have the power to order re-instatement. It can only make a recommendation that the applicant be reinstated. However, it does have the power to order reinstatement or re-engagement in unfair dismissal cases.[2]

Box 11– details of complaint

5.47 Great care should be taken when completing this part of the originating application as this is the applicant's first opportunity to set

---

1   See Chapter 9.
2   The Government's response to the Task Force recommendations proposes to allow employment tribunals to be able to order re-instatement or re-engagement and to hear complaints about discrimination by managers/trustees of occupational pension schemes.

out the case. Rather than trying to fit all the details of the applicant's case into the box provided, the details should be set out on a separate sheet attached to the ET1 form.

5.48 The details of the claim should be set out in numbered paragraphs, setting out concisely the grounds on which the claim is being brought including the section numbers of the relevant legislation, for example DDA 1995, ERA 1996. Advisers should have taken detailed instructions from their client (see Chapter 2) by this point and so should take care to ensure that any s 5(2) (failure to make reasonable adjustments) claim is made as well as a s 5(1) (less favourable treatment) claim where appropriate. The unrepresented client may, of course, have difficulty identifying the relevant sections of the legislation and so may not state them in the ET1. This can be remedied at the directions hearing stage when the tribunal will want to identify the issues in dispute (see Chapter 7). When drafting the statement, advisers should take care to state clearly, where appropriate, the following information.

In all cases
–   The nature of the applicant's disability and how the applicant meets the definition of disability contained in s 1 of and Sch 1 to the DDA 1995.
–   The relationship between the applicant and the respondent (eg employer/employee, principal/contractor, line manager/ employee or co-workers).
–   Details of the applicant's position and duties and the applicant's experience and qualifications for the job if appropriate.
–   The nature of the respondent, including whether or not it is a large organisation and the number of people it employs.
–   The law under which the claim(s) are being brought (eg the DDA 1995 and any other legislation such as the ERA 1996). Advisers need not at this stage give specific sections of the Acts if they are unsure of these.

Recruitment cases
–   Where the position was advertised and when, giving the job title.
–   How the applicant applied and details of the interview process if relevant.
–   The job description and the person specification and how the applicant met them.

–   Any reasonable adjustments the applicant requested, which were not made in the arrangements for offering him employment (eg information in an accessible form or an accessible venue for the interview).

–   The names and positions of the interview panel and details of the questions asked if these are alleged to have been discriminatory.

–   Details of the less favourable treatment afforded to the applicant (eg failure to be shortlisted or appointed to the post).

–   Details of the experience and qualifications of the person who was appointed to the post if known and whether or not that person has a disability.

–   Any reasons given by the respondent for the failure to shortlist or appoint the applicant.

In cases concerning dismissal or termination of contract

–   The date when notice (if any) was given and the date when employment ended.

–   All reasons given by the employer for the termination of the contract (eg redundancy on the basis of selection criteria which took into account the applicant's disability related sickness absence record).

–   The name and position of the person(s) who made the decision to terminate the contract.

–   Details of employees in circumstances similar to those of the applicant who did not have their contracts of employment terminated.

–   Any grievance or appeal procedures utilised by the applicant, including details of how the appeal was conducted and whether or not it is alleged that this was discriminatory.

–   Any reasonable adjustments the respondent failed to make for the applicant and whether or not provision of this adjustment would have affected termination of the contract.[1]

In cases of failure to make reasonable adjustments

–   The adjustments requested, of whom and on what date(s).

–   How the adjustments would remove or reduce the substantial disadvantage experienced by the applicant.

–   The date of refusal to provide the adjustments and details of the person who made that decision where appropriate.

---

1   See *Clark v Novacold Ltd* [1999] 2 All ER 977, [1999] ICR 951, [1999] IRLR 318, CA, [1998] IRLR 420, EAT concerning reasonable adjustments and dismissal.

– The likely cost of the adjustments and the disruption such adjustments are likely to cause (if there is no cost or likely disruption this should be stated).

– Details of any outside organisations that were, or were not but should have been, consulted about the adjustments (eg disability employment adviser, a disability organisation or technical specialists).

– The availability of financial and other assistance available to the respondent in making the adjustments.

In cases of less favourable treatment (other than dismissal)

– The treatment received by the applicant (eg failure to promote or denial of a benefit).

– How this less favourable treatment was for a reason relating to the applicant's disability.[1]

– How other employees have been treated.

– Details of the applicant's qualifications in comparison with others where appropriate (eg qualifications for promotion).

In cases of harassment

– The name and status of the person(s) alleged to have committed the acts of harassment.

– Specific details of the acts of harassment with dates. Where abuse is alleged the exact language used by the harassers should be stated.

– Details of the person to whom the applicant complained about the harassment. When and what action was taken by the person complained to and within what timescale.

5.49 If there are problems with the applicant's case, it is wise to set them out at this point in the statement. For example, if there is likely to be a dispute about whether or not the claim is being presented within time, the applicant's adviser should set out here why it is maintained:

– that the act of discrimination is in time;
– that the act of discrimination is a continuing one; and/or
– why it would be just and equitable for the tribunal to allow the claim to be heard out of time.

If this is not done, the respondent may not submit a full answer or defence to the allegations but simply allege that the tribunal cannot hear the applicant's claim because it is out of time.

---

1 See *Clark v Novacold Ltd* above.

5.50   It is important to set out within the details of complaint all the incidents upon which the applicant wishes to rely as acts of discrimination. This point was emphasised by the EAT in *British Gas Services Ltd v McCaull*.[1] The EAT held that the employment tribunal had erred in finding that the employers had discriminated against the applicant by failing to supply him with specific information about an alternative job when this failure had not been mentioned in his originating application. Mr McCaull's originating application said 'my employer dismissed me due to my medical condition, epilepsy. They failed to offer suitable alternative employment or to take reasonable steps to rearrange or alter my working conditions'. No mention was made in the originating application (or in later submissions to the tribunal at the hearing) that the employer had failed to provide enough information about a particular job although this did emerge at the hearing. The EAT said:

> 'it is important that tribunals in such cases should deal with the complaints of "less favourable treatment" as they are defined by the applicant and not as the tribunal subsequently chooses to define them. If a tribunal finds less favourable treatment in some act or omission of which the applicant has not complained there is a grave danger that there will have been a breach of the rules of natural justice because the other party will not have been put on notice that this might be held against it.'

Particular care will need to be taken when a client has submitted the originating application himself before seeking legal advice. An application to the tribunal for permission to amend the ET1 form may be needed in these circumstances. Close questioning of a client is often required to obtain details of every instance as clients frequently believe that important incidents, for example of harassment or abuse, are not worth mentioning to the adviser because they do not relate to the main claim or because they were commonplace. Failure to mention specific incidents may prevent reference to them at the hearing in the applicant's witness statement. In addition, if this statement does not sufficiently particularise each incident of discrimination claimed, the tribunal may order that further particulars or details be provided before the case can proceed. If the tribunal does not do this, the respondent is likely to ask for further particulars of the originating application. It is usually better for the applicant to set out all of the claim rather than trying to answer the respondent's questions about the claim. In this way the strengths of the applicant's case can be emphasised and the weaknesses of the respondent's case highlighted.

---

1   [2001] IRLR 60.

Once the originating application has been completed

5.51　　Where time permits, the client should be sent a draft copy of the originating application for comment. The final copy of the application should then be sent to the appropriate tribunal office together with a request for a directions hearing and a list of dates to avoid for this hearing.

For office use

Application to an Employment Tribunal

- If you fax this form you do not need to send one in the post.
- This form has to be photocopied. Please use CAPITALS and black ink (if possible).
- Where there are tick boxes, please tick the one that applies.

Received at ET

Case number

Code

Initials

---

1 Please give the type of complaint you want the tribunal to decide (for example, unfair dismissal, equal pay). A full list is available from the tribunal office. If you have more than one complaint list them all.

DISABILITY DISCRIMINATION

---

2 Please give your details

Mr [X]   Mrs [ ]   Miss [ ]   Ms [ ]   Other _____

First names   RAJESH

Surname   MISTRY

Date of birth   25/04/53

Address   79 ASTOR CLOSE
EALING
LONDON

Postcode   W5 6AZ

Phone number   020 8522622

Daytime phone number   020 8522622

Please give an address to which we should send documents if different from above

Postcode

---

3 If a representative is acting for you please give details
(all correspondence will be sent to your representative)

Name

Address
TO BE ADVISED

Postcode

Phone | Fax

Reference

---

4 Please give the dates of your employment

From _____ to _____

---

5 Please give the name and address of the employer, other organisation or person against whom this complaint is being brought

Name (1) ANDREW HOLDEN
(2) THE GOVERNING BODY OF THE

Address   WHITEMORE PRIMARY SCHOOL

WHITEMORE PRIMARY SCHOOL
PARKSIDE
EALING
LONDON

Postcode W5 9DS

Phone number   020 8767 444

Please give the place where you worked or applied to work if different from above

Address

Postcode

---

6 Please say what job you did for the employer (or what job you applied for). If this does not apply, please say what your connection was with the employer

MUSIC CO-ORDINATOR

IT1(E/W)

7 Please give the number of normal basic hours worked each week

Hours per week

35 HOURS

9 If your complaint is not about dismissal, please give the date when the matter you are complaining about took place

12 & 25 MARCH 1999

8 Please give your earning details

Basic wage or salary

£ **30,000** : **00** per **ANNUM**

Average take home pay

£ : per

Other bonuses or benefits

£ : per

10 Unfair dismissal applicants only

Please indicate what you are seeking at this stage, if you win your case

☐ Reinstatement: to carry on working in your old job as before (an order for reinstatement normally includes an award of compensation for loss of earnings).

☐ Re-engagement: to start another job or new contract with your old employer (an order for re-engagement normally includes an award of compensation for loss of earnings).

☒ Compensation only: to get an award of money

11 Please give details of your complaint

If there is not enough space for your answer, please continue on a separate sheet and attach it to this form.

PLEASE SEE ATTACHED

12 Please sign and date this form, then send it to the address on the back page of this booklet.

Signed

Rafmistry

Date

1 JUNE 1999

IT1(E/W)

CASE STUDIES

DETAILS OF COMPLAINT

(1) The Respondents are the Head Teacher and the Governing Body of a primary school, which has approximately 40 members of teaching and non-teaching staff.

(2) The Applicant has a BA (Hons) degree in Music and a Certificate in Education. He has been a fully qualified Music Teacher for just over 21 years. He has taught music in a variety of primary schools in and around the Liverpool area. For the last 6½ years he has worked as a Music Teacher in Liverpool. A curriculum vitae detailing the Applicant's qualifications and experience is attached.

(3) The Applicant has had a visual impairment since birth and is registered blind. He is a fluent Braille reader, which is his preferred method of written communication. He owns a personal computer and text printer which, when used in conjunction with a scanner and Braille embosser, enables him to access and produce printed materials in text and braille. When working, he also employs a Personal Assistant to read for him and to undertake administrative tasks such as photocopying.

(4) In early 1999 the Applicant was made redundant from his employment as a Music Teacher. He saw the position of Music Co-ordinator with the Respondent school advertised in the *Times Educational Supplement*, which he receives on tape. The Applicant applied for the post in February 1999 and was subsequently shortlisted for the position and invited to attend an interview.

(5) The interview took place on 12 March 1999 in the Head Teacher's office at the school. The Applicant travelled on his own to attend the interview. He did not know in advance who would be interviewing him. He was shown to the interview room by a receptionist. The Applicant was greeted at the start of the interview by one of the Respondents, the Head Teacher of the school, Mr Andrew Holden, who explained that he would be chairing the interview panel. The Applicant was not told who the other panel members were and so he asked Mr Holden if they could introduce themselves to him so that he could be aware of where they were seated. The other panel members were Mrs Alison Martin who is the Head of the English Department, Mr

Peter Wilson who is a Personnel Officer with the Local Education Authority and Mr George Harman who is the Chair of the Governing Body.

(6) During the course of the interview the panel members acknowledged that the Applicant had impressive qualifications and met the essential criteria for the position. Mrs Alison Martin then asked the Applicant how he would cope with the volume of paperwork involved with the work as the post holder would be required to plan the music curriculum and produce lesson plans as well as teach music. The Applicant stated that his preferred method of written communication is Braille and that it was possible for him, with a personal computer, scanner and Braille embosser, to produce and access printed material including, with the appropriate software, musical notation. Mr Holden interrupted the Applicant before he could explain that he had his own personal computer and text printer, to say that the school's budget would not be able to sustain the purchase of all this equipment. The Applicant reassured Mr Holden that there should be little or no additional expense to the school as the Applicant personally owns some of the equipment and the Access To Work Scheme would be prepared to provide a grant to cover the cost of the rest of the equipment. The Access To Work Scheme would also provide a grant to cover the cost of employing a Personal Assistant for the Applicant.

(7) The Applicant was told by Mr Holden at the end of the interview that the panel would make its decision in the next two weeks and that all candidates would be notified of the outcome by letter. The Applicant asked if he could be telephoned instead of receiving a letter. The Applicant was not telephoned but received a letter dated 25 March 1999 from Mr Holden notifying him that he had been unsuccessful in this application.

(8) The Applicant telephoned Mr Holden to ask why he had been unsuccessful but Mr Holden was unavailable. The Applicant spoke to Mr Holden's secretary and left a message asking Mr Holden to return his call. The Applicant did not receive a telephone call from Mr Holden and so wrote to him on 27 March 1999. On 1 April 1999 the Applicant received a letter from Mr Holden's secretary to say that he was out of the country during the Easter break and so could not reply to the Applicant's letter.

(9)   The Respondent unjustifiably discriminated against the Applicant by treating him less favourably for a reason relating to his disability within the meaning of s 5(1) of the Disability Discrimination Act 1995 in:

  (a) the arrangements which the Respondent made for the purposes of determining to whom the Respondent should offer employment; in particular, the manner in which the interview was conducted and the manner and behaviour of the Chair of the interview panel, Andrew Holden;
  (b) the failure to appoint him to the post when he was the most suitable candidate,

  contrary to s 4(1)(a) and (c).

(10) The Respondent also unjustifiably discriminated against the applicant by failing to take reasonable steps to prevent the Applicant from being placed at a substantial disadvantage within the meaning of s 5(2) and s 6 of the DDA 1995 in failing to let the Applicant know by whom he was to be interviewed contrary to s 4(1)(a) of the Disability Discrimination Act 1995.

(11) The Respondent's behaviour was humiliating to the Applicant and caused him distress.

(12) The Applicant seeks a declaration and an order for compensation.

Chapter 6

ANALYSING THE NOTICE OF APPEARANCE, DRAFTING REQUESTS FOR FURTHER PARTICULARS AND REQUESTS FOR DISCOVERY

THE ET3 – NOTICE OF APPEARANCE

6.1   When the employment tribunal receives the ET1, it will send a copy of it to the respondent together with the standard ET3 (notice of appearance) form. Although, as with the ET1, the respondent does not have to use this form, it is generally used. A notice of appearance must be in writing and should contain:

– the respondent's full name and address, with an alternative address for service of notice or other documents if appropriate; and
– whether or not the respondent will be resisting the claim, and if so, sufficient particulars to show on what grounds the claim is to be resisted.[1]

6.2   If the respondent believes that the applicant has not provided sufficient particulars to enable an adequate response to be made, it can ask the applicant to supply further particulars of the originating application,[2] whilst at the same time writing to the tribunal to apply for an extension of time to enter a notice of appearance. It is unusual for respondents to do this. They will more often merely enter an ET3 as a holding measure, stating that further details of the applicant's case have been sought and that once these have been obtained, the respondents will be able to provide fuller details of their grounds of resistance.

TIME-LIMITS

6.3   The notice of appearance should be submitted within 21days of the copy of the originating application being received from the

---

1   Employment Tribunals (Constitution and Rules of Procedure) Regulations 1993, Sch 1, para 3(1).
2   Ibid, Sch 1, para 4(1)(a).

tribunal.[1] However, if the claim is made against a foreign State, the time-limit is extended to 2 months.[2] In practice, there is far more flexibility with the time-limits for submitting the ET3 than there is in respect of the ET1. When a notice of appearance is presented after the expiry of the 21-day time-limit, it is expressly deemed to include an application for an extension of time under para 15(2), provided that it has supplied grounds in support of such an application.[3] By virtue of para 15(1), a respondent can specifically request an application for an extension of time. Technically, the tribunal can entertain an application for an extension of time at any stage[4] although it would have to be justified.

6.4   Where a request to submit a late ET3 is made, and the tribunal chair is satisfied that it was reasonably practicable to submit the claim within time, when granting the application the tribunal can order the respondent to pay costs.[5]

6.5   When the tribunal office receives the ET3, it will send a copy to all other parties to the proceedings. The applicant's adviser should diarise the expected date of receipt of the ET3, and if it is not received at the expected time, contact the tribunal to find out whether or not it has been received. If an application for extra time has been submitted, representatives may wish to write to the tribunal objecting to this, or asking for costs to be awarded against the respondent. This may be particularly pertinent when a questionnaire has already been served and answered, and the information required for completion of the ET3 has already been produced in the questionnaire response.

6.6   Where a respondent has failed to enter a notice of appearance, he will be debarred from taking any further part in the proceedings. However, in such circumstances the respondent can:

–   apply for an extension of time for entering an appearance;
–   apply for further particulars of the originating application.[6]

Where no application for an extension of time or further particulars is made, if the case proceeds to a hearing, the respondent can:

---

1   Employment Tribunals (Constitution and Rules of Procedure) Regulations 1993, Sch 1, para 3(1).
2   State Immunity Act 1978, s 12(2).
3   Employment Tribunals (Constitution and Rules of Procedure) Regulations 1993, SI 1993/2687, Sch 1, para 3(3).
4   *St Mungo Community Trust v Colleano* [1980] ICR 254, EAT.
5   Employment Tribunals (Constitution and Rules of Procedure) Regulations 1993, Sch 1, para 3(4).
6   Ibid, Sch 1, para 3(2)(a).

- apply for a review of the tribunal's decision on the grounds that the respondent never received notice of the proceedings;[1]
- be called as a witness by another person;[2]
- be sent a copy of the tribunal's decision.[3]

CONTENTS OF THE ET3

6.7 The ET3 will give the respondent's details of rates of pay, date of employment of the applicant, whether or not dismissal is accepted and, most importantly, whether or not the application is resisted and, if so, on what grounds. The applicant's adviser will need to study carefully the grounds for resistance and, in particular, to compare these with anything in the correspondence with the applicant and in the response to the questionnaire, if one has been received. The representative's principal concern at this stage will be to identify any contradictions appearing in the respondent's version of events. The adviser should note such contradictions separately, as they may be useful in forming questions for cross-examination at the substantive hearing. In addition, representatives will need to take full instructions from applicants so that any request for further particulars and discovery can be fully informed. In some cases, this will be the first time that an issue such as health and safety has been raised, and at this stage the adviser may have to obtain expert evidence or information regarding the health and safety risks in that particular workplace.

6.8 It is also at this stage that the respondent is likely to raise any jurisdictional points, for example that the company/organisation is not subject to the DDA 1995 as it has fewer than 15 employees or that the applicant is not disabled. The latter, as advisers will be aware, is one of the most contested areas of the DDA 1995, and preliminary hearings to determine such issues are extremely common. If a jurisdictional point is indicated at this stage, the respondent may have requested a preliminary hearing directly, or, if not, the tribunal will in any event note that there is a jurisdictional issue and will set a date for a hearing. The adviser will need to be prepared or preparing for the hearing from the moment that it appears that this will be an issue.[4]

---

1   Employment Tribunals (Constitution and Rules of Procedure) Regulations 1993, Sch 1, para 3(2)(c).
2   Ibid, Sch 1, para 3(2)(d).
3   Ibid, Sch 1, para 3(2)(e).
4   See Chapters 3, 7 and 8 for further details.

REQUEST FOR FURTHER PARTICULARS

6.9   To ensure that applicants and respondents are fully aware of the case they will have to put/answer at tribunal, parties can ask each other for further particulars of the notice of appearance or of the originating application. Well-drafted requests for further particulars and discovery at an early stage of the case can encourage settlement, particularly in view of the costs the respondent may incur in complying with these requests. In addition, further documentation can be provided which can be compared with the questionnaire responses, notice of appearance and ultimately the witnesses' evidence.

6.10   The employment tribunal can order these particulars to be supplied[1] either on the application of a party or of its own motion. For example, if an employer states that a disabled employee has been dismissed because that person had an unacceptably high level of sickness absence, the applicant would be entitled to ask for further particulars as to what is meant by 'unacceptably' and how many days it is alleged that the applicant took off sick in a given period. Advisers will need to bear in mind that the tribunal will not order further particulars to be supplied where they are unnecessary, for example when the purpose of such particulars is solely to ascertain what witnesses the other party is likely to call to give evidence[2] or where the particulars relate solely to compensation when liability has not yet been determined.[3] It is also useful to remember that the purpose of the particulars is not effectively to try the case on paper. Thus, advisers need to be wary of requesting information which is essentially a matter of evidence. If in doubt, however, advisers can always ask for the particulars and the respondent can object if they believe that it is a matter of evidence and not a further particular – ultimately, it will be for the tribunal to determine whether or not it should be given.

6.11   The most useful summary of the principle to be borne in mind in dealing with further particulars was given in the case of *Byrne v Financial Times Ltd,*[4] when Wood J stated:

> 'General principles affecting the ordering of further and better particulars include that the parties should not be taken by surprise at the last minute; that particulars should only be ordered when necessary in order to do justice in the case or to prevent adjournment; that the order should not be

---

1   Employment Tribunals (Constitution and Rules of Procedure) Regulations 1993, Sch 1, para 4(1).

2   *P&O European Ferries (Dover) Ltd v Byrne* [1989] IRLR 254, CA.

3   *Colonial Mutual Life Assurance Society Ltd v Clinch* [1981] ICR 752, EAT.

4   [1991] IRLR 417 at 419, EAT.

oppressive; that particulars are for the purpose of identifying the issues and not for the production of the evidence; and that complicated pleadings battles should not be encouraged.'

6.12 On receipt of the ET3, and having taken instructions from the applicant, the adviser should go through each paragraph to determine whether there is anything in it requiring clarification. The request for particulars should be made by setting out each paragraph on which particulars are being requested, with the particulars sought listed after the relevant paragraph. A draft copy should be sent to the applicant beforehand, to ensure that he is happy with this and to see if there is anything else he would like to have raised. The request should be sent, together with the request for discovery,[1] directly to the respondent or respondent's representative, allowing them 14–21 days to respond. A copy should be sent to the tribunal, for its information. If the respondent neither responds within the time-limit nor asks for further time, the adviser should write to the tribunal requesting that an order be made. The request should include information as to why the particulars are necessary and an explanation that the respondent has been given a number of days to supply these particulars but has not done so.

6.13 If the respondent fails to comply with the order within the specified time-limit set by the tribunal, either all or part of the notice of appearance can be struck out, and the respondent can be barred from taking any further part in the proceedings. Accordingly, advisers should diarise the relevant date for the replies to be received, and if no response is forthcoming, apply to the tribunal for the ET3 to be struck out. The tribunal will have to give the respondent the opportunity to show why the proceedings should not be struck out.

QUESTIONS

6.14 Parties to the proceedings can also clarify the issues further by requesting written answers to questions. Schedule 1, para 4(5) to the Employment Tribunals (Constitution and Rules of Procedure) Regulations 1993, which provides for this process, states that an order may be made for the provision of such answers if the tribunal considers:

'(a) that the answer of the party to that question may help to clarify any issue likely to arise for determination in the proceedings, and
(b) that it would be likely to assist the progress of the proceedings for that answer to be available to the tribunal before the hearing.'

---

1 See **6.17**.

Since it is not compulsory to answer the respondent's questionnaire, this procedure may be particularly useful where a respondent has refused to do so.

6.15   Where an applicant has not received a response to the questionnaire, it may be worth submitting as questions some, if not all, of the queries contained in question 6 of the questionnaire. This should be done in writing to the respondent, with a copy to the tribunal, with a time-limit for response. If no response is forthcoming, then, as with the request for further particulars, advisers should write to the tribunal requesting it to exercise its power under Sch 1, para 4(3) to make an order, detailing why the answers are necessary for the fair determination of the case. If an order is made, the tribunal will specify a period of time within which the questions must be answered. If they are not, the tribunal can order part or all of the ET3 to be struck out and debar the respondent from taking further part in the proceedings. The respondent must be given notice that this is being considered. Again, the adviser should diarise the expected date of response, and, if none is forthcoming, apply to the tribunal for the ET3 to be struck out.

6.16   Where a questionnaire was never submitted, advisers need to be aware that the tribunal may decide that it is more appropriate for the applicant to seek leave to serve a questionnaire out of time than to proceed directly to the questions procedure.

DISCOVERY AND INSPECTION

6.17   Documentation is crucial to any case but particularly to a discrimination case, as it will often be the only evidence from which to draw an inference or direct proof of discrimination. Discovery is the process by which advisers may access documents which can then be used to bolster their case. These documents are then examined to identify any weaknesses or particular strengths, and/or to request further discovery and to assist in any negotiation.

6.18   There is no obligation, as there is in other legal arenas, for the parties to disclose voluntarily all relevant documentation in their possession. The applicant will have to make very careful use of the discovery process. It will be important to find out from the applicant what documents there may be that are relevant to the case – no one knows the job and the workplace better than the client. Such documents include:

– the contract of employment;
– the grievance and disciplinary procedures;

- the sick leave procedures/sickness absence policy;
- any equal opportunities policy and disability policy;
- the personnel file;
- internal and external memos, emails and any correspondence relating to the discriminatory incident (employers often forget that emails constitute correspondence, so it will be necessary to mention them specifically);
- copies of any correspondence between the employer and the lessor of its premises (where there is an issue as to a refusal of consent to make a reasonable adjustment to the physical features of premises);
- any risk assessments or health and safety assessments;
- the health and safety policy;
- any medical or expert reports (medical reports may not have been seen by the applicant prior to tribunal proceedings, and, although the respondent may argue that confidentiality means that such a report should not be disclosed, advisers can equally argue that in order for the applicant to have a fair trial, disclosure is essential;[1] in such a case, advisers should request an oral hearing to determine disclosure[2]);
- any comparative evidence (eg sales figures or commission of (non-disabled) colleagues);
- the redundancy criteria;
- the appraisal forms;
- the annual report and accounts of the company/organisation;
- job application forms (these can be copied with names and personal details deleted); and
- any notes of interviews with details of those involved in the interview process.

6.19 To ensure that advisers have full disclosure, it may be useful to add as a 'catch all' 'all documents relevant to the issues in the case'. In addition, advisers will certainly want to see all documents that the respondent intends to rely upon.

6.20 Discovery entitles the applicant to a list of documents held by the respondent (and vice versa); inspection is the process by which the documents are inspected and details taken or copies obtained. Respondents can supply a list of documents by way of

---

1   Particularly in light of the Human Rights Act 1998, Sch 1, Art 6 – right to a fair hearing. See also *London Borough of Hammersmith and Fulham v Farnsworth* [2000] IRLR 691.

2   In some cases, a tribunal may consider it appropriate to delete irrelevant parts of a report, or to limit disclosure to legal advisers: *DHSS v Sloan* [1981] ICR 313, EAT.

discovery and can ask the applicant's representative to arrange a mutually convenient time for inspection. This will mean that the applicant's representative will have to visit the respondent's premises or the premises of the respondent's representative in order to inspect the documents and take copies as necessary. This is only likely to happen, however, where there are vast numbers of documents, as it is usual practice for discovery and inspection to take the form of copies of documents being made, with, in some cases, photocopying charges being asked of the other party. So long as these charges are reasonable, they should be met. It is worth remembering that 'documents' is not restricted to print alone – the term includes tape recordings and photographs.

Privileged documents

6.21   Neither party can be asked to disclose privileged documents. 'Privilege' arises in the following instances:

–   **Legal privilege**   The first form of legal privilege is legal advice privilege. This covers communications between a client and legal adviser which are confidential and are made for the purpose of obtaining or providing legal advice. This privilege lasts indefinitely. The second form is legal proceedings privilege, which protects communications between a client, legal representative and third parties which are made for the purpose of existing or contemplated legal proceedings. Such privilege ends when the proceedings come to an end. 'Legal representative' means a barrister or a solicitor, solicitor's employee or other authorised litigator (as defined in the Courts and Legal Services Act 1990) who has been instructed to act for a party in relation to a claim. Advisers need to be aware that unless they are qualified lawyers, their communications may not be covered by privilege. If there is an issue about this, advisers will need to argue before the tribunal that such communication, although not privileged, is confidential and should not be disclosed because of the relationship between the client and adviser. It will be for the tribunal to decide whether or not such documentation is to be disclosed.

–   **'Without prejudice' communications**   These should not be disclosed to a court.[1] They most commonly take the form of correspondence between the parties about settlement. Parties can enter into dialogue about settling the case without their case being

---

1   *Cutts v Head* [1984] Ch 290, CA; *Independent Research Services Ltd v Catterall* [1993] ICR 1, EAT: this case held that this rule applies as much to proceedings before employment tribunals as it does to proceedings in a court of law.

compromised by ensuring that all communications are marked 'without prejudice'.

– **Public interest immunity** This protects certain documents from discovery on the ground that disclosure would be damaging to the public interest. Where this is claimed, the tribunal has to balance the potential damage against the importance of the documents to the proceedings, the extent of injustice caused by their non-disclosure and the public interest in fair administration of justice.[1] It is possible, however, that the Human Rights Act 1998, and in particular Art 6 which guarantees the right to a fair trial, may make further inroads into 'public interest immunity' as a justification for withholding documents.

– **National security** Where a minister believes that the disclosure of any information would be contrary to the interests of national security, any disclosure of that information is prohibited.[2]

Documents held by third parties

6.22 Where a third party holds a document (eg a report prepared by a disability employment adviser) and the report is not disclosed voluntarily, the employment tribunal has the power (under Employment Tribunals (Constitution and Rules of Procedure) Regulations 1993, Sch 1, para 4(2)(b)) to order any person and therefore the holder of the document to attend at an appointed place at an appointed time and to produce any document relating to the matter to be determined. The power can be exercised either on request by either party or of the tribunal's own motion. Whilst this power is useful where an essential document is being held by another party, advisers will need to be certain that such documentation will assist them, and that they will not obtain a document which is damaging but which will be in the public arena by this time. This tribunal power can be used prior to the hearing, as the order does not have to be for the party to attend the substantive hearing, but could be to attend a preliminary hearing. It will be better to have such documents disclosed at the earliest possible opportunity.

Ordering discovery

6.23 The tribunal has the power (under Employment Tribunals (Constitution and Rules of Procedure) Regulations 1993, Sch 1, para 4(1)(b)) to order discovery, either on the application of either party or of its own motion, or to order inspection of documents

---

1   *D v NSPCC* [1977] 1 All ER 589, HL.
2   Employment Rights Act 1996, s 195.

(including photocopying) such as may be granted by the county court. The county court can order discovery of documents which have been in the possession of a party and which relate to any question in the proceedings. When considering disclosure, county courts will take into account all the circumstances of the case and, in particular, the overriding objectives in Part 1 of the Civil Procedure Rules 1998 (Practice Direction 31). These overriding objectives include ensuring that parties are on an equal footing, saving expense, and ensuring that the case is dealt with expeditiously and fairly (Civil Procedure Rules 1998, r 1.1). Tribunals will often give directions for the exchange of documents on which parties will be relying and for the production of an agreed bundle of documents that can be used at the hearing. However, it is useful to seek discovery as early as possible, and specifically of documents that the respondent is unlikely to rely upon, as they may be of most help to the applicant's case.

6.24   When requesting discovery, advisers should send a letter to the respondent, with a copy to the tribunal, asking for the list of documents and giving a particular period of time within which a response is expected. If there is no response, advisers should write to the tribunal, trying to give at least a broad outline as to why documents are required and how they are relevant, as well as indicating that voluntary disclosure has already been sought.

6.25   Advisers may find it useful to look at – and potentially quote from – the case of *West Midlands Passenger Transport Executive v Singh*,[1] where the Court of Appeal held that, when deciding whether information sought in a discrimination case was relevant, the special features of discrimination proceedings should be taken account of. The court stated that:

–   the documents in question need not prove conclusively that the employer has discriminated; for the purposes of the discovery application it need only be established that the documents may tend to prove that such discrimination has taken place;

–   direct discrimination means that the complainant has not been assessed according to individual merit but has been treated less favourably as a member of a particular group (statistical information may establish a discernible pattern in the treatment of a particular group, for example under-representation in certain jobs or lack of promotion, which may in turn give rise to an inference of discrimination against members of the group);

---

1   [1988] ICR 614, [1988] IRLR 186, CA.

– if a practice is being operated against a group, then, in the absence of a satisfactory explanation, it will be reasonable to infer that the complainant as a member of that group, has been treated less favourably on the grounds of race or sex;

– evidence of discrimination against a group in relation to promotion may be more persuasive evidence of discrimination in the particular case than previous treatment of the applicant which may be indicative of personal factors peculiar to the applicant;

– as suitability can rarely be measured solely by objective means but will generally involve subjective judgements, evidence relating to the success or failure of members of a particular group may indicate that the real reason for failure is a conscious or unconscious discriminatory attitude which involves stereotyped assumptions about members of that group; and

– as employers are permitted to adduce evidence demonstrating that in practice they operate a policy of non-discrimination, the employee must be entitled to seek evidence to the contrary.

6.26 In *Sivanandan v London Borough of Enfield and Others*,[1] the applicant appealed against an employment tribunal decision to confine an order for discovery to documents in existence when the applicant, who was complaining of direct discrimination and victimisation, was dismissed. The EAT held that it was consistent with the approach to the evidential difficulties in discrimination cases that tribunals should be prepared to be 'generous' in the orders for discovery that they make in such cases. In a direct discrimination or victimisation case, it should be understood that there may well be documents which come into existence after the events that immediately gave rise to the complaint which may be pertinent and shed light on the difficult questions regarding inferences to be drawn or decisions made about the motivation of the parties in a victimisation case.

6.27 When the documents are received, copies should be sent to the client, and each document should be studied for any information that would be relevant to the case and which support the applicant's position. It may be that further documents are referred to in the disclosed documents, which will then need to be sought if it appears that they may be relevant.

Documents which are damaging to the applicant's case

6.28 At this stage, advisers may, for the first time, receive documents which are potentially damaging to the client's case. For example, it is

---

1   2 February 1999, EAT 450, 628, Case No 1351/98.

not uncommon for job applicants to have to complete an application form that has a medical questionnaire attached. This questionnaire may ask about any disabilities and many applicants may not view their particular condition as a disability, or, if they do, will be concerned about not getting an interview if they disclose it. They might not therefore disclose any disability on the medical questionnaire. When applicants are first seen by an adviser, they might not mention such a form (although obviously the adviser should question the applicant closely about this at the first meeting) and so this may be the first indication that the respondent may impugn the applicant's credibility by use of this form. On receipt of such information, advisers need to take full instructions from the applicant about the circumstances surrounding the document. It need not be fatal to a claim to have such information in existence – the important thing is to ensure that the applicant addresses the existence of this information in her witness statement, and to stress to the tribunal the reasons for non-disclosure at that stage.

6.29   If there are any documents which considerably undermine the applicant's case, advisers will need to consider carefully whether the case is so damaged that it is no longer worth pursuing.

6.30   Once all the documents have been received, advisers will need to review the case to ensure that everything necessary has been obtained (eg receipt of documents may raise the need for further documents) and to ensure that the case still has the same prospects of success as anticipated previously. If not, the adviser and applicant will need to discuss the way forward (eg whether to continue, accept a settlement offer or withdraw).

CASE STUDIES

NOTICE OF APPEARANCE

(1)   The first Respondent is the Head Teacher employed by the second Respondent. The second Respondent is the Governing Body of a relatively small, grant-maintained school with 300 pupils and a total of 30 teaching and non-teaching staff.

(2)   In January 1999, the Music Co-ordinator employed at the Respondent's school tendered her resignation. The job of Music Co-ordinator involves planning the music curriculum, producing lesson plans and providing music for school assemblies, productions and special events as well as teaching music. The Respondent advertised in the *Times Educational Supplement* for a replacement. A large number of applications of a high calibre were received in response to the advertisement and nine candidates were shortlisted for interview, including the Applicant.

(3)   The first and second Respondents were not aware of the Applicant's visual impairment prior to the interview on 12 March 1999. The Applicant did not complete the part of the Application form that asked if he had any disabilities or serious illnesses. This question had been placed on the form to ensure that the Respondents could comply with their duties under the provisions of the Disability Discrimination Act 1995.

(4)   The interview took place on 12 March 1999. It is denied that the Applicant did not know in advance who would be interviewing him. With the letter inviting the Applicant for interview he was sent a map giving directions to the school, which on the reverse stated the time of the interview, the room it would be in and the names of the interview panel.

(5)   In any event, the first Respondent was happy to introduce the Applicant to the panel members and did so when requested to by the Applicant.

(6)   It is denied that the panel members acknowledged during the course of the interview that the Applicant met all the essential criteria for the post.

(7)   Mrs Alison Martin did not ask the Applicant how he would cope with the volume of paperwork, but rather how he would cope with the work – this was a question asked of all candidates.

(8)   It is denied that the first Respondent said that the school's budget would not stretch to the purchase of additional equipment or that he raised the question of cost at all. The first Respondent merely

enquired as to how much extra room might be needed for the equipment.

(9)   The panel members decided to appoint to the post the candidate who was the best qualified and most suited to the post. This was not the Applicant.

(10) It is denied that the first Respondent did not telephone the Applicant to let him know the outcome of the interview. The first Respondent's secretary was instructed to telephone all of the shortlisted candidates and to confirm the call with a letter.

(11) The first Respondent did not receive a telephone message from the Applicant. This may have been because his secretary was away at that time and a temporary secretary was working for him. The first Respondent was out of the country for a period from 29 March to 12 April 1999.

(12) It is denied that the Respondents discriminated against the Applicant in either the arrangements made for the purpose of determining to whom employment should be offered or in refusing or deliberately not offering employment, or at all.

(13) In particular, it is denied that the Respondents discriminated against the Applicant in:

 (a)   the manner in which the interview was conducted or by the behaviour of any panel member including the first Respondent or by failing to let the Applicant know who was on the interview panel;

 (b)   the failure to appoint the Applicant to the post – the standard of applications was very high and the position was offered to the best-qualified and most suitable candidate for the position.

(14) If, which is denied, the first Respondent is found to have acted contrary to the provisions of the Disability Discrimination Act 1995, the second Respondent will aver that it is not liable for such breach in accordance with s 58(5) of the Act, in that it has taken such steps as were reasonably practicable to prevent the first Respondent from doing such acts or from doing, in the course of his employment, acts of that description.

(15) The Respondents deny that their behaviour caused the Applicant any humiliation or distress.

**IN THE EMPLOYMENT TRIBUNAL
CASE NUMBER: 23450/99**

BETWEEN

MR R MISTRY

Applicant

And

(1) ANDREW HOLDEN

(2) GOVERNORS OF WHITEMORE PRIMARY SCHOOL

Respondent

REQUEST FOR FURTHER PARTICULARS OF NOTICE OF APPEARANCE

Paragraph 2

OF

'A large number of applications of a high calibre were received in response to the advertisement and nine candidates were shortlisted for interview, including the Applicant.'

STATE

1. How many applications were received – please provide copies of all applications.
2. What is meant by the term 'high calibre'.

Paragraph 3

OF

'This question had been placed on the form to ensure that the Respondents could comply with their duties under the provisions of the Disability Discrimination Act 1995.'

STATE

1. The precise wording on the form.
2. The use to which any answers given on this form would be put.

Paragraph 4

OF

'With the letter inviting the Applicant for interview he was sent a map giving directions to the school, which on the reverse stated the time of the interview, the room it would be in and the names of the interview panel.'

STATE

1. On what date the letter was sent to the Applicant.
2. Please supply a copy of the letter inviting the applicant to interview and a copy of any accompanying literature.

Paragraph 6

OF

'It is denied that the panel members acknowledged during the course of the interview that the Applicant met all the essential criteria for the post.'

STATE

1. What was said to the Applicant during his interview about his qualifications and experience.

Paragraph 7

OF

'Mrs Alison Martin did not ask the Applicant how he would cope with the volume of paperwork, but rather how he would cope with the work – this was a question asked of all candidates.'

STATE

1. Whether there were set number of questions asked of all candidates. If so please provide a copy of the list of questions.

Paragraph 8

OF

'The first Respondent merely enquired as to how much extra room might be needed for the equipment.'

STATE

1. Precisely what the first Respondent said to the Applicant about extra room.

Paragraph 9

OF

'The panel members decided to appoint to the post the candidate who was the best qualified and most suited to the post. This was not the Applicant.'

STATE

1. Whether the decision to appoint was unanimous; if not, who dissented and reasons for this.
2. In what way was the person appointed the best qualified and most suited to the post; in what way did s/he meet the person specification; and what criteria were used to judge whether or not s/he was the best qualified and most suited to the post.

Paragraph 10

OF

'The first Respondent's secretary was instructed to telephone all of the shortlisted candidates and to confirm the call with a letter.'

STATE

1. Whether or not the first Respondent's secretary was given specific instructions to telephone the Applicant because of his request.
2. Whether or not the secretary instructed to make the call to the Applicant was the first Respondent's usual secretary.
3. Whether or not the secretary did make the call to the Applicant and if s/he did:
   (a) on what date the call was made,
   (b) at what time the call was made,
   (c) to whom if anyone s/he spoke,
   (d) how many times s/he tried to make the call,
   (e) whether or not a message was left and if so what the message was,
   (f) whether or not s/he was asked to confirm to Mr Holden or anyone else that she had made or tried to call the Applicant and if so whether or not this was done.

Paragraph 11

OF

'This may have been because his secretary was on leave at that time and a temporary secretary was working for him.'

STATE

1. The dates during which the temporary secretary was working for the first Respondent.

Paragraph 14

OF

'... it has taken such steps as were reasonably practicable to prevent the first Respondent from doing such acts or from doing, in the course of his employment, acts of that description.'

STATE

1.   What steps the second Respondent has taken to prevent the first Respondent from doing such acts or from doing, in the course of his employment, acts of that description.

NOTE   Some of the questions may of course have already been answered in the reply to the questionnaire.

REQUEST FOR DISCOVERY IN THE CASE OF *RAJ MISTRY v ANDREW HOLDEN AND WHITEMOOR PRIMARY SCHOOL*

List of documents requested

(1) Copy of job description and person specification for the post of Music Co-ordinator.
(2) Copies of all application forms for the above post.
(3) Copies of all application forms held by all those shortlisting and interviewing for the above post.[1]
(4) Copies of all notes of shortlisting.
(5) Copies of all notes of interview.
(6) Copies of equal opportunities policy.
(7) Copies of recruitment and selection policy.
(8) Copies of disability policy.
(9) Copies of training materials for any equal opportunities courses/ disability courses which the interviewers have attended.

---

1   Some employers will keep the original application forms in personnel and give each shortlister their own copies. These may have notes on them and so it is important to obtain copies of these if possible.

Chapter 7

INTERLOCUTORY MATTERS

THE DIRECTIONS HEARING

Directions

7.1 In *Goodwin v The Patent Office*,[1] the EAT indicated that there should be a directions hearing in every case under the DDA 1995. Therefore, advisers should be prepared for a directions hearing as soon as the originating application has been submitted. In some cases, the tribunal will notify the applicant of the date for the directions hearing at the same time as providing the applicant with the respondent's notice of appearance. If the tribunal does not, of its own motion, list a directions hearing, a request for directions can be made to the tribunal by either party under the Employment Tribunals (Constitution and Rules of Procedure) Regulations 1993, Sch 1, para 16(2). It is sensible to make such a request because directions hearings are a useful means of ensuring that the advisers are fully prepared for the main hearing.

7.2 Some tribunals are now prepared to conduct directions hearings by way of a conference telephone call which can save travelling and waiting time for often relatively short hearings. An applicant representing herself could ask for this as a reasonable adjustment if travelling to the tribunal or accessibility is difficult.

7.3 In November 2000, the Secretary of State for Trade and Industry announced proposals to reform tribunals. Among the amendments to the employment tribunal rules of procedure will be a new statement of the principles guiding the tribunals, which will explain the overriding objective of the tribunals to deal with cases justly, including, so far as practicable, ensuring the parties are dealt with equally; saving expense; acting in proportion with the complexity of the case; and dealing with cases fairly and expeditiously. The parties will have a duty to assist the tribunal in furthering the overriding objective. In addition, tribunals will be able to further the overriding objective by giving such directions

---

1   [1999] IRLR 4, EAT.

to the parties as appear to them to be appropriate. These changes are due to be implemented in July 2001. They are likely to mean that directions hearings will become more common in all cases.

7.4   It is sensible to agree directions with the respondent before the hearing. In practice, this usually means telephoning or writing to the respondent's representative to ask her views on such matters as the length of the hearing, witnesses, the issues in dispute and to ask if directions can be agreed to save time. Respondents are usually amenable to agreeing directions as this is likely to mean that the hearing will be shorter and so less expensive. It is also a good way of discovering the issues that can be agreed and the issues that are in dispute before the directions hearing so as not to be taken by surprise at the hearing itself by the other party. Alternatively, directions can always be agreed at the tribunal just before the directions hearing itself.

7.5   Directions hearings are before a Chairman sitting alone who will deal with:

(1)   the issues that are not in dispute (eg the respondent might agree that the applicant meets the definition of disability or that the applicant was dismissed and so that there was less favourable treatment under s 5(2) of the DDA 1995);[1]

(2)   the issues that are in dispute – advisers should be prepared to set out for the Chairman the main issues of the case and the sections of the DDA 1995 relied upon, for example less favourable treatment (s 4 and s 5(1)), failure to make reasonable adjustments (s 4, s 5(2) and s 6), justification or victimisation (s 4 and s 55);

(3)   whether or not there is a need for a preliminary hearing – the Chairman is likely to order a preliminary hearing if there is a dispute about such issues as whether or not:
    (a)   the applicant meets the definition of disability;[2]
    (b)   the claim was presented in time;[3]
    (c)   the DDA 1995 applies to the applicant or the respondent, for example:
        (i)   is or was the applicant in excluded employment?,
        (ii) does the respondent have 15 employees including or excluding associated companies, branches, etc?,
        (iii) was or is the applicant an 'employee'?, and
        (iv) was or is the applicant a 'contract worker'?;
    (d)   the tribunal has the jurisdiction to hear the claim;

---

1   *Clark v Novacold Ltd* [1998] IRLR 420.
2   See Chapter 3.
3   See Chapter 5.

(4) the number of witnesses both parties are going to call and witness orders if necessary; however, in practice, advisers may not be aware at the directions hearing stage that a witness order will be necessary, therefore witness orders may be applied for at the directions hearing or at a later stage in writing.

The proposed amendments to the employment tribunal rules of procedure (see **7.3** above) will give tribunals the power to order costs; strike out the whole or part of the originating application or notice of appearance; or direct that a respondent be debarred from defending altogether for failure to comply with any directions issued by the tribunal (subject to opportunity to show cause why this should not be done). In addition, the tribunal will have the power to strike out, at any stage in the proceedings, an application or response on the grounds that it has no real prospect of success.

Orders

7.6   Under the Employment Tribunals (Constitution and Rules of Procedure) Regulations 1993, Sch 1, para 4(2), a tribunal, which can be a Chairman sitting alone,[1] may on application by any party to the proceedings or of its own motion order any person within Great Britain to attend as a witness. The order will specify the time and place at which the witness concerned must attend, ie the preliminary hearing or main liability hearing.

7.7   When applying for a witness order, the adviser will need to show that the witness in question can give evidence which is relevant to the issues in dispute and that it is necessary to issue the witness order.[2] In order to show that a witness order is necessary, advisers should write to the witness inviting her to attend to give evidence voluntarily. If the witness fails to reply to this letter or refuses to attend, an order may be applied for. A witness may also indicate that it would be much easier for her to attend the hearing to give evidence if she was served with a witness order, for example because an employer is unwilling to release her. In these circumstances, a witness order may be sought.

7.8   In most cases, a witness order will not be necessary. This is not least because a witness who is reluctant to attend is unlikely to co-operate before the hearing in the drafting of the witness statement or at the hearing itself and so may not be a good witness to call at all. As a general

---

1   Employment Tribunals (Constitution and Rules of Procedure) Regulations 1993, Sch 1, para 13(8).
2   *Dada v Metal Box Co Ltd* [1974] ICR 559, [1974] IRLR 251; *Eagle Star Insurance Co Ltd v Hayward* [1981] ICR 860, EAT.

rule, if the adviser is unsure about what a witness might say in evidence, it is unwise to call that witness. It would be better for the other side to call the witness so that there will be the opportunity to cross-examine the witness. Thus, it is vital to name all the relevant respondents in the originating application as naming particular individuals is likely to ensure that they will appear to give evidence.[1]

7.9   If a witness order is made against a person in his absence, that person may apply to the tribunal to vary or set aside the order by writing to the Secretary of the tribunals. The Secretary will then serve notice of the application to set aside or vary the order to all the other parties to the proceedings. The power of the tribunal to order a witness to attend is similar to the power of the High Court to subpoena a person to attend before it. If a person who is subject to a tribunal witness order fails to comply with its terms, that person is liable on summary conviction to a fine.[2]

7.10   The tribunal's power to order a witness to attend is discretionary and so it is difficult to appeal against the tribunal's decision. As the application for a witness order is an interlocutory matter, there is no power to review the witness order. It is important, therefore, for advisers to ensure when applying for an order that all the facts and reasons why the order is sought are set out clearly in the application. This may be another reason for not making the application at the directions hearing stage. However, it is also important not to leave the application for a witness order too late as the witness must have sufficient time to apply to set aside or vary the order, by way of an oral hearing if necessary.

7.11   If the witness order is granted at the directions hearing or early in the proceedings, advisers should make a note on the file reminding themselves to make an application to vary the order if the date or time of the hearing changes if the wording of the order granted does not take this into account. An application to vary the order will also be needed if the hearing goes part-heard before all of that witness's evidence has been heard. Finally, when the witness has finished giving his evidence, the adviser or representative will need to ask the tribunal to 'release' the witness so that the witness will not be in breach of the order by leaving the tribunal before the expiry of the time period specified in the order.

Exchange of witness statements

7.12   Tribunals are increasingly asking that all witnesses give their evidence from prepared witness statements, copies of which should be

1   See Chapter 5 on drafting the originating application.
2   ETA 1996, s 7(4).

supplied to the respondent and members of the panel at the hearing. This is usually better for representatives as well, but advisers should ensure that it is appropriate for their client. For example, it might be better for an applicant with learning disabilities to be asked clear and simple questions by his or her representative rather than reading from a prepared statement. If this is the case, the applicant's adviser should ask for permission for the applicant to give his evidence in this way at the directions hearing.

7.13 It is also usual for the Chairman to order that witness statements be exchanged before the hearing unless there is good reason why they should not be. It is in the interests of both parties to know the other's whole case by the date of the hearing. This means that there is less likely to be something unexpected at the hearing for which the representative is unprepared. It is usually ordered that witness statements will be exchanged at least 7 days before the hearing.

7.14 The applicant's representative should ask for exchange to take place more than 7 days in advance of the hearing if the applicant needs the statements in an alternative format (eg braille) and the respondent is unable to supply them in such a format but the applicant is able to convert statements given on the disk to braille. This is worth doing even though, in practice, exchange of witness statements rarely takes place a full 7 days before the hearing. Asking for this adjustment may mean that exchange takes place at least a few days before the hearing and, if it has not, this can be drawn to the tribunal's attention at the hearing.

The length of time the hearing is likely to last

7.15 The Chairman is likely to want to set a date for the next hearing, whether a preliminary hearing or the main hearing at the directions hearing and so advisers should come prepared with suitable dates for themselves, their clients and witnesses. Increasingly, tribunals are directing that this date will not later be postponed other than in exceptional circumstances.[1] It may also be necessary to consider whether or not the applicant is likely to require any reasonable adjustments under Part III of the DDA 1995 from the tribunal which will mean that the hearing will take longer. Such adjustments could include extra or longer breaks if the applicant's disability means that she tires easily or finds it difficult to concentrate for long periods of time. The use of a reader, signer or interpreter by the applicant is also an adjustment that will mean that the hearing will take longer as all documents will

---

1   See Chapter 8.

have to be communicated to the applicant by a third party. In addition, the signer or interpreter will need regular breaks.

7.16 Advisers should give careful consideration to how long the hearing is likely to last and give as accurate an assessment as possible. It is much better to overestimate the time needed and leave a day free than to underestimate and risk the case being 'part heard'. If all the evidence cannot be heard in the time allocated, the tribunal will order that the case be re-listed to continue at a later date. In busy areas this can be 6 months later by which time the impact of the applicant's evidence, which is usually heard first, may be forgotten. The case may settle in the intervening period, but if it does not the client will have to wait for often a considerable period for a remedy and this may cause grave hardship.

7.17 It is the applicant's adviser's duty to tell the client about the procedure at the hearing and to ask if the applicant will need any such adjustments. The adviser should ask the Chairman for these reasonable adjustments at the directions hearing and be prepared to give an estimate of how much extra time the applicant is likely to need. Advisers and applicants should be prepared to be imaginative and ask for adjustments that will genuinely assist the applicant, the respondent and the tribunal. Tribunals have little experience of making such adjustments and most will be willing to accommodate reasonable requests. For example, if a sign language interpreter is unavailable or the applicant has difficulty using speech, it may be a reasonable adjustment to use a palantypist who can type what is said. This can then be projected onto a screen or wall to be read. A speech to text synthesiser may also be used in a similar manner although accuracy may not always be as good as with a palantypist.

7.18 Other reasonable adjustments under Part III of the DDA 1995 (and Sch 1, Art 6 to the HRA 1998) needed by the applicant at the hearing or from the tribunal might include:

– holding the hearing at an alternative accessible venue;
– holding the hearing at a venue near to the applicant's home as opposed to where the respondent is based if the applicant cannot travel long distances because of a disability;
– speech-to-text machines or palantypists; or
– correspondence from the tribunal in an accessible format (eg tape, braille or of a specified type and size of font).

7.19 The Chairman may direct that the tribunal discuss the need for reasonable adjustments such as additional breaks with the parties before the start of the main hearing. This should be recorded in the Chairman's directions.

7.20 If the Chairman refuses to make such reasonable adjustments for a disabled person, advisers will need to consider an appeal to the EAT under Sch 1, Art 6 to the HRA 1998 on the basis that a fair hearing is impossible. There may, of course, also be a possible claim against the tribunal under Part II of the DDA 1995 in the county court, although an appeal to the EAT is likely to be a more appropriate way forward.

Exchange of documents and the preparation of the hearing bundle

7.21 It is usual for the Chairman to order that each party let the other have all the documents intended to be relied upon at the hearing at least 14 days before the hearing and that six copies of an agreed, indexed bundle be produced at the hearing. If the applicant has difficulty accessing standard print documents, the applicant's adviser should consider asking for exchange of documents to take place more than 14 days before the hearing unless the respondent can supply them in the applicant's preferred format. This would mean, for example, that unless the respondent can supply the documents in braille, it should supply them at least 21 days in advance so that they can be scanned or typed up and translated into braille or read out to the applicant.

7.22 The applicant's advisers can also ask for all correspondence from the respondent to be supplied in an accessible format. This could be on tape, disc or in braille or of a specified type and size of font and the Chairman should be asked to order this.

Further particulars

7.23 If either party has not sufficiently particularised their case, the Chairman is likely to direct that further particulars be supplied.[1] If further particulars have already been requested from the respondent (or vice versa) and have not been supplied by the date of the directions hearing, the Chairman can be asked to order that they be provided. Advisers should take copies of the request for further and better particulars to the hearing for the Chairman to read.

7.24 If the applicant drafted the originating application without the benefit of legal advice, the applicant's adviser should consider asking the Chairman for permission to submit an amended originating application setting out the case in full. The Chairman may be willing to give such permission provided the amended originating application is

---

1 Employment Tribunals (Constitution and Rules of Procedure) Regulations 1993, Sch 1, para 4(1). See also Chapter 6.

submitted by a specified date, especially if it can be argued that this will expedite the case. In these circumstances, the Chairman will allow the respondent to submit an amended notice of appearance in response. In some cases, the Chairman may order this without it being requested by the parties.

Discovery of documents

7.25   If the applicant is aware of a document in the possession of the respondent that the respondent will not provide to the applicant, say for confidentiality reasons, the applicant's representative should ask the Chairman to order its supply. This may be done only where it is known that a specific document exists. The Chairman will not allow a 'fishing expedition'. The applicant's representative will also have to convince the Chairman that this document is relevant to the case and will assist the proceedings. If confidentiality of third parties is an issue, the Chairman can be asked to order that all names and addresses are deleted and that the third parties are known only by numbers or letters of the alphabet.

Expert evidence and cost

7.26   If a medical expert is to be called, the tribunal should be asked to meet the cost of this. In complex cases where each party intends to call expert witnesses, the respondent may ask for directions specifying dates by which the applicant is to supply his expert evidence on which the respondent will then ask its expert to comment. The respondent may also ask for the applicant to be examined by the respondent's medical expert. Advisers should not agree to such a direction without first taking specific instruction from the client on whether or not they are prepared to attend such an examination. Advisers may also need to make it clear that the applicant does not consent in any way to such an examination or to any form of treatment or invasive test being administered by the respondent's medical expert. Advisers will have to bear in mind the guidance issued by the EAT in *De Keyser*.[1]

Restricted reporting orders

7.27   Under the Employment Tribunals (Constitution and Rules of Procedure) Regulations 1993, Sch 1, r 14(1A), the tribunal can, either of its own motion or on application from a party, make a restricted reporting order if evidence of a personal nature is likely to be heard by

---

1   *De Keyser Ltd v Miss L Wilson*, 1 March 2001 EAT No 1438/00. See Chapter 3 for further details.

the tribunal.[1] It is not essential that the application for a restricted reporting order be made at the directions hearing stage, but this is a good opportunity to raise the issue. The application for such an order can be made at any time before the promulgation of the tribunal's decision, ie the date on which the determination of the originating application is sent to the parties. Therefore, it should be possible to ask for a restricted reporting order at the main hearing itself.

7.28 The tribunal will not make a restricted reporting order unless it has given each party an opportunity to advance oral arguments at a hearing if they so wish.

7.29 Where the tribunal does make a restricted reporting order, it will:

–   specify the persons who may not be identified;
–   specify that the order shall remain in force until the promulgation of the decision unless it is revoked earlier; and
–   ensure that a notice of the fact is displayed on the noticeboard of the tribunal with any list of the proceedings taking place before the employment tribunal, and on the door of the room in which proceedings affected by the order are taking place.

The tribunal may revoke a restricted reporting order at any time.

7.30 Advisers should consider asking for a restricted reporting order where any personal evidence about a client's health or ability to cope with the effect of the disability on personal day-to-day activities is to be given to the tribunal. This may be particularly pertinent in preliminary hearings when deciding whether or not the applicant meets the definition of disability. Advisers should also consider requesting a restricted reporting order where evidence about how the applicant became disabled is to be given. In the case of '*A*' *v* '*B*'[2] the evidence given by the applicant about her depression and mental health problems included evidence about how she had been raped in November 1997.

Applications for the hearing to be held in private

7.31 A tribunal may be reluctant to hold a hearing in private. It will need to balance the need to have a fair and open hearing with the need to protect the privacy of the applicant. Nevertheless, under the Employment Tribunals (Constitution and Rules of Procedure) Regulations 1993, Sch 1, para 8, the tribunal can hear evidence in private from any person if the information to be given as evidence has been

---

1   ETA 1996, s 12 'restriction of publicity in disability cases'.
2   Case No 2600067/99.

communicated to that person in confidence. This could apply to evidence to be given by a doctor seen by the applicant where the applicant has not disclosed full details of his disability to his family.

JOINDER

7.32 Another interlocutory matter that might be dealt with by the tribunal in a case under the DDA 1995, either by way of a hearing or by making directions or orders, is joinder.

7.33 As discussed in Chapter 5, advisers should take care to ensure that all respondents are correctly named at the outset. However, if this has not been done on the originating application, it is still possible to join another party to the proceedings at a later stage. The tribunal has the discretion to join a party to the proceedings as a respondent at any time[1] including after the time-limit for presenting a claim against a new respondent has expired.[2] A party can even be joined after the decision on the merits has been made. This was done in *Linbourne v Constable,*[3] where the EAT held that an amendment should be allowed to substitute a respondent even though the decision had already been given.

7.34 When hearing an application to join another party to the proceedings the tribunal will take into consideration the following guidelines laid down in the case of *Cocking v Sandhurst (Stationers) Ltd.*[4]

– The tribunal should ask whether the originating application complied with the rules relating to the presentation of originating applications (see Chapter 5) and if it was presented within the relevant time-limit (ie within 3 months). If it was not, a new originating application must be submitted within the relevant time-limit.

– If the original application did comply with the rules on presentation of originating applications, the tribunal has the discretion to allow a party to be joined or substituted for an existing party. However, the tribunal is likely to do so only if there has been a genuine mistake which parties are now trying to correct. The mistake must not be misleading or likely to cause reasonable doubt about the identity of the person claimed against or the person making the claim.

---

1   Employment Tribunals (Constitution and Rules of Procedure) Regulations 1993, Sch 1, para 17(1).
2   *Drinkwater Sabey Ltd v Burnett* [1995] ICR 328, [1995] IRLR 238, EAT; following *Gillick v BP Chemicals Ltd* [1993] IRLR 437, EAT.
3   [1993] ICR 698. See also *Watts v Seven Kings Motor Co Ltd* [1983] ICR 135.
4   [1974] ICR 650.

– When deciding whether or not to exercise its discretion, the tribunal should consider all the circumstances of the case including any injustice or hardship which may be caused to any of the parties or potential parties if the amendment is either allowed or refused. If allowing the amendment is likely to cause unnecessary additional cost to one party, the tribunal might order the party seeking the amendment to pay the additional costs caused by the late amendment. This is another reason to name the correct respondent at the outset.

7.35 In *Sivanandan v London Borough of Enfield and Others*,[1] the EAT held that the tribunal had erred in law by refusing to allow the applicant to join as respondents members of the executive committee of an unincorporated association whom she claimed had knowingly aided and abetted her employer in an act of unlawful race discrimination. The applicant had made the application for joinder because she had named the unincorporated association as a respondent on her originating application. However, the tribunal had dismissed the unincorporated association as a party because it did not exist as a legal entity and so could not be sued. The EAT said that the tribunal should have readily acceded to the application for joinder, bearing in mind that the application had sued the association at the outset. There was a manifest error of law and an obvious injustice to the applicant in the tribunal's approach.

7.36 However, the tribunal can only join a party against whom relief is sought. In *Sandhu v Department of Education and Science*,[2] an order joining the DES as a respondent to a race discrimination claim was refused on the basis that it was not the applicant's employer; nor was there any evidence to show that it had aided the employer in any discriminatory act. Therefore, no relief could be granted against the Department of Education and Science and it could not be joined as a party to the proceedings.

7.37 The tribunal can also order that a respondent be dismissed from being a party to the proceedings[3] or that one party represent a number of parties who have the same interests.[4] Such orders can be made by the tribunal of its own motion or on application by a party and will usually be decided by the Chairman alone.

---

1 2 February 1999, EAT 450, 628, Case No 1351/98.
2 [1978] IRLR 208, EAT.
3 Employment Tribunals (Constitution and Rules of Procedure) Regulations 1993, Sch 1, para 17(2).
4 Ibid, Sch 1, para 17(3).

Bankruptcy and insolvency

7.38   If one of the parties is bankrupt, the trustee in bankruptcy will have an interest in the outcome and so will be entitled to apply to be joined as a party.

Striking out

7.39   An application for striking out may be made by either party at any stage up to and including the main hearing.

Want of prosecution
7.40   The respondent may apply to have the originating application struck out for want of prosecution by the applicant.[1] In considering such an application, the tribunal will apply the guidelines as laid down by the House of Lords in *Birkett v James*[2] which referred to two types of case.

(1)   The first case is where the applicant has failed to comply with an order of the tribunal and it was made clear that the application would be struck out unless the applicant complied with the order within the time allowed. This could be an order for further particulars, discovery or written answers. However, before the tribunal strikes out the originating application, the applicant must be given the opportunity to show cause why such an order should not be made. The tribunal will normally serve a notice on the applicant giving him the opportunity to show cause orally or in writing why such an order for striking out should not be made.[3]
(2)   The second case is where there has been an inordinate and inexcusable delay on the part of the applicant or the applicant's representative and the delay means that there is a substantial risk that it will not be possible to have a fair trial of the issues or it is likely to cause serious prejudice to the respondent.

Scandalous, frivolous or vexatious applications
7.41   At any stage of the proceedings, the tribunal can order that all or any part of the originating application or notice of appearance be struck out or amended on the basis that it or the conduct of the party is scandalous, frivolous or vexatious.[4] Before exercising its power to strike out, however, the tribunal must give the party against whom the order is proposed the opportunity either to show cause orally why the order

---

1   Employment Tribunals (Constitution and Rules of Procedure) Regulations 1993, Sch 1, para 13(2)(f).
2   [1978] AC 297.
3   Employment Tribunals (Constitution and Rules of Procedure) Regulations 1993, Sch 1, para 13(3).
4   Ibid, Sch 1, para 13(2)(d) and (e).

should not be made or send notice to that party giving them an opportunity to show such cause orally or in writing.[1]

7.42 The words 'frivolous' and 'vexatious' may be widely interpreted and are not limited to dishonest claims or those made in bad faith. They may, for example, include an attempt to re-litigate an issue which has already been fully litigated and so the application is an abuse of process. They could also be used as a threat against a respondent who will not supply further and better particulars of a brief notice of appearance despite orders for such particulars. However, it should be noted that to date it has been relatively rare for tribunals to strike out proceedings.

7.43 In *Telephone Information Services Ltd v Wilkinson*,[2] the employer had made an offer to pay the employee bringing a claim for unfair dismissal the maximum statutory compensation which could then be awarded. The employee, however, was not prepared to withdraw the originating application. The EAT upheld the tribunal's refusal to strike out on the basis that the employee was entitled to pursue the claim in the expectation that a finding of unfair dismissal might be made regardless of monetary compensation. This is an even stronger argument in a claim for discrimination, as with social legislation of this kind the applicant should be entitled to pursue a claim for a declaration of discrimination.

7.44 An individual may be classed as a vexatious litigant if that person persistently and unreasonably makes applications to the tribunal or institutes appeals to the EAT. In these circumstances the EAT has the power, by way of a restriction of proceedings order, to prevent proceedings by that person being instituted or continued in either the tribunal or the EAT unless leave is given to do so.[3]

PRE-HEARING REVIEWS

7.45 Pre-hearing reviews under Sch 1, para 7(4) of the Employment Tribunals (Constitution and Rules of Procedure) Regulations 1993 are usually used to weed out particular contentions, claims or even whole cases which 'have no reasonable prospect of success'. They are usually instigated by respondents to raise the threat of costs against applicants. There is no reason, however, why pre-hearing reviews cannot be instigated by applicants against respondents. The tribunal can also instigate the process of its own motion by giving notice to the parties.

---

1   Employment Tribunals (Constitution and Rules of Procedure) Regulations 1993, Sch 1, para 13(3).
2   [1991] IRLR 148, EAT.
3   ETA 1996, s 33.

However, it is arguable that pre-hearing reviews are not appropriate in discrimination claims because so much is dependent on oral evidence and documents which are unlikely to be obtained until the case nears the full hearing.

7.46   The tribunal must provide an opportunity for the parties to be heard and to make written and oral representations at the pre-hearing review which may take place before a Chairman alone. A pre-hearing review shall not take place unless the secretary of the tribunal has sent notice to the parties giving them the opportunity to submit representations in writing and to advance oral argument at the review if they so wish. Advisers should resist any attempt by respondents to turn directions hearings into a pre-hearing review as notice *must* be given for this. The material available to the tribunal at the hearing and the matters that it can consider are strictly limited to:

- the contents of the originating application and notice of appearance;
- any representations in writing; and
- any oral argument.[1]

7.47   No live evidence can be heard at a pre-hearing review and so evidence may be submitted only by way of written representations, but these can include all or part of the witness statements to be used at the main hearing.

7.48   If, on consideration of the above, the tribunal concludes that a particular claim of the applicant or defence of the respondent has no prospect of success, it must record its reasons in summary form and send them to the parties. There is no obligation on the tribunal to provide extended reasons. The tribunal will then usually make a deposit order as a condition of a party being allowed to continue with a contention or the case as a whole. The order is that the party must pay a deposit of up to £500 (an increase from the previous £150) as a condition of being permitted to continue to take part in the proceedings 'relating to that matter'.[2] However, the tribunal must take reasonable steps before making the order to ensure that the party can comply with the order, including taking account of information about the parties' means and ability to pay the deposit.

---

1   Employment Tribunals (Constitution and Rules of Procedure) Regulations 1993, Sch 1, para 7(1).
2   By virtue of the Employment Tribunals (Increase of Maximum Deposit) Order 2001, SI 2001/237, amending s 9(3) of the Employment Tribunals Act 1996, the maximum deposit which can be required at a pre-hearing review is to be increased to £500. This is due to be implemented in July 2001.

7.49 The party on whom the order is served must pay the deposit within 21 days, although if further representations are made within that 21-day period a further 14 days in which to pay the deposit will be granted. If the order is not complied with, the tribunal has no discretion and must strike out the originating application or notice of appearance or the relevant part to which the order relates.

7.50 The deposit is refundable:

(1) if the originating application is withdrawn, as proceedings would then be at an end;
(2) if the offending part of the originating application or notice of appearance is removed – this is not provided for in the Employment Tribunals (Constitution and Rules of Procedure) Regulations 1993, but will usually happen in practice if the tribunal has not already declined to make the order for the deposit at the pre-hearing review on an assurance or undertaking that the document will be amended;
(3) at the end of the proceedings,[1] unless an award of costs is made against that party, when the deposit is paid in full or part settlement of the award.[2]

---

1   Employment Tribunals (Constitution and Rules of Procedure) Regulations 1993, Sch 1, para 7(8).
2   Ibid, Sch 1, para 12(8).

Chapter 8

EVIDENCE AND HEARINGS

PRELIMINARY HEARINGS

8.1   Employment tribunals have the power to hold what are commonly referred to as preliminary hearings, either of their own motion or on application by any of the parties.[1] Preliminary hearings determine any issue relating to the entitlement of any party to bring or to contest the proceedings to which the ET1 relates. At these hearings, the tribunal will usually consist of a legally qualified Chair and two lay members. Discrimination, as well as other cases can be heard by a Chair alone where both parties have given consent,[2] but advisers should ensure that a full tribunal hears the applicant's case. It should be noted that where a majority decision is given, it may have been that the two lay members outvoted the Chair.

8.2   Certain features of disability discrimination cases will lead to particular issues being determined by means of a preliminary hearing.[3] These issues include:

–   the meaning of 'disability', ie whether the applicant is a disabled person within the meaning of s 1 of the DDA 1995 and therefore whether the tribunal has jurisdiction to hear the claim;
–   the number of people employed by the respondent, and so whether the respondent falls within the exemptions contained in s 7 of the DDA 1995;
–   whether or not the applicant was/is an employee;
–   whether the claim has been brought against the correct respondent;
–   whether or not the claim is out of time; and, if it is, whether or not the tribunal should exercise its discretion under Sch 3, para 3(2) to the DDA 1995.

---

1   By virtue of Employment Tribunal (Constitution and Rules of Procedure) Regulations 1993, Sch 1, para 6.
2   Employment Tribunals Act 1996, s 4.
3   See Chapter 7.

8.3   Advisers should be aware of any issues which could give rise to a preliminary hearing, either from the client's instructions or from the respondent's ET3. If there are any dates that need to be avoided for the preliminary hearing, advisers should notify the tribunal as soon as it becomes apparent that there will be such a hearing. Advisers will also need to ensure that they are aware of dates on which any witnesses may not be able to attend. The hearing should be fixed and an estimate given of the likely length. The hearing itself may sometimes take almost as long as the full hearing (this is particularly the case where disability is in issue).

8.4   For each hearing, advisers will need to consider carefully the evidence necessary to meet the relevant burden of proof to ensure that the claim can proceed to a full hearing. This chapter now deals with the nature of the evidence that will need to be gathered and presented to the tribunal.

Definition of disability

8.5   This is one of the most common areas of jurisdiction to be determined in preliminary hearings, and often the respondent will either not admit or will deny that the applicant has a disability so that the applicant has to meet another hurdle in pursuing the claim. Research carried out by the Institute of Employment Studies[1] into the workings of the DDA 1995 in the first 19 months of its implementation found that there was some evidence of a tendency for respondents and their advisers to adopt a deliberate strategy of challenging the applicant on each part of the definition.

8.6   The evidence that may be necessary to prove that a client has a disability for the purposes of the DDA 1995 can be summarised as:

- a full statement from the client;
- any reports from the GP and specialist consultants;
- the occupational therapist's report, if any;
- information from disability organisations/charities;
- witnesses, other than medical, to the effects on the client's day-to-day activities;
- information from the World Health Organisation;
- research papers from journals or the internet;
- proof of receipt of disability benefits or a blue badge (driving); and
- case-law.[2]

---

1   Meager et al *Monitoring the Disability Discrimination Act 1995* (NDC/DfEE, London, 1999).
2   See Chapters 1, 3 and Appendix 2.

See Chapter 3 for a detailed consideration of these requirements.

Number of employees and associated companies

8.7 The employment provisions of the DDA 1995 do not apply to employers with fewer than 15 employees.[1] There have already been a number of cases involving disputed numbers of employees, particularly where the applicant is employed by a company with fewer than 15 employees but the company is associated with another company with a greater number of employees. In general, the tribunal will not lift the 'corporate veil' to determine that two companies are one and the same, unless the individual companies have been set up as some form of sham. Whilst associated companies can be taken together for the purposes of the SDA 1975, this is not so for cases pursued under the DDA 1995.[2]

8.8 As the number of employees is fundamental to the jurisdiction of a tribunal in a case under the DDA 1995, when the issue arises either the tribunal itself will order a preliminary hearing or the respondent is likely to ask for one. Where the number of employees is at issue, advisers will need to gather the following evidence:

– the number of employees – a list of all those people employed by the company/organisation and the hours they work;
– a list of all temporary and contract workers and any volunteers;[3]
– the company's annual report or brochures;
– a company search will indicate the names of the directors, details of any associated companies and often the number of employees;[4]
– National Insurance records; and
– details of any associated companies or branches abroad. It is unclear whether, for the purposes of s 7, employees to be counted as forming the 15 minimum have to be employed in the UK; it may be worth arguing that, where there are branches of a company abroad, these employees should be included in the number of company employees.

8.9 Advisers can ask the respondent for discovery of some of the above documents, either in the questionnaire served upon the respondent or,

---

1   Section 7 of the Disability Discrimination Act 1995, as amended.
2   See *Hardie v C D Northern Ltd* [2000] IRLR 87 and *Colt Group Ltd v Couchman* [2000] ICR 327, EAT. See also *Murray v Newham CAB* EAT No 1096/99 for the position regarding volunteers as employees.
3   See *Murray v Newham CAB* EAT No 1096/99.
4   This can be checked with Companies House by means of a company search.

if this issue has arisen only after submission of the ET1, by means of a request for discovery in advance of the preliminary hearing.[1]

Employee covered by the DDA 1995/correct respondent

8.10   The respondent may argue that the applicant is not covered by the DDA 1995 because the employment does not fall within the definition at s 68(1), or because the applicant is not a contract worker[2] within the terms of s 12(6). This situation may arise where an applicant is a volunteer, or where there is a dispute about the nature of any contract the applicant has.

8.11   There may be a dispute about whether or not the named respondent is the respondent to whom liability would attach if there were discrimination. This is particularly common in contract cases, where the issue of principal and contract worker can often be confused.[3] Again, advisers will need to make use of discovery procedures to request copies of documents such as contracts entered into between the applicant and the respondent, or any other party to the proceedings and National Insurance records.

Out of time cases

8.12   The issues arising in connection with time-limits include:

–   whether or not discrimination is continuing, and therefore within the time-limit[4] or whether it was a one-off act of discrimination and, therefore, out of time; and

–   whether or not the tribunal should exercise its jurisdiction to hear the claim out of time because it is 'just and equitable' to do so.[5]

8.13   Where there is a dispute as to whether or not an act is a continuing act or a one-off act with continuing consequences, advisers should consider whether it would be more appropriate for the issue of jurisdiction to be dealt with at the substantive hearing. It is likely that any preliminary hearing on this issue would require evidence to be given about the acts and their nature, with the respondent possibly calling contradictory evidence. Thus, it may be more sensible for all of this to be done at a substantive hearing. This has an advantage in that if the

---

1   If the respondent will not provide such documents on request, advisers should write to the tribunal requesting an order for discovery – See Chapter 6.
2   See *Abbey Life Assurance Co Ltd v Tansell* [2000] IRLR 387, (2000) IDS Brief B661/5, CA; *sub nom MHC Consulting Services Ltd v Tansell* [1999] IRLR 677, EAT.
3   Ibid.
4   DDA 1995, Sch 3, para 3(3).
5   See Chapter 4 for a detailed consideration of these issues.

tribunal is likely to find in the applicant's favour, having heard all the evidence, it is more likely to find it just and equitable to accept jurisdiction if the claim is out of time.

8.14 Where the issue is one of a claim being made out of time, and the tribunal is being asked to exercise its jurisdiction, advisers should obtain evidence:

- from a doctor/consultant as to any medical reasons for the client's failure to submit the claim on time (this may be particularly relevant to applicants who are newly diagnosed as having a disability, as they may have difficulty coming to terms with their disability and tribunals may look leniently on such situations);
- as to whether or not the client had access to information (tribunals have been understanding of the fact that the DDA 1995 is a relatively new piece of legislation about which there is little knowledge); and
- of negligence of any previous advisers (where a client's previous advisers have failed to recognise a case under the DDA 1995 or have advised negligently that there was not a case under that Act, the tribunal may be willing to accept jurisdiction).[1]

Procedure at and preparation for the preliminary hearing

8.15 The preliminary hearing is conducted in the same way as the main hearing.[2] One would normally expect the party with the burden of proof to proceed first (usually the applicant, unless it is a case in which the employer claims to have fewer than 15 employees), but ultimately the tribunal will determine how the hearing is to run. Having read the papers in the case, the tribunal will often take a view of which party it wants to hear first. Advisers will need to prepare for the hearing in the same way as the substantive hearing by preparing:

- a bundle, agreed if possible but, if not, just the applicant's bundle;
- witness statements (these may or may not have been ordered, but it is useful in any event to have them to submit to the tribunal; it will also make it easier for the applicant); and
- a written outline of the relevant law, evidence and submissions supporting the applicant's case (whilst it is not always possible to include all of the evidence, as advisers may not have had copies of the respondent's witness statements prior to the hearing, it is nevertheless useful to prepare a written submission so that the

---

1   See Chapter 5 for a more detailed consideration of this issue.
2   See **8.18**.

tribunal can look at it during the hearing and during their decision making).

8.16   Representatives for the applicant and the respondent may be invited to make opening comments, outlining their case in relation to the jurisdictional issue. The evidence is then called, with both parties having an opportunity to cross-examine. Finally, the tribunal will invite closing submissions from both parties. The tribunal will then retire, with decisions either being made the same day or sent on to applicants.

8.17   If this decision goes against an applicant, the applicant must consider whether or not to appeal. The appeals process is dealt with in Chapter 10. It is important to remember that advisers can appeal against *any* decision of the tribunal, and not only a decision after the main hearing.

MAIN HEARING

8.18   The tribunal at the main hearing will consist of a legally qualified Chair and two lay members. These lay members used to be drawn exclusively from nominations submitted by the TUC and the CBI, but this process has now been broadened to draw people from all parts of the community. The tribunal will often include a mix of ethnic backgrounds and genders. It does not always follow that there will be a disabled person among the tribunal members. As the legislation is at a comparatively early stage, the members concerned may not have heard a disability case before; however, they will have heard other discrimination cases.

Preparation for the main hearing

8.19   By this stage, advisers will have amassed evidence relevant to their client's case. This will include witness statements. The applicant's witness statement will be the most important document. Advisers will have taken full instructions at the first meeting with the applicant, and this should form the basis of the witness statement. It will detail the circumstances of the case in chronological order. Advisers will need to go through any issues which have arisen in the ET3, the questionnaire responses or the response to the request for further particulars and questions. If there are any awkward issues, for example if a client failed to disclose disability on an application form when specifically asked to do so, it is advisable to deal with these in the statement, so that the applicant can put their explanation forward before being forced to do so in cross-examination by the respondent.

8.20   Statements should be finished – or started – with the wording 'this statement is true' (as in civil court proceedings). Statements should be double-spaced and the type size should be 14 point as this is easier to read and is the recommended point size in the RNIB's clear print guidelines, unless of course anyone requires it to be larger. If possible, the applicant should have read out the statement to himself to check that he is happy with it and so that it does not sound as though it has been written by someone else and uses, for example, unfamiliar words. It is often useful to indicate in the statement when reference is being made to a document which will be in the bundle. Although at the time at which the statements are exchanged it might not be possible to give a precise page number, reference can be made to 'the document at page x of the bundle', as this page number can be inserted prior to the hearing, with these copies of the statement being given to the tribunal members.

8.21   Advisers will have taken details of any other potential witnesses at an early stage – when first interviewing the client or subsequently if it emerged that a particular witness would be useful. Advisers will need to meet witnesses or, if not practicable, to talk to them at length over the telephone, both to find out exactly what they can say which is of use to the applicant and also to get an idea of how good a witness they will be. The witnesses should be challenged as they would be in cross-examination, to ensure that they are not likely to be damaging to the applicant's case at the actual hearing. A full witness statement should be taken, and sent to the witness for approval and signature.

8.22   As above, the statement should contain the wording that 'this statement is true', and should be double-spaced, in 14 point as a matter of good practice but larger if necessary. It will need to cover the issues about which the witness is going to give evidence in a logical and chronological order. Expert witnesses should ensure that their qualifications and experience are detailed in the statement. Advisers should ensure that witnesses have read the statement to ensure that they are happy not only with the content but also with the language. The statements may have to be exchanged, and it is to be hoped that applicants will have obtained a directions order to this effect. If not, it is worth in any event asking the respondent if he would be willing to exchange witness statements in advance of the hearing, even if this is only in the waiting rooms before the hearing.

8.23   Where a witness is the subject of a witness order, tribunals will not expect a witness statement to be in existence. However, if possible, it is advisable to obtain a statement that the witness is prepared to sign, for the adviser's own benefit. Advisers need to be very careful about calling such a witness – if she does not give the evidence expected, she cannot be cross-examined by the party calling her, and such a situation can be damaging for the applicant. Clients need to be made fully aware of the risks of calling such a witness.

8.24   Where the case concerns the need for a reasonable adjustment, advisers may wish to consider calling the disability employment adviser (DEA) to give evidence. The DEA is part of the Disability Services Team, which operates out of the Job Centre and supplies information and assistance to disabled people seeking work or those in work. The DEA is considered to be neutral, and there is a variation across the country in terms of what a DEA will be prepared to say at a tribunal hearing. DEAs may be able to give information either about an individual case, particularly if they have been involved in any report, or generally about their services. If advisers do decide to call a DEA, they are likely to require a witness order. Advisers should speak to the DEA beforehand about what he can offer to the hearing, and whether or not he would be prepared to give a witness statement in advance. If he is not willing to give any written statement of any sort, advisers should consider carefully whether such a witness might benefit or damage the case.

8.25   Advisers can also consider calling evidence from disability organisations, such as the Royal National Institute for the Blind (RNIB), or the Royal National Institute for the Deaf (RNID). These organisations often have employment workers who can provide practical information about various adjustments that can usefully be made in the workplace. They can also produce reports on an individual in the workplace.

8.26   The cost of expert witnesses may be an issue for advisers and their clients. Costs can be sought from the tribunal on the basis that the evidence is essential.[1] Alternatively, it may be worth approaching a specific disability organisation for assistance with funding.

8.27   As well as support from the Access to Work Scheme, other organisations may be willing to contribute towards the costs of any reasonable adjustments. Organisations such as the Shaw Trust and Rehab UK should be contacted about this for either a witness statement from an employee or, more practicably, a written information sheet on their services and financial provision. Certain organisations can provide technical evidence, for example, Remap[2] is an organisation which specialises in adapting equipment for disabled people (eg a forklift truck which needs to be adapted for use by someone with only one arm).

---

1   See Chapter 3 at **3.24**.
2   See Chapter 2 at **2.13** and Appendix 1.

8.28 Where the case concerns reasonable adjustments, the applicant should also ensure that the bundle contains information about the Access to Work Scheme, so that the tribunal is fully aware of the financial assistance that employees can obtain for adjustments.

The bundle

8.29 Relevant documents in an agreed bundle will include the ET1 and ET3, the questionnaire and its response, any requests for further particulars and their responses, and any documents already disclosed (eg appraisals and memos and e-mails concerning the applicant). The tribunal may already have ordered that an agreed bundle be prepared for the hearing, but if not, it may be worth agreeing this in any event. Advisers should contact the respondent or the respondent's representative to agree which documents should go in the bundle. An agreed bundle does not necessarily mean that the applicant is agreeing to the content of the documents – just that they agree their existence.

8.30 Where a respondent is represented, the respondent's representative may offer to draw up an index which applicant advisers will need to scrutinise and amend as appropriate, adding anything the respondent has omitted, and then make up the necessary six bundles. Applicants may be asked to pay photocopying charges and, so long as these are reasonable, they must meet them. Advisers should ensure that they check all the bundles on the day of the hearing to ensure that nothing has been omitted.

8.31 If advisers have to index the documents themselves, it is usually preferable to put the tribunal documentation (eg the ET1, ET3, questionnaire, responses and further particulars) at the front of the bundle, with other documents so far as possible in chronological order. Alternatively, they can be in subject headings, for example pleadings, disability, employment etc. Each document will need to be numbered, usually in the top right-hand corner of the page for ease of use and the index drawn up from this. If further documents have to be added at a later stage, such as at the hearing, these can be inserted (numbered) either at the end of the bundle or as supplementaries (eg 36(a) and 36(b)).

8.32 On the day of the hearing, advisers will need to ensure that there are sufficient copies of the bundle, case-law and any written submissions for the tribunal, the witness stand and the respondent as well as themselves. This means that at least six sets of everything will be needed. There is a lack of photocopying facilities at most tribunals, so it is important to take spare copies of documents, just in case.

8.33   In complex cases, a chronology and a list of the people involved in the case may be helpful. If the tribunal does not order this, it is open to the parties to agree this between them prior to the hearing. If the chronology cannot be agreed by both parties, two separate chronologies may be presented to the tribunal.

8.34   Advisers may find that the respondent attempts to settle prior to the hearing. If this happens, extra time can be requested from the tribunal to facilitate this.

Postponements and adjournments

Postponements
8.35   Where a date has been fixed for a hearing, but it is unsuitable for either the adviser or one of the witnesses, it will be necessary to seek a postponement.[1] Where a tribunal has fixed a date without seeking dates to avoid from the parties, it will be more inclined to re-list the hearing, specifically when this is done within 14 days of receiving notice of the hearing. In any event, advisers will need to give reasons as to why the dates are unsuitable and provide alternative dates.

8.36   In *Cook v Thorne House Autistic Community*,[2] an appeal was brought against the decision not to allow a hearing to be postponed. In this case the originating application was lodged on 24 January 1998. The Notice of Appearance, which disputed that the applicant's dyslexia was a disability for the purposes of the DDA 1995, was entered on 19 February 1998. The tribunal listed the matter for a hearing on 23 February 1998, but granted a request for a postponement and listed the hearing again for 11 May 1998. On 23 March 1998 the applicant instructed an expert at the Institute of Dyslexia to prepare a report for the preliminary hearing. On 26 March 1998 the expert indicated that he would be unavailable until 16 June 1998 and so on 27 March 1998 the applicant asked for a further postponement of the hearing.

8.37   On 30 March 1998 the tribunal refused this request stating that: 'It is unreasonable to request apparently important medical reports so late in the day. The hearing must proceed as listed.' The applicant appealed to the EAT against this decision on the basis that it was perverse. The EAT allowing the appeal said that:

'It is a matter of crucial importance in the case that the applicant be given a reasonable opportunity to put forward the best medical evidence to

---

1   The employment tribunal Chair may postpone the day or time fixed for, or adjourn, any hearing – Employment Tribunals (Constitution and Rules of Procedure) Regulations 1993, Sch 1, para 13(7).
2   [1999] Disc LR 100, EAT.

address her complaint. It is a critical question for her and she is to be given the opportunity ... under the Disability Discrimination Act, tribunals will have to come to terms with the fact that there may be occasions when the medical profession have to assist ... the tribunals may need to adjust their timescales so as to adjust to the requirements of the medical profession. This is not automatic but where as here the doctor simply cannot deal with the tribunal case, it would be contrary to justice if the tribunal were not to give full weight to his unavailability.'

8.38 Tribunals are more inclined to grant postponements where a witness is unavailable for good reason rather than where the applicant's representative cannot attend on the given date. This is because tribunals take the view that where solicitors are representing, an alternative or agent can be instructed. Where the representative works for a voluntary organisation such as a Law Centre, it should be argued that they are not in the same position as a commercial enterprise. Applicants can refer to the case of *Yearwood v Royal Mail and Others*,[1] where the applicant was represented by Wellingborough Racial Equality Council which had only one person who could represent people at tribunals. This case had been listed by the Bedford tribunal for the same day as another case which the representative was dealing with at the Leicester tribunal. The Leicester case was part heard and so the Leicester tribunal refused to postpone, saying that the Bedford case should be postponed. The Chairman at Bedford refused the request for a postponement and this decision was appealed. The EAT stated that it was mindful of the difficulties which listing problems can cause for organisations such as the Racial Equality Council which provides useful assistance to the community and so allowed a postponement where it would not have done so had the applicant been represented by a firm of solicitors. In addition, representatives can cite Sch 1, Art 6 to the HRA 1998, in arguing that without a postponement the applicant will be unrepresented and, in a type of case which is often complex, will not have a fair hearing.

Adjournments
8.39 A tribunal can adjourn a hearing which has already started[2] and is likely to do so at its own motion or at the request of a party where, for example:

- there is insufficient time to hear outstanding evidence;
- one of the witnesses has become unexpectedly unavailable for good reason (eg ill health);

---

1   (Unreported) EAT No 843/97.
2   *Yearwood v Royal Mail and Others* (unreported) EAT No 843/97.

–   if the Chair or one of the lay members becomes unavailable.

If a document or witness is produced at the hearing, the existence of which the applicant had no prior knowledge, a request for an adjournment may be made. This may be granted for a short period but if more time is required because, for example, of the client's disability and the extended time required to take instructions, the tribunal may be inclined to grant this (again, bearing in mind Sch 1, Art 6 to the HRA 1998).

The proceedings

8.40   It is useful for the applicant to visit a tribunal before the date of the hearing itself in order to get an idea of the procedure and layout. Most hearings are open to the public and tribunal reception staff will usually show members of the public who wish to watch to the appropriate hearings. At the hearing, the applicant and the applicant's representative invariably sit on the right. Advisers will need to ensure that applicants are given breaks when necessary, for example someone with a hearing impairment may require frequent breaks when signing answers. This should have been raised at any directions hearing or the Chair at the directions hearing may have directed that this be dealt with immediately before the main hearing. If it has not already been dealt with, a request should be made at the outset of the main hearing. If the tribunal is reluctant to allow this, attention should be drawn to the tribunal's obligations in this respect under Part III of the DDA 1995 (as a service provider) and also to its obligations under Sch 1, Arts 6 and 14 to the HRA 1998 to allow a fair and non-discriminatory trial.

8.41   If the only cause of action that the applicant has is one of discrimination, then she will generally have to present her case to the tribunal first. It is usually an advantage for the applicant to present her case first, as it will create a picture of the employer that will then have to be dispelled. However, tribunals have the power to regulate their own proceedings[1] and they may decide that they wish to hear evidence in a particular order, particularly where a respondent admits less favourable treatment for a reason relating to a disability but is claiming justification (in which case, the burden of proof lies with the respondent). Advisers may have to make representations as to their client being heard first, although it is important not to alienate the tribunal and, if the tribunal is not receptive to any such representations, it is best not to pursue them.

---

1   Employment Tribunals (Constitution and Rules of Procedure) Regulations 1993, Sch 1, para 9.

Opening remarks

8.42   There is no right as such to an opening speech in a discrimination or unfair dismissal case. The Employment Tribunals (Constitution and Rules of Procedure) Regulations 1993[1] make reference only to 'addressing' the tribunal, but this could be at any stage, and is subject to the tribunal's ability to regulate its own proceedings as it wishes. However, most tribunals do give the parties an opportunity to do this and advisers need to make the most of it. Advisers need to outline the legal and factual issues in the case, explaining the legal basis on which the case is brought, and making reference to any major case-law to which the tribunal should have regard during the course of the hearing. Advisers may also wish to identify the witnesses who will be called, and, very briefly, what their evidence will prove.

8.43   In a particularly complex case, it may be useful to outline the chronology of events and to give an explanation of who the main players in the case are.

8.44   The tribunal may begin – particularly where no directions hearing has been held – by trying to clarify any areas of agreement or of dispute between the parties.

The hearing of evidence

8.45   Although tribunals are intended to be informal, they have become increasingly formal, particularly as many parties are legally represented.[2] Tribunals are bound by the rules of natural justice and so each party must be given the opportunity to present its case fully and effectively. This rule of natural justice is underpinned by the requirements regarding the right to a fair hearing in Sch 1, Art 6 to the HRA 1998. This will be particularly pertinent where an unexpected document or witness has been produced at the last moment. It will be important to seek an adjournment to deal with any such issues and, if necessary, to reschedule the hearing for another day. For example, if an applicant has a visual impairment and the document has to be read to him, this may take extra time. In order for the hearing to be fair, this time must be allowed. The tribunal may be invited to make a costs order against the respondent where documents are produced at the 'eleventh hour' and proceedings have to be adjourned.

---

1   Employment Tribunals (Constitution and Rules of Procedure) Regulations 1993, Sch 1, para 9.
2   *Aberdeen Steak Houses v Ibrahim* [1988] ICR 550 at 557 laid out not only what was required of tribunals under the rules of natural justice but also made it clear that total informality was not desirable and would be counter-productive.

8.46   It is important to estimate the correct length of a hearing in order to avoid a case being heard only in part. A hearing in part means not only that the evidence will not all be heard together, but it is likely to increase the stress experienced by the applicant.

Witnesses

8.47   Witness evidence is likely to be given, as indicated above, by means of witness statements, in conjunction with the bundle of documents. The statement becomes evidence once the witness has read it out or the tribunal has read it. Having been sworn in or affirmed (tribunals have the power to administer oaths[1]), witnesses will generally read their own statements. Advisers need to have ensured before the hearing that if there are likely to be any problems with this, they have been addressed. For example, if a client is dyslexic, and does not wish to read the document out, the adviser will need to ask the tribunal's leave to read the document out or for the tribunal to read it themselves. Similarly, statements may have to be put into large formats for some visually impaired people or in braille for braille users.

8.48   Hearsay evidence – a statement made by someone who is not a witness at the hearing, but which is being stated as the truth – can be admitted in civil proceedings such as tribunal hearings, subject to the provisions of the Civil Evidence Act 1995. Representatives can object to the admission of such evidence, but tactically it may be best merely to alert the tribunal to the fact that the evidence is disputed, and that it will be commented upon in closing. During closing, advisers can ask that little or no weight be given to the evidence because of its being hearsay.

Conduct of the hearing

8.49   As the witnesses give their evidence in chief (generally by means of a witness statement), representatives will need to refer at particular points to documents in the bundle. To ensure that their contents are fully aired, it will usually be best to read them out. For example, if the applicant refers to having received a letter from the employer, the representative can ask if it is the letter at page x of the bundle. When the applicant confirms that it is, the letter can be read out by the applicant or the representative. If the tribunal is not happy with this being done (and this sometimes happens when running short of time), it will indicate this. As tribunals have a wide discretion as to how the proceedings are run, it may be difficult to challenge their decision. Representatives will have to ensure that the final decision takes into

---

1   By Sch 1, para 9(4) to the Employment Tribunal (Constitution and Rules of Procedure) Regulations 1993.

account the written evidence in the bundle and, if this is not the case, it may form the basis for an appeal against the decision.

8.50 Without prejudice communications (eg letters trying to negotiate a settlement before the hearing) should not be raised in evidence. If they are, the opposing party may legitimately ask that the tribunal be stopped and reconvened with a new panel as the evidence should not have been heard.

8.51 It is rare that the tribunal will order that *all* evidence must be contained in the witness statements (and it is doubtful whether such a decision would be upheld) and so advisers may ask supplementary questions. It is usually sensible, however, for representatives to indicate that they intend to do this, with the tribunal's permission, before the witness starts to give her evidence.

8.52 The witness will then be cross-examined. The representative should have prepared witnesses for the areas about which they are likely to be questioned. This may include not only questions about the documents in the bundle, and any contradictions in the ET3, questionnaire etc, but also about relevant passages of the employment Code of Practice and any sector specific guidance on the DDA 1995. Representatives will need to make detailed notes of the questions and answers, as these will be used for re-examination. When cross-examining, representatives should ensure that questions are fairly short, and should not bully or intimidate the witness.

8.53 Following cross-examination, the person calling the witness will be able to re-examine. This will be confined to those areas arising out of cross-examination. Following this, the tribunal will have an opportunity to ask the witness questions. If a representative forgets to ask a question, it is best to ask the tribunal's leave to ask a further question, rather than have it unasked. It is also useful to ask the client if there is anything that they feel has not been addressed. If possible, there could be a method of communication such as writing notes, although obviously tribunals should give representatives time to take instructions from their client. If necessary, this may take the form of a 'reasonable adjustment' where the client has a signer and needs extra time for communication.

Closing
8.54 Following the general procedure, the person who called evidence second will be the first to close. In discrimination cases, (depending on whether or not there is an unfair dismissal claim as well) the applicant will be the last to close. At this stage it is important to deal with the law, case-law and, most importantly, the evidence. Here advisers can use the questionnaire, ET3 and witnesses' evidence to highlight any

inconsistencies, and to invite the tribunal to accept the applicant's evidence. It will be useful to have a skeleton submission to hand to the tribunal, with the details from live evidence to be supplemented at the hearing. The skeleton submission should deal broadly with the relevant law; an outline of the claim under this law; relevant case-law and how it applies to the case; the evidence including any adverse inferences to be drawn prior to the questionnaire; and finally, an invitation to the tribunal to find in favour of the applicant. Reference should also be made to the Code of Practice where relevant.

Problems during the hearing

8.55   As indicated above, problems such as the introduction of new evidence may occur during the hearing. The representative must ensure that these issues are raised with the tribunal. If the tribunal then decides to overrule any objection, it may form the basis of an appeal against its subsequent decision. However, if it is not raised as an issue, it cannot be used in any appeal. Where the problem lies in the sudden unavailability of a witness, advisers may need to request an adjournment, having discussed the issue and the potential cost implications with the client.

8.56   Where a witness order has been made, the witness attends the hearing and, having spoken to the witness, it becomes apparent that her evidence is not useful, there will be difficulties in not calling that witness at that stage. Representatives can ask the tribunal to release the witness, but it is likely that the tribunal would wish to hear directly from the witness about being released, and this may in the end prove damaging to the case. This is one of the dangers of obtaining a witness order. It may be best simply to proceed with the witness, having explained the situation fully to the client, but to ask as few questions as possible.

The decision

8.57   The decision of a tribunal may be given on the day of the hearing, with written reasons to follow, or it may be reserved. The Employment Tribunals (Constitution and Rules of Procedure) Regulations 1993[1] sets out the specific requirements of the decisions. In discrimination cases, reasons must be in extended form.[2]

Costs

8.58   Costs in a tribunal hearing can be awarded only in very limited circumstances:[3]

---

1   At Sch 1, para 10.
2   Ibid, Sch 1, para 10(4).
3   Ibid, Sch 1, para 12.

– where the party bringing or conducting the proceedings has acted frivolously, vexatiously, abusively, disruptively or otherwise unreasonably;
– where a hearing has had to be adjourned or postponed due to the conduct of a party;
– where a respondent has failed to respond to a request for reinstatement; or
– where a pre-hearing review has been held, and a deposit has had to be paid as a result.

8.59 The tribunal can order costs to be paid in one of three ways:

– that the party must pay a specified sum not exceeding £500;
– that the party must pay a sum which has been agreed between the parties;
– or the party must pay the whole or a specified part of the costs to be taxed.[1]

The costs can include the cost of witness allowances and an independent expert's report.[2]

8.60 Whilst the maximum which can be awarded in costs at the time of writing is £500, amendments have been proposed to the employment tribunal rules of procedure to raise this ceiling to £10,000. This is due to come into force in July 2001, and is something which may have the effect of deterring disabled people from bringing their claims. In addition, it is proposed that a tribunal will be able to order costs against a party where its representative has acted vexatiously or unreasonably in conducting the case. The proposal is further that the tribunal will be required to consider imposing costs where in its opinion a party, or a party's representative, has acted vexatiously or unreasonably.

8.61 Where a tribunal is considering an award of costs against an applicant, advisers must defend this vigorously. Discrimination cases are very difficult to win and often it is only possible to assess prospects of success after all the evidence has been heard. In addition, the DDA 1995 is relatively new, and advice as to prospects of success will vary considerably. Applicants should not be penalised for bringing a case for which the prospect of success is uncertain. Advisers must be aware, however, that a 'party' refers not only to the applicant, but also to the representative and the representative's conduct of the proceedings will be taken into account in determining whether or not to award costs.[3]

---

1   Employment Tribunals (Constitution and Rules of Procedure) Regulations 1993, Sch 1, para 12(3).
2   Ibid, Sch 1, para 12(1) and Sch 2, para 8A.
3   *Beynon and Others v Scadden and Others* [1999] IRLR 700.

Witness expenses

8.62   The applicant and any witnesses attending the tribunal hearing can claim an allowance to cover travel costs, accommodation (if necessary) and the cost of a carer (if necessary).[1] The allowances are on a fixed scale and are usually announced by the Secretary of State annually. An allowance can also be paid for the attendance of a medical expert if necessary, and in such cases the amount payable is not fixed but must be 'reasonable'. Where costs are ordered, it is possible for the tribunal to order that these allowances are repaid to the Secretary of State by a party against whom the order for costs has been made.

---

1   The Secretary of State can determine these allowances: ETA 1996, s 5(3).

Chapter 9

REMEDIES

INTRODUCTION

9.1 For the applicant, the most important aspect of the case is the remedy. At the earliest opportunity, advisers will need to calculate what compensation they believe the client may obtain from tribunal proceedings. This should be sent to the client in an appropriate format so that the client is clear about what is likely to be achieved from the case if it is successful. A case may settle before going to a full hearing. Alternatively, following the successful tribunal hearing, the applicant may be asked by the tribunal to consider reaching an agreement on remedy. If no agreement is reached, a hearing will be held to determine compensation, a declaration of discrimination and recommendations.

WHAT REMEDIES ARE AVAILABLE?

9.2 By virtue of s 8(2) of the DDA 1995, where a tribunal thinks it 'just and equitable', it can make:

- a declaration of discrimination;
- a compensation order; or
- recommendations.[1]

9.3 There is no power as yet to order reinstatement or re-engagement, but a tribunal may recommend that course. However, if an applicant also has a claim for unfair dismissal, she would be able to ask for reinstatement or re-engagement within that claim.[2]

---

1   See Chapter 1 at **1.53**.
2   ERA 1996, s 113. Note that if a tribunal orders reinstatement or re-engagement in a case where there has been both unfair dismissal and disability discrimination, and an employer fails to comply with such an order, a higher additional award may be made due to the original dismissal being also an act of disability discrimination (Employment Rights (Disputes Resolution) Act 1998, s 14).

9.4   The Government's response to the Task Force recommendations propose that tribunals should in future be able to order reinstatement or re-engagement.

Financial compensation

9.5   Financial compensation under the DDA 1995, unlike unfair dismissal, has no upper limit and so thorough preparation of the compensation claim is extremely important. The compensation claimed can be for any financial loss which is attributable to the unlawful act of discrimination. See *Coleman v Skyrail Oceanic Ltd.*[1] In the case of *Sherrif v Klyne Tugs (Lowestoft) Ltd*,[2] the Court of Appeal stated that the claimant does not have to prove that the loss was 'reasonably foreseeable', but only that a causal link has been established. A tribunal will have to determine whether any intervening act has broken the chain of causation.

9.6   The monetary compensation to be awarded in a case under the DDA 1995 can be divided into three parts:

– compensation for actual financial loss to the date of hearing;
– compensation for future loss of earnings; and
– compensation for injury to feelings and personal injury.

Financial loss to the date of hearing – or special damages

9.7   This is perhaps the most straightforward part of the compensation calculation. Advisers will need to calculate what the net loss to the client is per week, and multiply this loss by the number of weeks from the date of the act of discrimination up to the date of the tribunal hearing, depending upon the factors to be taken into account as detailed below.

9.8   Advisers will need to include in the weekly loss:

– net salary loss (unlike unfair dismissal, there is no limit on the weekly earnings figure);
– overtime, where this is contractual;
– pension loss;
– any other benefits which would have been earned in that time (eg contractual bonuses or commission likely to have been accrued); and
– the disabled person's tax credit, where the employment would be paid at a level which would have afforded this.

---

1   [1981] IRLR 398, CA.
2   [1999] IRLR 481.

9.9 Advisers will need to deduct from this any income the applicant has received, for example earnings from another job, income-based incapacity benefit the applicant has received during the period for which the loss is awarded and any sick pay paid by the employer pursuant to the employment contract.

Recruitment cases

9.10 The amount of compensation for loss to the date of the hearing in a recruitment case will depend upon whether or not the employment tribunal believes that the applicant would have succeeded in obtaining the job but for the discrimination. Advisers will need to demonstrate that the applicant had the highest chance of being appointed, using all the documentation disclosed by the respondent and any other pertinent evidence. The tribunal may reach a percentage decision on this chance, for example that there was a 50 per cent chance of an applicant being given the job. In this case, the loss until the date of the hearing will be calculated in full, divided by half and the remaining figure will be the loss to the date of the hearing.

Dismissal cases

9.11 In a dismissal case, the tribunal will have to decide whether or not the employee would have been retained in the post but for the discrimination. Whilst in a straightforward dismissal this may be relatively easy to demonstrate, it is likely to be more difficult in, for example, a redundancy case. Advisers in such a case will need to demonstrate that, had the redundancy criteria been correctly applied, the applicant would have remained in the post.[1]

Reasonable adjustment cases

9.12 Where an applicant is claiming a failure to make reasonable adjustments, the calculation of damages will depend upon the loss which has resulted from the failure. If an applicant is still employed by the respondent, this is likely to consist of compensation for injury to feelings, for any physical injury incurred as a result of the failure and potentially for any losses such as a failure to obtain promotion, where this can be directly attributable to the failure (eg where an adjustment does not enable an individual to carry out a particular type of work and that work is required for a promotion to a higher grade for which the applicant would otherwise have been perfectly suited).

---

1   *Kirker v British Sugar*, Case No 2601249/97, Nottingham Employment Tribunal. For an example of such a case, refer to the employment tribunal decision, not the later EAT decision.

Future loss of earnings

9.13   This is the part of remedies in discrimination cases which is most difficult to determine, as it may depend on a number of factors. Generally speaking, tribunals will decide upon a figure which represents the annual loss to the employee, including contractual bonuses and benefits but less any income actually received. This is known as the multiplicand. The tribunal multiplies this by another figure known as the multiplier. The multiplier is based on the number of years of loss of earnings for which the tribunal decides to compensate the applicant.

9.14   Income received by the applicant will be taken into account and so reduces the annual loss unless it results from payments made by the applicant, for example from a contributory pension scheme. This was reaffirmed by the case of *Kerrigan v Rover Group Ltd.*[1] In that case, Mr Kerrigan won his employment tribunal claim for disability discrimination. In calculating the compensation that should be awarded to Mr Kerrigan, the payments he was receiving from a contributory pension scheme were deducted from the loss of earnings figure. The decision on calculation of his compensation was appealed against by Mr Kerrigan. The EAT reaffirmed that:

> 'It is the undisputed fact that pension payments are not to be taken into account when calculating damages for personal injury or wrongful dismissal.'[2]

9.15   If the applicant has new employment, income from that will also be taken into account. The tribunal will consider the length of time the applicant is likely to work in the new job, and, if it pays less than the job for which she applied or from which she was dismissed, the tribunal will calculate the loss of income for that period.

Length of future loss
9.16   Calculation of the period of future loss is often difficult, and will depend on the following factors.

Future employability
9.17   In a recruitment case, the tribunal will first have to decide whether or not the employee would have been recruited to the post in dispute, as with the determination of loss of earnings to the date of the tribunal. Whatever percentage figure is reached, this will be the basis for the future loss calculation.

---

1   EAT No 1185/98.
2   This is a well-established principle, as referred to in the case of *Hopkins v Norcros* [1994] IRLR 18.

9.18 Where the case concerns a dismissal, as with the determination of loss of earnings to the date of the tribunal, the tribunal will have to determine whether or not the employee would have been kept on in the post were it not for the discrimination.

Length of time of future employment
9.19 Where an employee has applied for a post and the tribunal has decided that the employee would have been offered the post but for the discrimination, or where the tribunal has determined a percentage chance of this, it will then have to decide for how long to award future loss of earnings.[1] This will depend on:

– the applicant's age and the nature of the work (thus, the likelihood of the applicant remaining in that job);
– how long the job itself was likely to last (eg whether it was a short-term contract or was for a specific project);
– the nature of the industry and the client's previous work record (if the industry is one which experiences a high turnover of staff, it may be more difficult to argue that a person might have a 'job for life'; and if the applicant has chosen to move jobs frequently, the respondent may be able to argue that the applicant was unlikely to remain for long in any event); and
– the usual retirement age in that type of employment.

9.20 Even if the tribunal believes that the applicant would have stayed in the job for the rest of her life (in a recruitment case, it will be more difficult to argue that someone would have been in a job for life), the tribunal will still have to consider whether the applicant is likely to find alternative employment. If the tribunal decides that this is likely, it will award compensation only up to the date by which they believe other employment would be obtained. Obviously, age will be a factor in this, as will the local employment conditions (ie in an area of high unemployment there is likely to be less chance of obtaining employment, particularly for a disabled person). In addition, if the applicant is trained in a specific area of work, this will obviously limit job prospects. Advisers will need to ensure that applicants keep details of all job applications and rejections, as well as obtaining details of local employment, perhaps from the Employment Service or Job Centre or local newspapers to show what had been or is available. Up-to-date statistics on unemployment, both national and regional, are also

---

1   See *Ministry of Defence v Wheeler* [1998] IRLR 23, where the Court of Appeal considered the order in which to apply the percentage chance to lost earnings and earnings on the amount which should have been earned by way of mitigation.

available on the National Statistics website at http://www.statistics. gov.uk.

9.21 As disability will affect future employability, the adviser should obtain reports from disability organisations and/or the Disability Rights Commission[1] as to the unemployment rates of disabled people. For example, in the case of *Kirker v British Sugar*,[2] a visually impaired shift chemist was made redundant by means of a scoring system which discriminated against him. In determining future loss of earnings, the tribunal used a report by the RNIB,[3] which stated that blind and partially sighted people were 2.5 times more likely to be unemployed than those without sight problems. Thus, the tribunal decided that Mr Kirker was unlikely to ever find work again for the rest of his working life. He obtained the highest amount of compensation awarded so far by a tribunal (£103,146.49)[4] in a DDA 1995 case.

9.22 In *McLaughlan v Stolt Commex Seaway Ltd*,[5] a loss prevention manager who worked for an oil company and had a terminal illness was awarded £77,696 plus interest for unlawful disability discrimination. Mr McLaughlin was diagnosed as having a malignant tumour in his gullet in May 1997. Although chemotherapy reduced the tumour it was clear that his illness was terminal which his employers knew. He returned to work in January 1998 but was summarily dismissed the following July, ostensibly for poor performance. The compensation the tribunal awarded him was made up of:

£40,300 for past loss
£32,936 for future loss
£5,000 for injury to feelings
£2,012 interest
Total £80,248

With regard to the future loss, the tribunal held that the medical evidence from Mr McLaughlin's consultant oncologist was 'crucial'. After considering the consultant's statistical evidence regarding Mr McLaughlin's life expectancy, the tribunal rejected his legal representative's submission that he should be awarded 4 years' future loss. The tribunal decided that 8 months' was appropriate.

9.23 Other disability charities, such as RNID, have produced similar reports and advisers should contact the Disability Rights Commission for relevant statistics. In addition, an employment consultant's report may be extremely useful.

---

1   www.drc-gb.org
2   Case No 2601249/97, Nottingham Employment Tribunal.
3   RNIB, *Blind in Britain – the employment challenge* (1996).
4   But see **9.55** for eventual amount obtained.
5   Case No S/200809/99, EOR DCLD No 41 August 1999.

9.24   The same factors will apply to dismissal cases, with one further consideration: the tribunal will take into account the length of time that the applicant has worked for the employer. The longer the applicant's service, the more likely that they would have stayed in the job for a considerable amount of time, and possibly for life.

The multiplier

9.25   Having decided upon a number of years for future loss of earnings, the tribunal will convert that figure into an appropriate 'multiplier'. The principle derives from personal injury cases, to which discrimination cases are akin. The multiplier will not be the number of years determined, because this would mean that the applicant would have benefited in excess of the actual loss and would amount to accelerated receipt. The multiplier used in cases where a person is unlikely to work again until retirement age is usually that shown in the Ogden tables. These can be found in publications concerning personal injury or, occasionally, employment. The use of these tables is supported by the EAT decision in *Ministry of Defence v Mutton*.[1] Where the loss will continue for a period ending before retirement, it will not necessarily be appropriate to use the Ogden tables. Instead, advisers can use the CPID tables,[2] which give fixed rates for the number of years of earnings. These multipliers do not allow for contingencies, such as retirement taken prior to retirement age because of ill health, which can instead be dealt with by reducing the multiplier by an appropriate percentage amount or by reducing the final overall amount.

9.26   An example of a calculation of compensation in a DDA 1995 case can be found in the case of *Kirker v British Sugar plc*.[3] At the remedies hearing, the tribunal found that Mr Kirker, who was visually impaired, would have on the balance of probability retained his job had the redundancy procedure been carried out without discrimination. Mr Kirker, who was 40 at the time of the hearing, had attempted to find employment since his redundancy but had not been successful: he had previously worked as a shift chemist but was not professionally qualified. Taking into account the research by RNIB, which stated that visually impaired people face an unemployment rate of 2.5 times the national average, it was held that Mr Kirker was unlikely to find alternative employment for the rest of his working life. As employees of British Sugar tended to retire between the ages of 55 and 60, it was decided that his working life would be to 55 – a period of 15 years. It was also decided

---

1   [1996] ICR 590.
2   See *Nelson-Jones on Multipliers* (Butterworths, 1998).
3   Case No 2601249/97.

that, as his condition was one with which he was born and for which had received treatment for most of his 40 years, the risk of having to take ill health retirement because his eyesight had deteriorated to the extent that he could no longer perform his duties would be 20 per cent. Mr Kirker's weekly salary of £323 was taken, with a reduction for DLA,[1] plus an annual figure of £1,347.50 for the employer's contribution to pension, which was at 5.5 per cent of salary. This produced an annual loss of £15,699.50. With a projected working life of 15 years, the tribunal made an allowance for accelerated payment and took the appropriate multiplier at eight.[2] This produced a figure of £125,596 which was then reduced by 20 per cent to produce a figure of £100,476.80.

9.27   As the pension scheme was a final salary scheme, there was an award for loss representing the difference between the deferred pension he would receive and that part of the pension he would have received had he stayed with the company. This was calculated by applying to his existing deferred pension of £6,853.64 a multiplier to reflect the normal retirement age of 65 and the applicant's current age – in this case of 1.5. Consideration was then given to the applicant having to withdraw early from the pension scheme for reasons other than death or disability, and a 40 per cent reduction was taken to reflect the difference between 15 years – the predicted length of working life – and 25 years, the time until retirement of 25 years. This produced a total of £6,168.28 under this head.

9.28   Mr Kirker was also compensated for loss of the ability to take ill health early retirement. Under the employer's scheme, an employee was entitled to take early retirement at the age of 50 or above. In that event, his pension would be calculated on pensionable service and salary to the date of early retirement and then reduced by 4 per cent per annum for every year and month early before age 60. If the applicant had retired at 55 because of ill health, then his retirement pension would not suffer the 4 per cent deduction and would be based on the greater of service to date and two-thirds potential service to normal retirement date. In Mr Kirker's case, it was held that the former would prevail. Thus the tribunal calculated the difference between a pension taken at that age based upon the applicant's existing salary – the difference between 35 sixtieths of his existing salary of £24,500 (£14,291.66) and that product reduced by 20 per cent (£11,433.33),

---

1   This is in the author's opinion not something which should have been deducted, as this would have been paid regardless of his being in or out of employment. See also **9.55** for further details of the challenge subsequently made to the taxation of salary in this case.

2   There did not appear to be any use of multiplier tables in this case.

being 4 per cent for each of the five years between 55 and 60. To the resulting figure (£2858.33) the tribunal applied a multiplier of eleven in order to account for a life expectancy of 20 years thereafter. 20 per cent was applied to that result (£31,441.63) to represent the chance which the tribunal applied to the earlier calculation to reflect what might be a supervening ocular crisis. The product of those calculations was £6,288.33, which was rounded down to £6,250, to acknowledge the rough and ready nature of such an exercise.

Pension loss
9.29   Pension loss is an important part of the applicant's claim for loss, and may feature in both recruitment and dismissal cases. It is likely to be decided in one of a number of ways:

–   where the client is not likely to be unemployed for long and thus the loss is small, a tribunal may make an award for pension losses based on the loss of the employer's pension contribution;
–   in cases involving a higher salary or greater loss, the tribunal can award compensation which represents the cost of purchasing the pensionable benefits – lost benefits – in the marketplace; or
–   the loss can be determined by taking the net value of the applicant's loss and applying an appropriate multiplier using the Ogden tables (see **9.25**).

9.30   Calculations will also depend upon whether the pension scheme the applicant has lost is based on money purchase or final salary. In a money purchase scheme, a pension fund is established for the employee and contributions are paid into it. In due course, the fund is used for the purchase of retirement annuities and for the payment of a lump sum on retirement. When the employee leaves, the fund will continue to grow, and the employee's loss will essentially comprise the employer's contributions and any growth from those contributions.

9.31   Final salary schemes provide a pension based on the year's pensionable pay immediately before retirement or from some time before. There may also be entitlement to a lump sum. With such a pension, the employer must ensure that the scheme is adequately funded to provide these sums. Where an individual leaves employment before retirement age, they are likely to lose some of the benefits of such acquired pension rights.

9.32   Unless the applicant is unlikely to find employment before retirement age, loss of pension, as with loss of earnings, will be awarded up to the likely date of obtaining other employment, which the tribunal is likely to assume will also provide a pension scheme. Advisers must remember that if an applicant finds employment with no pension scheme, and thus has to join a private pension scheme as opposed to an occupational one, this is not likely to be as beneficial. There are considerable 'up front' charges in private as opposed to occupational schemes.

9.33   Calculating pension loss is both complex and difficult. Advisers may find a useful starting point in the booklet *Industrial Tribunals: Compensation for Loss of Pension Rights.*[1] This offers guidelines for tribunals in calculating pension loss, although tribunals are not bound by it. Alternatively, and particularly where an applicant's or independent actuaries' losses are likely to be great, advisers can contact insurance companies for estimates of the value of purchasing the pensionable benefits, or to determine the applicant's loss.

Loss of the chance of being able to take retirement through ill health
9.34   Where there is a pension scheme, and the applicant may have been able to take early retirement through ill health, the applicant can claim compensation for not being able to take this.

9.35   Where the applicant has been deprived of an opportunity to take permanent ill health insurance, a claim can also be made in this respect. It may be more appropriate to make a claim for this by way of breach of contract in the county court or – depending on the sum at stake, which is likely to be substantial – High Court than in the tribunal. Public funding (depending on the client's income and capital) may be available for a breach of contract claim in the courts as opposed to the tribunal.

Reduction for future contingencies
9.36   Once the tribunal has determined the number of years of loss of earnings, with the appropriate multiplier, this will then be multiplied by the salary at the date of leaving/applying for the job, minus any reduction for the percentage chance of not getting the job/remaining in employment. The reduction for future contingencies – for the percentage chance of the applicant being made redundant (lawfully), resigning or having to leave due to ill health – can either be built into the multiplier or be deducted at this stage. In this respect, it is important to have medical evidence to support a contention that the applicant's disability is unlikely to deteriorate within a certain number of years.[2]

Mitigating loss

9.37   Applicants have a duty to mitigate their losses, ie they have to take reasonable steps to keep their losses as low as possible. Tribunals will

---

1   C Sara, D Pugsley and D Crump (HMSO, 1991).
2   See *McLaughlan v Stolt Commex Seaway Ltd* at **9.22**.

want to be assured that applicants have done all they can to obtain other work and to minimise financial loss. Respondents will often raise what they see as a failure to mitigate loss as a way of reducing the damages awarded. Applicants need to keep details of all job applications, with any rejection letters. It is also useful to obtain evidence of the local unemployment rate, and how many jobs are advertised. The Employment Service Office will have these details. It is for the respondent to show that the duty to mitigate has not been discharged,[1] although in reality it is sensible for the applicant to compile evidence that they have been mitigating their losses.

9.38   One problem that may arise in this respect is that the respondent may have offered the applicant another job. An applicant would be advised to consider this, as a tribunal will be loath to hold that an applicant has taken steps to mitigate loss where an alternative job has not been taken up. Whilst it is understandable that an applicant may not wish to have anything more to do with a discriminatory employer, the tribunal will want to be certain that there has not been a failure to mitigate.

9.39   In the case of *Kerrigan v Rover Group Ltd*,[2] Rover wrote to Mr Kerrigan after he had left their employment to offer him three alternative positions. Mr Kerrigan rejected the offer. The tribunal stated that in rejecting the respondent's offer without any attempt to investigate it, the applicant had not discharged his duty to mitigate his loss. It further found that if the respondent's offer to discuss alternative employment had been taken up, this would have resulted in the applicant either concluding that the offer was not genuine or finding himself re-employed. The tribunal felt that the latter was the more likely result, and thus imposed a cut-off date on the amount of compensation to be paid. The decision was upheld by the EAT.

9.40   Where an adviser has made the consequences clear to the applicant – in writing or another appropriate format – but the applicant does not wish to investigate the possibility of re-employment, advisers must marshal whatever evidence they can that the applicant has acted reasonably. There may be particular reasons for a failure to respond to an offer, for example the workplace is too far away or the job would involve contact with a person who has harassed the applicant and that there has been an irreversible breakdown in the employment relationship. These reasons should have been put to the respondent at the time and they will have to be put before the tribunal.

---

1   See *Gardner-Hill v Roland Berger Technics Ltd* [1982] IRLR 498.
2   EAT No 1185/98. See also *Wilding v British Telecommunications plc* 25 January 2001 EAT No 901/99.

Injury to feelings and personal injury

Injury to feelings

9.41 Although compensation for injury to feelings is awarded in almost all discrimination cases, it is not automatic, and advisers must ensure that they prepare carefully for this aspect of the remedies hearing. Witness evidence will be useful, not only from the applicant but often also from a partner, friend or relative (or from a medical expert, eg a GP) who has witnessed the effects of the respondent's discriminatory behaviour upon the applicant.

9.42 The guidelines for awards relating to injury to feelings were given in *Armitage Marsden and HM Prison Service v Johnson*[1] and are as follows.

(1) Awards for injuries to feelings are compensatory. They should be just to both parties. They should compensate fully without punishing the tortfeasor (ie the respondent). Feelings of indignation at the tortfeasor's conduct should not be allowed to inflate the award.

(2) Awards should not be too low, as that would diminish respect for the policy of the anti-discrimination legislation. On the other hand, awards should be restrained.

(3) Awards should bear some broad similarity to the range of awards in personal injury cases.

(4) In exercising their discretion in assessing a sum, tribunals should remind themselves of the value in everyday life of the sum they have in mind. This may be done by reference to purchasing power or by reference to earnings.

(5) Tribunals should bear in mind the reference of Lord Bingham MR to the need for public respect for the level of awards made.

9.43 Whilst there is no minimum or maximum figure for an award for injury to feelings, some cases have indicated that where an award for injury to feelings is made, it should not be for less than £500.[2] Awards for injury to feelings in disability discrimination cases averaged £3,635 in 1999,[3] however, there have been a few sizeable awards – £15,000 for injury to feelings in the case of *Ninsiima v London Borough of Waltham Forest*[4] and £25,000 in the case of *Harling v CL Plastics Ltd*.[5] The award

---

1   [1997] IRLR 162.
2   *Sharifi v Strathclyde Regional Council* [1992] IRLR 259, EAT and *Noone v North West Thames Regional Health Authority* [1988] IRLR 530.
3   See *Equal Opportunities Review*, No 93, September/October 2000.
4   Case No 3201853/98, Stratford Tribunal. See also *Bridges v Sita GB Ltd*, Case No 2301175/99, London South Tribunal.
5   Case No 18404928/99 (January 2000), Leeds Tribunal. See **9.46**.

may be increased by any psychological harm that has been experienced by the applicant. In such a case, particularly where the applicant is being treated for an illness such as depression, evidence from a doctor or psychiatrist will be invaluable.

Aggravated damages

9.44   The tribunal in *Armitage Marsden and HM Prison Service v Johnson*[1] held that as a matter of principle 'aggravated' damages could be awarded in a case of discrimination on the basis of race or gender. Obviously, this will also apply to cases of disability discrimination. Aggravated damages represent additional compensation for injury to feelings where the manner or the motive of the respondent has increased that injury. In the case of *Broome v Cassell,*[2] Lord Diplock stated that an award for aggravated damages could be made where the applicant's 'sense of injury resulting from the wrongful … act is justifiably heightened by the manner in which or motive for which the [respondent] did it'. An example of an award of aggravated damages in a case of racial discrimination is that of *Armitage Marsden and HM Prison Service v Johnson* (above), where the applicant's claims of racial discrimination were not properly investigated by the prison, and £7,500 was awarded as damages.

9.45   There have been some cases under the DDA 1995 involving awards of aggravated damages, for example *Calvert v Jewelglen Ltd.*[3] Mr Calvert, who has epilepsy, was offered employment at a nursing home. The matron and deputy were fully aware of his medical history. When he had a dizzy spell which he reported, he was sent home and told that he was not wanted. The tribunal awarded a total of £6,940 compensation, including £2,500 for injury to feelings. The tribunal found that the applicant was extremely hurt by the demeaning and degrading treatment he received. The tribunal also awarded £100 for aggravated damages 'by reason of the manner in which he was handled and the way in which the dismissal was carried out'.

9.46   More recently, the case of *Harling v CL Plastics Ltd*[4] concerned an applicant with dyslexia which gave him a spelling and reading age of 6 years 5 months. He was subjected to both verbal and physical abuse; he was told to 'piss off and learn' by both colleagues and some shift leaders, as well as being beaten about the head and ears. The applicant left employment, having suffered severe emotional distress. The tribunal

---

1   [1997] IRLR 162.
2   [1972] 1 All ER 801.
3   Case No 2403989/97.
4   Case No 1804928/99 (January 2000), Leeds Tribunal.

took £15,000 as a starting point for injury to feelings. It held that there were considerable aggravating factors, including the period over which the bullying was allowed (18 months), the fact that junior members of management either took part in the abuse or stood by and watched it, and the fact that the respondent's witnesses treated some of the questions put to them with contempt and insolence and attacked the applicant's character in their evidence. Hence a final award for injury to feelings including aggravated damages of £25,000 was made.

Personal injury

9.47 Following the decision of *Sheriff v Klyne Tugs,*[1] it is clear that tribunals will be determining issues of personal injury in certain cases. Where an applicant's personal injury has arisen out of discriminatory treatment, this will have to be assessed as a personal injury in an ordinary tort case would be. A client may believe that an existing disability has been aggravated by the respondent's failure to make reasonable adjustments (eg a client whose back problem has been worsened by a failure to provide an appropriate chair). As this book is not a guide to personal injury issues, advisers should seek expert advice. However, in general, medical evidence will be necessary as to the nature of the injury and its likely cause, the effect of the injury on the applicant and the prognosis. An amount will be awarded for pain, suffering and loss of amenity, as well as for future loss of earnings caused as a result of the injury.

9.48 In the case of *Ninsiima v London Borough of Waltham Forest,*[2] the award of £15,000 for injury to feelings included compensation for a back injury caused by the respondent's failure to make reasonable adjustments.

Compensation for the employer's failure to make an adjustment to the physical features of the premises

9.49 Where there has been a failure to make a reasonable adjustment involving physical alteration to premises, the tribunal can join the lessor of the premises to the tribunal proceedings.[3] Where the tribunal determines that there was an unreasonable refusal by the lessor to consent to alterations to the premises, or that the conditions were unreasonable, it may:

– make a declaration which it considers appropriate;

---

1   [1999] IRLR 481.
2   Case No 3201853/98, Stratford Tribunal.
3   DDA 1995, Sch 4, para 2, and see Chapter 1.

– make an order authorising the occupier of the premises to make the alteration specified in the order; and/or
– order the lessor to pay compensation to the complainant.

If the tribunal orders the lessor to pay compensation, it cannot also order the employer occupier to pay compensation. There are no guidelines for payment of such compensation, but it is likely that awards will follow the general pattern as outlined above.

Recoupment

9.50 Where a claim is made for unfair dismissal, or one of a number of other claims (excluding discrimination), the Department of Social Security (DSS) can recover the cost of any jobseeker's allowance or income support paid to the applicant prior to the ending of the tribunal proceedings. In these circumstances, the tribunal has to disregard jobseeker's allowance or income support in determining compensation. The tribunal then specifies in its decision the amount of the award and the amount of the 'prescribed element' (loss of earnings etc in the period up to the conclusion of the tribunal). The tribunal also states the date to which the prescribed element relates, and the amount, if any, by which the compensation exceeds it. The tribunal then notifies the DSS of the award that has been made which includes a prescribed element and the DSS can serve a recoupment notice on the employer. The employer pays the sum subject to the notice to the DSS, with the remainder going to the applicant. The DSS may not always recoup; if it does not do so, and notifies the employer of this, the full sum may be paid to the applicant.[1]

9.51 In calculating the award of compensation, where the recoupment provisions do not apply (ie there is no unfair dismissal claim alongside the disability discrimination claim), the tribunal will take into account any income the applicant is receiving.

Interest

9.52 The tribunal has the power to award interest on sums awarded in discrimination cases.[2] If the tribunal does not award interest, it must give reasons for its decision not to do so.[3] Interest is calculated as simple interest which accrues from day to day.

---

1   See, generally, the Employment Protection (Recoupment of Jobseeker's Allowance and Income Support) Regulations 1996, SI 1996/2349.
2   Employment Tribunals (Interest on Awards in Discrimination Cases) Regulations 1996, SI 1996/2803.
3   Ibid, regs 2(1) and 7(2).

9.53 No interest is paid on compensation awarded for any loss or matter which occurs outside the period beginning with the discrimination complained of and ending with the day when the tribunal calculates the interest (the relevant period). Interest can be awarded for the whole of the period for injury to feelings, but all other types of awards attract interest for only half that period.

Taxation

9.54 Money received as a settlement for loss of employment, including any statutory redundancy payment or basic award up to the value of £30,000 is not taxable.[1] Anything in excess of this figure is taxable. It is arguable that money paid for injury to feelings is akin to a personal injury award for damages, and so should not be taxed.

9.55 Where awards are made at a tribunal, the basic award (or redundancy payment) should be tax free. Tax is normally taken into account in assessing the amount of the award and so normally it would be received tax free.[2] However, in the case of *Kirker v British Sugar*[3] the tribunal found that Mr Kirker had been discriminated against in being made redundant and awarded him £103,146.49 in compensation based on his net salary. The respondent's solicitors took advice from their accountants and entered into correspondence with the Inland Revenue. The view of the accountants and the Inland Revenue was that s 148 of the Income and Corporation Taxes Act 1988 applied to that part of the award relating to both past and future loss of earnings, subject to the first £30,000 being exempt from a charge to income tax. Thus, the monies were paid to the applicant, excluding £24,004.26 which was paid to the Inland Revenue. Mr Kirker wrote to the employment tribunal about this because his compensation had been calculated on his net salary on the assumption that income tax would not, therefore, be payable on the award and the matter was listed for a review hearing. At the review hearing, the tribunal decided to hold a further hearing to consider grossing up the award (ultimately the case was settled without the further hearing with British Sugar agreeing to pay Mr Kirker a total of £167,000 including interest). To ensure that applicants are not left with less than the tribunal intended, advisers should ensure that at any hearing the respondent is asked to indemnify the applicant against any tax which may be claimed by the Inland Revenue in respect of the award.

---

1   Income and Corporation Taxes Act 1988, s 148.
2   See *Ministry of Defence v Mutton* [1996] ICR 590.
3   Case No 2601249/97, Nottingham Employment Tribunal.

RECOMMENDATIONS

9.56 The tribunal can make recommendations:

'that the respondent take, within a specified period, action appearing to the tribunal to be reasonable, in all the circumstances of the case, for the purpose of obviating or reducing the adverse effect on the complainant of any matter to which the complaint relates.'[1]

9.57 Where the respondent fails to comply with a recommendation, without 'reasonable justification', the tribunal can, where it thinks it just and equitable to do so, increase the amount of compensation to be paid where an order was made for compensation, or, where compensation was not awarded, it can award compensation.[2]

9.58 Advisers can request recommendations such as the drawing up and implementation of a disability policy, but this power will be particularly useful to request any reasonable adjustments required by the applicant in respect of which a finding of discrimination has been made.

9.59 In *Bush v Rolls Royce*,[3] a case concerning harassment, the tribunal recommended that Rolls Royce should take the following actions before 1 September 1999.

'(a) provide disability awareness training for the existing members of the drawing office; and
(b) amend their equal opportunities policy and their harassment policy to make specific reference to the Disability Discrimination Act 1995 and the subsidiary legislation and Code and Guidance.'

The recommendations were made because of the tribunal's concerns about Rolls Royce's approach in the case – it had never specifically addressed the issues raised by the DDA 1995, there was no evidence that any training had been given on the DDA 1995 or its ramifications for managers. When Mr Bush's general allegations of harassment were first made they were not investigated under Rolls Royce's harassment policy. The tribunal also awarded compensation of £4,000, all for injury to feelings.

---

1 DDA 1995, s 8(2)(c).
2 Ibid, s 8(5)(a) and (b).
3 9 July 1999, Case Nos 1401054/98 and 1401495/98, EOR DCLD No 44, Summer 2000.

THE REMEDIES HEARING

9.60   It is clear from the guidance laid down in *Buxton v Equinox Design*[1] that remedies hearings in most disability discrimination cases need to be held separately so that all the issues can be dealt with. The EAT stated:

> 'The remedies hearing in discrimination cases requires careful judicial management. When the compensation is uncapped, the relatively brief and informal hearing on remedy appropriate in unfair dismissal cases may not be appropriate and it will often be the case that the remedies hearing should involve the parties in careful pre-preparation under the management of the tribunal. For this purpose directions may be required involving an exchange of statements of case and any witness statements.'

9.61   Advisers will need to be as thorough in preparing for the remedies hearing as for the substantive hearing. The nature of evidence required may include the following.

–   A statement from the applicant which is vital to the case, and must cover details of:
  (a) the effect of the discrimination on the applicant;
  (b) any physical injury sustained as a result of the discrimination (eg a physical injury to an applicant's back sustained as a result of a failure to provide the requisite chair by way of complying with the duty under s 6 of the DDA 1995 to make reasonable adjustments);
  (c) any psychiatric injury (ie injury to feelings);
  (d) any attempts to obtain alternative employment, with copies of applications, rejection letters, etc; and
  (e) any particular difficulties in applying for work (eg limits of particular skills, mobility problems or family reasons for having to stay in a particular area).
–   A statement from a member of the applicant's family or a friend will be useful as it is often those closest to the disabled person who will be most acutely aware of the effect that discrimination may have had upon them (eg a lack of confidence or exacerbation of the effects of the disability).
–   Details of the local job market.
–   Where the claim is for an injury (whether psychological or physical), a report from a relevant medical expert (consultant or GP) is essential.
–   Where it is argued that due to disability the applicant is unlikely to gain employment for some time, it is useful to obtain a specific report from an employment consultant, such as one from a

---

1   [1999] IRLR 158.

particular disability charity. As a less expensive alternative, advisers can obtain one of the charities' general reports, which can give an overall picture of the difficulties encountered by people with particular disabilities in the workplace. For example, reports from the RNIB[1] and RNID indicate (respectively) that blind and hearing impaired people are 2.5 times more likely to be unemployed than those without sight/hearing impairments.

– In certain extreme cases, where the respondent has caused a personal injury requiring care, a specialist report on the cost of that care would be required.

Advisers may need to seek discovery of documents to prepare fully, such as those relating to a pension scheme, or permanent health insurance documents. A schedule of loss, outlining exactly what the applicant is claiming, and on what basis, should be submitted to the respondent and the tribunal.[2]

9.62 Where the tribunal has made an award, and the respondent has failed to pay it within the requisite time, the applicant will have to register the judgment with the county court and enforce it as a breach of contract.

SETTLEMENTS

9.63 Many of the cases brought under the DDA 1995 have been settled prior to hearing. There are a number of advantages to settlement before hearing:

– the client will not have to give evidence (appearing in a tribunal can be a difficult and distressing experience, particularly if the disability is being disputed);
– the recoupment provisions will not apply (in an unfair dismissal claim);
– the applicant may obtain more in settlement than would be possible in the tribunal (eg reinstatement or re-engagement or particular reasonable adjustments); and
– the applicant may obtain compensation more quickly than waiting for the tribunal case to conclude.

9.64 There are only two ways in which an individual can waive the right to bring a claim against an employer in an employment tribunal: by means of a settlement through ACAS (the Advisory Conciliation and

---

1   Used in *Kirker v British Sugar*, Case No 2601249/97.
2   See **9.78** and the case study at the end of this chapter for further details.

Arbitration Service) or by signing a compromise agreement under s 9 of the DDA 1995 and s 203 of the ERA 1996.

Compromise agreements

9.65 Section 203 of the ERA 1996, as amended, provides that an agreement reached between the parties which seeks to circumvent the jurisdiction of an employment tribunal will be void unless it satisfies the requirements of a compromise agreement. These requirements are that:

– the agreement is in writing;
– it must relate to the particular complaint;
– the complainant must have received independent legal advice from a relevant independent adviser (s 203 specifies that 'relevant' includes officers, official employees or members of a trade union, advice centre workers and qualified solicitors and barristers);
– the independent adviser must have a current insurance policy covering the risk of a claim by the complainant in respect of loss arising as a consequence of the advice; and
– the agreement must identify the adviser and must state that the statutory conditions regulating compromise agreements have been satisfied.

Where a compromise agreement has been breached, it can be enforced in the county court in the same way as any breach of contract claim.

9.66 Compromise agreements cannot exclude potential complaints which have not yet arisen, although they are not limited to complaints which have been presented to an employment tribunal.

Settlement sums

9.67 It is often extremely difficult to ascertain the appropriate settlement sum. As always, the starting point is the client. What does the client want from the case: a job, apology, or compensation? Advisers may find that clients have unrealistic expectations of the sum that they might expect from an employer in a case under the DDA 1995, due in part to the publicity attracted by the big awards. The adviser must explain to the client how awards are calculated and why, and perhaps highlight any differences between their situation and the situation of those who have received higher awards.

9.68 Determining how much compensation a client should settle for can also be a difficult exercise. One means of arriving at an appropriate figure is to calculate the actual financial loss from the date of discrimination to the date of the hearing/likely hearing, as well as future loss, as discussed above. An amount for injury to feelings should be added, thus providing the best possible scenario should the case be successful at hearing. For this should be deducted an amount representing the risk of litigation, ie what chance there is of not succeeding if the case goes to tribunal. This may then be a reasonable sum at which to settle. The stronger the case, the smaller the deduction. In any event, advisers will need to have prepared a schedule of loss at the earliest possible stage.[1]

9.69   Some clients may choose to settle for a sum which advisers think is too low. Of course, so long as the adviser has laid out clearly the potential settlement figures and the risks involved in litigation, it is the client's decision whether or not to accept the offer.

9.70   There is also the possibility of obtaining a 'commercial settlement', which is based on the cost to the respondent of defending the case (eg the cost of lawyers' fees and the attendance of employee witnesses at the tribunal).

9.71   Applicants may also want a reference. The tribunal cannot order an agreed reference and where an applicant is relatively young and is likely to be employed again, it may be a valuable part of the settlement.

9.72   In addition, there may also be the issue of reasonable adjustments if the client is still employed. Any settlement must include these adjustments.

ACAS

9.73   ACAS provides conciliation services in employment cases. If requested by the respondent or if they consider there is a reasonable prospect of success, the conciliation officers employed by ACAS must try to promote a settlement of a complaint under the DDA 1995.[2] Anything communicated to a conciliation officer is not admissible in evidence other than with the consent of the person who communicated it.[3]

9.74   Once a tribunal application is lodged, ACAS is automatically sent copies of correspondence between the parties and the tribunal, as well as the ET1 and ET3. An ACAS officer will be assigned to the case and will write to the parties to advise of their availability to assist in a settlement. Advisers should remember that when an offer has been made to an ACAS officer, communicated to the applicant and accepted by either the applicant or the person acting on his behalf, ie the adviser, it will be

---

1   See the case study at the end of this chapter.
2   Schedule 3, para 1.
3   Ibid, Sch 3, para 4.

binding (and equally for respondents). Clients need to be fully aware of the implications of dealing with ACAS officers and it may be best to ensure that this is reiterated in writing.

9.75 Where it has been involved in the settlement, ACAS (or sometimes the respondent or the applicant's representative) will draw up a COT3 form on which are entered the details of any settlement. The COT3 agreement may be signed on behalf of the applicant and the respondent by their respective legal advisers. However, in *Gloystarne & Co v Martin*,[1] the EAT held that a COT3 settlement form signed by a representative who was not shown as the representative on the originating application did not bind the applicant. In these circumstances, the applicant will personally need to sign the COT3 agreement. The ACAS officer will inform the tribunal office that settlement has been reached, and the proceedings will be stayed. If proceedings are stayed, they can be revived if the terms of the settlement are not adhered to. In some cases, the tribunal may dismiss the claim upon receipt of settlement details. However, it is preferable for there to be a stay instead so that the applicant may resurrect the proceedings if the agreement is not adhered to.

9.76 Whilst views as to the helpfulness of ACAS officers vary, a settlement through ACAS can offer advantages otherwise unavailable, for example, any reinstatement or re-engagement through a COT3 will have continuity of employment preserved.[2]

9.77 Advisers can take the initiative and contact the ACAS officers with a view to their contacting the respondent and considering settlement. Whilst acting through ACAS, the adviser is not prohibited from contacting the respondent, but ACAS will not want to merely rubber stamp an agreement reached between the adviser and the respondent without its input. Thus, it is best to keep ACAS informed.

Negotiating with the respondent

9.78 Although much of the negotiation with the respondents may be done through ACAS,[3] applicants' advisers may also contact respondents directly. Advisers should remember to ensure that any correspondence about settlement is marked 'without prejudice', so that it cannot be referred to in the tribunal should the case proceed. It is advisable to draw up a schedule of loss[4] at the earliest opportunity and to send a copy

---

1 [2001] IRLR 15.
2 Employment Protection (Continuity of Employment) Regulations 1996, SI 1996/3147.
3 See **9.73–9.77**.
4 See the case study at the end of this chapter.

of this to the respondent. The schedule should set out all the applicant's losses and the amount for injury to feelings he is seeking. An accompanying letter can indicate any lower amount the applicant is willing to accept in settlement; this should be marked 'without prejudice'.

9.79 Advisers should remember to include the provision of references, which may be crucial for an applicant when attempting to re-enter the job market. The wording of the reference should be negotiated between the two parties, with any settlement agreement ensuring that the respondent does not provide references other than the agreed one.

9.80 Advisers must remember that some clients (eg those with learning difficulties or mental health problems) will require extra time to consider settlement offers. It may be advisable to make this clear to the respondent's representative at the earliest possible opportunity, in order to avoid an offer of settlement made the day before the hearing, or even at the hearing itself, at which point the client will be unable to give full consideration to the offer. In any event, this will ensure the respondent focuses on settlement at an earlier stage.

Confidentiality clauses

9.81 Respondents will often wish to insist on a confidentiality clause being included in any settlement, by which the applicant employee cannot disclose any details of the case and the settlement arrived at to anyone other than, for example, a spouse or immediate family. There are two issues to remember in relation to this. First, many applicants may wish to take a case partly to have some public acknowledgement of the discrimination which they have suffered. A confidentiality clause will obviously stifle this and the nature and extent of the clause must be fully explained to the client, particularly that if they breach the clause they will be in breach of contract.

9.82 If a clause is to be accepted, it may be worth negotiating on the extent of it: for example, a clause could prevent an applicant from disclosing the sum settled for and from disclosing the name of the employer, but this would leave the details of the discrimination to be used by, for example, a disability organisation in promoting the effectiveness of the DDA 1995.

9.83 Secondly, as the desire to keep an alleged incident of discrimination confidential may often motivate an employer to settle, the applicant's adviser should use this as a negotiating tool to obtain increased damages. Any settlement put to the respondent can be indicated as being on the basis of there being no confidentiality clause: if one is required, then the applicant should be compensated for being unable to disclose the details of the case.

9.84   It should also be explained to clients at the outset of the case that if they wish to publicise the fact that they are bringing a claim against their employer, this is likely to have an effect on any later confidentiality clause or even perhaps that the respondent will not settle at all.

Points to remember when considering the contents of the COT3

9.85   Advisers should remember the following points when considering the contents of the COT3.

–   It is usual for respondents to require full and final settlement of all outstanding claims. It is important to ensure that claims as to pension rights are excluded from this general term and also that any personal injury claims being run sumultaneously are not compromised.

–   When including the making of reasonable adjustments in the body of the agreement, advisers should ensure that these are drafted with sufficient precision to cover all eventualities. For example, if training on a particular computer package is to be afforded, that training must happen within a particular time and there should be provision made in case the applicant has to reschedule the training.

9.86   Where a COT3 has been breached, the means of enforcing it will depend upon whether the tribunal has dismissed the application or stayed it. The former is the most usual way in which a tribunal will deal with a claim that has been settled. Where the application has been dismissed, the applicant will have to enforce the agreement in the same way as a breach of contract in the county court or High Court depending on the amount of money involved. Public funding may be available, depending upon the size of the claim and the applicant's circumstances.

9.87   Where the tribunal application has been stayed, the applicant can reinstate it. Alternatively, she can pursue the breach of agreement in the county court, in the same way as for a breach of contract claim. Where the COT3 contains terms for the provision of reasonable adjustments within a specified time frame, it is advisable to get the tribunal to stay the application rather than dismiss it, at least until the specified time period has expired so that it can be reinstated if the adjustments are not provided.

Consent order

9.88 Although applicants do not waive their right to bring tribunal proceedings by way of a consent order, these can be used to settle tribunal cases. Essentially, a consent order consists of a contract between the applicant and the respondent whereby, in consideration for the applicant withdrawing the claim from the tribunal, the respondent agrees to a particular course of action and/or payment of compensation. If either side breaches the agreement, the injured party can take action in the county court in the same way as with a breach of contract case. A consent order cannot prevent the applicant from continuing with a claim in the employment tribunal, but if the applicant does so, the respondent can sue him for breach of the order.

CASE STUDIES

IN THE EMPLOYMENT TRIBUNAL
CASE NUMBER: 23450/99

BETWEEN

MR R MISTRY

Applicant

And

(1) ANDREW HOLDEN

First Respondent

(2) GOVERNORS OF WHITEMORE PRIMARY SCHOOL

Second Respondent

SCHEDULE OF LOSS

---

1. **Loss of earnings from the date on which the applicant would have started work (5 April 1999) to the date of hearing (29 August 1999)**
    Net salary £24,000 divided by 52 (weeks) = £461.54 per week
    20 (weeks) × 461.54 = £9,230.80.[1]
    Total £9,230.80

2. **Plus pension contributions**
    10% of gross salary (£30,000) = £3,000 divided by 52 weeks = £58
    20 (weeks) × £58 = £1,160
    Total £10,390.80

3. **Minus income received**
    Incapacity benefit of £50.35 per week, × 20 (weeks) = £1,007.[2]
    Total: £9,383.80

---

1   Gross salary of £30,000, net salary of £24,000. Following *Kirker*, advisers can use gross salary figures or ask the tribunal to direct that the respondent enter into an undertaking that they reimburse any tax should the award be subject to same; where a settlement is made, such an undertaking for sums in excess of £30,000 should also be written into the settlement agreement.

2   Income which derives from contributions paid by an employee such as an occupational pension are not taken into account as income. It could be argued that incapacity benefit, which is a contributory benefit, should be viewed in this way. The applicant has also been in receipt of disability living allowance for a number of years, and, although it is not a contributory benefit (as he would have been awarded this in any event), this should not be deducted.

4. Plus injury to feelings
£4,000.[1]
Total: £13,383.80.

5. Plus future loss of earnings
Future loss of earnings for 5 years with a multiplier applied of 4.65.
Multiplier $= 4.65 \times £24,000 = £111,600.$[2]
Total: £124,983.80

6. Plus future loss of pension
£3,000 per year (see above) $\times$ 4.65 (same multiplier as above) $=$ £13,950.
Total: £138,933.80.

7. Plus interest
Interest on the amount for injury to feelings – from the date of discrimination to the date of tribunal.
25 March 1999 (date of the letter stating that the applicant did not get the job) to 29 August (date of the hearing) $=$ 21.5 weeks
Interest of 8% on £4,000 $=$ £320
£320 divided by 52 $= 6.15 \times 21.5 =$ £132.22
Interest on compensation, excluding future loss
Payable from the mid point (the day falling half-way between the act of discrimination and the date of calculation)
21.5 divided by 2 (mid point) $=$ 10.75

---

1   The average amount awarded for injury to feelings in disability cases in 1999 was £3,636 (see *Equal Opportunities Review* September/October 2000). This figure has been used as the starting point. In this case the applicant might argue that the injury to feelings was aggravated by the failure to contact him about the result of his interview or to give him proper feedback.

2   This calculation is based on Mr Mistry having been the best candidate for the job and the person who would have been given that job had it not been for the discrimination. Therefore, there is no percentage chance calculation. The local job centre estimates that the average length of time that a male of 50 is unemployed is 2 years. If possible, figures specific to the applicant's occupation should be obtained. The tribunal might expect the applicant to retrain or obtain alternative employment if the prospects for obtaining employment in his occupation are poor. The RNIB report *Blind in Britain* indicated that blind and partially sighted people are 2.5 times more likely to be unemployed than sighted people; $2.5 \times 2 = 5$, being the number of years of future loss being claimed. The tribunal would be likely to make some reduction for the chance of early retirement or retirement through ill health from the figure for future loss of earnings. The multiplier is based on the fixed-term multipliers in *Nelson-Jones on Multipliers* (Butterworths, 1998).

Interest of 8% on £9,383.80 = £750.70

£750.70 divided by 52 = £14.42 × 10.75 = £155.02

Total interest: £288.04[1]

Total amount claimed £139,220.24[2]

---

1   Alternatively, advisers can calculate the daily interest payable and multiply by the number of days.

2   In a recruitment case, it is likely to be difficult to persuade a tribunal to award a significant amount for future loss of earnings, but in any dealings with the respondent it is important to set out the full potential claim and reasons for it.

Chapter 10

REVIEWS AND APPEALS

REVIEWS

10.1   Reviews of decisions are rare, but the tribunal can review its decision under the Employment Tribunals (Constitution and Rules of Procedure) Regulations 1993, Sch 1, para 11(1) if:

(a)   the decision was made wrongly because of an error on the part of the tribunal staff (this does not include the Chairman or other members of the panel);

(b)   a party did not receive notice of proceedings leading to the decision;

(c)   the decision was made in the absence of a party;

(d)   new evidence has become available since the conclusion of the hearing, providing that at the time of the hearing it could not reasonably have been known or foreseen that such evidence existed; or

(e)   it would be in the interests of justice to review the decision.

10.2   A decision is defined by reg 2(2) of the Employment Tribunals (Constitution and Rules of Procedure) Regulations 1993 as including 'a declaration, an order, including an order striking out any originating application or notice of appearance' made under Sch 1, para 4(7) or 13(2), a recommendation or an award of the tribunal' and a determination under Sch 1, para 6 'entitlement to bring court proceedings'. Advisers should note that an interlocutory order is not a decision and so it is not possible to ask the tribunal to review any decision made as an interlocutory matter such as orders for further particulars, discovery or joinder. In these cases, the only course of action open to the parties is to appeal to the EAT.[1]

10.3   An application for a review must be made within 14 days after the date on which the decision was sent to the parties, and it must state the

---

1   See *Peter Simper & Co Ltd v Cooke* [1984] ICR 6, EAT; *Casella London Ltd v Banai* [1990] ICR 215, EAT; *Reddington v Straker & Sons Ltd* [1994] ICR 172, EAT.

grounds for the review in full.[1] The tribunal Chair has the discretion both to extend the time-limit[2] and to refuse an application made in time if in the Chair's opinion 'it has no reasonable prospect of success'.[3] An application for a review can either be made orally at the hearing or in writing to the Secretary (or Regional Secretary) at any time between the date of the hearing and 14 days after the decision has been sent to the parties. An application made in writing must state the grounds for the review in full.

APPEALS

The EAT

10.4   An appeal to the EAT can be made against a decision of the employment tribunal either after a preliminary hearing (eg on whether or not the applicant meets the definition of disability) or after the main liability hearing. Community legal funding (legal aid) may be available for EAT cases.

10.5   The EAT hearing an appeal will consist of a judge and two lay members. The lay members are appointed by the Queen on the recommendation of the Lord Chancellor and the Secretary of State and they must have 'special knowledge or experience of industrial relations, either as representatives of employers or representatives of workers'. There is no formal system of advertisement, nomination by representative bodies or training, although the EAT has recently indicated that it wishes to have training in issues concerning disability and disability awareness.

10.6   An appeal from a decision made by a tribunal Chairman sitting alone (eg striking out of proceedings, postponements, adjournments or extensions of time, directions or joining parties) can be heard by a judge sitting alone.[4]

10.7   Appeals against a decision made by a Chairman and lay members must be heard by a judge and two members, one as a representative of employers and one as a representative of workers, and occasionally by a

---

1   Employment Tribunals (Constitution and Rules of Procedure) Regulations 1993, Sch 1, para 11(4).
2   Ibid, Sch 1, para 15(1).
3   Ibid, Sch 1, para 11(5).
4   ETA 1996, s 28(4).

judge and two members from each side.[1] Parties may consent to a hearing with one member absent.[2]

10.8   The EAT must follow judgments of the Court of Appeal, but it is not bound by judgments of the divisions of the High Court or by a decision of the Court of Session (unless it is hearing a Scottish appeal), although these are highly persuasive. The EAT usually sits in London and Edinburgh, but can sit anywhere in England, Wales and Scotland, and its decisions are binding on tribunals throughout Great Britain. Its decisions are not binding on tribunals in Northern Ireland, but they are usually followed there. If an appellant or defendant with a disability cannot travel to or access the usual offices of the EAT either in Edinburgh or London, an application could be made to have the EAT sit at a more accessible venue as reasonable adjustment under Part III of the DDA 1995.

In what circumstances can an appeal be made to the EAT?

10.9   An appeal can only be made to the EAT on a question of law, ie that there has been an error of law. An appeal cannot be made against a finding of fact made by the employment tribunal. It is a finding of fact, for example, if after hearing all the evidence the employment tribunal decides that it prefers the evidence of one witness over that of another where their evidence is contradictory. It is sometimes difficult to distinguish between a question of fact and a question of law, but as a general rule an appeal to the EAT is only possible if at least one of the following apply to the decision.

Misapplication of law
10.10   An error of law occurs if the employment tribunal misdirects itself or if it misapplies or misunderstands the law. It is also an error of law if the tribunal fails to ask itself the right legal question, misconstrues a statute.[3]

Perversity
10.11   An appeal based on perversity must argue that no reasonable tribunal properly considering the evidence before it and directing itself according to the law *could* have reached the decision that it did. If an adviser intends to run an appeal on the basis of perversity,[4] she should obtain the Chairman's notes so that a complete record of proceedings

---

1   ETA 1996, s 28(3).
2   Ibid, s 28(4).
3   See *Abbey Life Assurance Co Ltd v Tansell* [2000] IRLR 387, CA.
4   See *Vicary v British Telecommunications plc* [1999] IRLR 680, EAT.

before the employment tribunal, as well as all the documents in the hearing bundle, are before the EAT.[1]

10.12   It is not easy to prove that the tribunal has been perverse in reaching its decision. The test to prove perversity is stringent. It will not be enough to show that the tribunal's decision was made against the weight of the evidence before it or that it did not consider a particular aspect of the evidence. This is because it is for the tribunal to decide how much weight it should give to each part of the evidence and the EAT should not interfere with this.[2]

No evidence

10.13   There may be an overlap with perversity here, but it is also an error of law for the tribunal to make a decision for which there is no supporting evidence. To rely on this ground, however, the adviser will have to show that there really was no evidence at all. If there was some evidence, however little, dealing with the subject-matter in question, then an appeal on this ground is likely to fail. If evidence on a particular subject given by one party is challenged by the other, the tribunal is entitled to decide whether or not to accept or reject the evidence. If the evidence offered by one party is not challenged, the tribunal should accept it, and if it makes a decision contrary to that evidence then its decision will have been made on the basis of there being no evidence in support and so is open to appeal.

Wrongful exercise of discretion

10.14   For an appeal to be based on the wrongful exercise of discretion the adviser will have to show that the tribunal either took into account a factor that it was improper for it to take into account or that it failed to take into account a factor that it should have considered.[3] The discretion exercised by the tribunal or Chairman must be beyond that of any reasonable tribunal or Chairman and to this extent this ground is akin to perversity.

Bias

10.15   Bias or apparent bias is a ground for appeal and is an error of law because it is a breach of the rules of natural justice. It may also be a breach of the HRA 1998, Sch 1, Art 6(1) – the right to a fair hearing. A specific complaint of bias with full particulars should be made in the

---

1   *Piggott Brothers & Co Ltd v Jackson* [1992] ICR 85, [1991] IRLR 309, CA; *Ministry of Defence v Hunt* [1996] IRLR 139.

2   *Hollister v National Farmers Union* [1979] ICR 542, [1979] IRLR 238, CA.

3   *Cook v Autistic Community* (unreported) Case No 465/98, EAT.

notice of appeal. The appellant will also have the opportunity to make the allegations by way of an affidavit and have that referred to the tribunal the appellant is complaining about.

Time-limits

10.16 In order to appeal against a decision of the employment tribunal, the notice of appeal and a copy of the extended reasons of the decision of the employment tribunal must be served on the EAT 'within ... 42 days from the date on which extended written reasons ... were sent to the appellant'.[1] If the employment tribunal gives only summary reasons, the adviser should apply to the tribunal for extended reasons as soon as possible so as to be able to submit the notice of appeal within time. It is possible to apply for an extension of time within which to serve the notice of appeal, but a justifiable excuse will have to be given for the delay.

Out of time appeals

10.17 Like the employment tribunal, the EAT has the discretion to extend time under r 37 of the Employment Appeal Tribunal Rules 1993, but it exercises this discretion reluctantly. In *United Arab Emirates v Abdelghafar*,[2] the EAT said that it would exercise its discretion only to extend the time-limit in exceptional cases.

10.18 The appeal is instigated by serving on the tribunal:

(a) a notice of appeal, substantially the same as Form 1 or 2 in the Schedule to the Employment Appeal Tribunal Rules 1993;
(b) a copy of the decision/order which is the subject of the appeal;
(c) a copy of the extended written reasons of the EAT.[3]

The forms and notes of guidance can be downloaded from the EAT website (www.employmentappeals.gov.uk). The tribunal will direct the time within which the respondent to the appeal must submit an answer to the appeal.[4]

Procedure

10.19 When the appeal has been registered, the parties will be sent a PHD form to be completed and returned to the EAT within 14 days. Failure to do so may result in the applicant not being allowed to pursue

---

1   Employment Appeal Tribunal Rules 1993, SI 1993/2854, r 3.
2   [1995] IRLR 243.
3   Employment Appeal Tribunal Rules 1993, r 3.
4   Ibid, r 6.

the appeal, or the respondent not being allowed to defend the appeal or cross-appeal. The defaulting party may also be ordered to pay costs. The EAT must have these forms at the preliminary hearing so that directions can be given at that stage.

Preliminary hearings

10.20 If the Registrar of the EAT believes that the EAT has the jurisdiction to hear the case, it will be listed for a preliminary hearing. The hearing is ex parte, that is the respondent does not have to attend but may do so, and at the discretion of the judge the respondent may be heard. At the hearing the appellant will have to show that there is an arguable point of law that should be heard. If the appellant can do this, the matter will be listed for a hearing before a full EAT on another date. If the EAT decides that there is no arguable case, judgment will be given with reasons for rejecting the appeal.

Directions

10.21 The EAT can give directions[1] on such matters as the duration of the hearing, amendments to pleadings and documentation. It is rare for the EAT to hear live evidence, although it does have the power to require attendance. If the EAT is going to hear live evidence from a witness, directions could deal with any necessary reasonable adjustments in the same way as directions in the employment tribunal.

The main hearing

10.22 The parties will be asked to give an estimate of the time the hearing will take and will be consulted about appropriate dates for the hearing.

10.23 The parties to the hearing will be asked to produce skeleton arguments and a chronology for the hearing. These should be served on the EAT and the parties should exchange them 14 days before the hearing. No later than one day before the hearing, the parties should also send the EAT a list of authorities. This is a list of the cases that are going to be referred to and relied upon. It is a good idea for the adviser to take copies of these cases to the hearing.

10.24 The EAT will prepare an index of the main documents and the decision of the tribunal against which appeal is being made. The parties will have to make up the bundles themselves using this index.

---

1   Employment Appeal Tribunal Rules 1993, r 24.

10.25   At the hearing itself, it is not possible to raise new points of law that have not been raised at the tribunal hearing. However, the EAT will hear additional or new arguments on how a particular aspect of the law should be interpreted if this is simply a matter of construction and will not require additional evidence to be heard.

10.26   New evidence will be allowed on appeal only if:

−   a reasonable explanation can be provided as to why the evidence was not put before the tribunal;
−   the new evidence is credible; and
−   had the evidence been put before the tribunal it would have had a decisive effect upon its decision.

10.27   The EAT usually gives its judgment orally after hearing the arguments, although it can reserve judgment. If judgment is not reserved, it will later make available a written judgment. The judgment of the EAT takes effect from the time it is given rather than from the time it is published.

Costs

10.28   The EAT does not normally award costs, but it does have the power to do so where 'proceedings were unnecessary, improper or vexatious or ... there has been unreasonable delay or other unreasonable conduct in bringing or conducting proceedings'.[1] Advisers should note that community legal funding (legal aid) is available for EAT cases.

Reviews and appeals

10.29   The EAT can review its own decision[2] either of its own motion or on the application of a party within 14 days of the decision. The EAT will do so if it made an error, if proper notice was not given to a party or it is in the interests of justice to do so.

10.30   Appeals from the EAT must be made to the Court of Appeal or Court of Session. However, it is only possible to appeal if the EAT gives leave or permission to do so. An application for leave should be made as soon as judgment has been given.

---

1   Employment Appeal Tribunal Rules 1993, r 4.
2   Ibid.

Appendix 1

USEFUL ADDRESSES

Ability Net
PO Box 94
Warwick CV34 5WS
Advice line 0800 269 545
Tel 01926 312847
Makes mainstream computer technology accessible to people with disabilities.

ACAS
Enquiries:
Tel 020 7396 5100 (London)
Tel 0141 204 2677 (Glasgow)
Tel 029 2076 1126 (Cardiff)
www.acas.org.uk

Ankylosing Spondylitis Society, National
PO Box 179
Mayfield East
Sussex TN20 6ZL
Tel 01435 873527

Arise
The Graham Hill Unit, Royal National Orthopaedic Hospital Trust
Brockley Hill
Stanmore HA7 4LP
Tel 020 8954 8939
Information on scoliosis for patients and professionals.

Arthritis Care
18 Stephenson Way
London NW1 2HD
Helpline 0808 8004050
Tel 020 7916 1500

Arthritis Research Campaign
St Mary's Gate
Chesterfield
Derbyshire S41 7DT
Tel 01246 558033
Range of free information booklets and leaflets available.

Association for Spina Bifida and Hydrocephalus
ASBAH House
42 Park Road
Peterborough PE1 2UQ
Tel 01733 555988

Asthma Campaign, National
Providence House
Providence Place
London N1 0NT
Helpline 0845 701 0203
Tel 020 7226 2260

Autistic Society, National
393 City Road
London EC1V 1NG
Tel 020 7833 2299
Offers information and advice to people with autistic spectrum disorders.

Back Care
16 Elmtree Road
Teddington
Middlesex TW11 8ST
Tel 020 8977 5474

Blind, Guide Dogs for the
Hillfields
Burghfield Common
Reading
Berkshire RG7 3YG
Tel 0118 983 5555

Blind, National Federation of the
The Old Surgery
215 Kirkgate
Wakefield WF1 1JG
Tel 01924 291313

Blind People, Action for
14–16 Verney Road
London SE16 3DZ
Tel 020 7732 8771
Employment, grants, information and
benefits advice.

Blind, Royal National Institute for
the (RNIB)
224 Great Portland Street
London W1N 6AA
Helpline 0845 766 9999
Advice, assistance and information on
benefits, equipment, employment and
support.

Braille Producers, UK Association of
108 High Street
Hurstpierpoint
West Sussex BN6 9PX
Tel 01273 834321
Fax 01273 833744
Offers advisory services on Braille
production.

Brain and Spine Foundation, British
7 Winchester House
Kennington Park
Cranmer Road
London SW9 6EJ
Helpline 0808 808 1000
Tel 020 7793 5939
Information and support by people
trained in understanding neurological
disorders.

Breast Cancer Care
Kiln House
210 New Kings Road
London SW6 4NZ
Helpline 0808 800 6000
Tel 020 7384 2984
Information and support.

Brittle Bone Society
30 Guthrie Street
Dundee DD1 5BS
Tel 01382 203336/7

Cancer, Association for New
Approaches to
St Peter's Hospital
Guildford Road
Chertsey
Surrey KT16 0PZ
Tel 01932 879 882
Information on therapies.

Cancer Research Campaign, The
10 Cambridge Terrace
London NW1 4JL
Tel 020 7224 1333

Citizens Advice Bureaux, National
Myddleton House
115–123 Pentonville Road
London N1 9LZ
Tel 020 7833 2181
Will provide details of local Citizens
Advice Bureaux.

Colitis and Chrohn's Disease,
National Association for
4 Beaumont House
Sutton Road
St Albans
Hertfordshire
AL1 5HH
Answer phone 01727 844296
Administration 01727 830038

Colostomy Association, British
15 Station Road
Reading
Berkshire RG1 1LG
Freephone helpline 0800 328 4257
Advice on living with a colostomy and returning to a full life after surgery.

Continence Campaign
c/o LSA
110 St Martin's Lane
London WC2N 4DY
Tel 020 7841 5447

Continence Foundation
307 Hatton Square
16 Baldwins Gardens
London EC1N 7RJ
Helpline 020 7831 9831

Counselling, British Association for
1 Regent Place
Rugby
Warwickshire CV21 2PJ
Tel 01788 550899
Information 01788 578328
Minicom 01788 572838
Lists of counselling agencies and local agencies available on receipt of A4 SAE.

Cranio Facial Support Group
c/o Steve Moody
44 Helmsdale Road
Leamington Spa
Warwickshire CV32 7DW
Tel 01926 334629
Advice, support and information for anyone dealing with Craniosynostosis or Aperts, Crouzon's Pfeiffers, Cloverleaf Skull, Saethre-Chotzen syndromes.

Cued Speech, National Centre for
Cornerhouse
Bay View
Stoke Fleming
Dartmouth
Devon TQ6 0QX
Tel 01803 770944
Training and information about cued speech, spoken language accessed through vision, for deaf people.

Cystic Fibrosis Trust
11 London Road
Bromley
Kent BR1 1BY
Tel 020 8464 7211

Davies Associates
Glebe House
Llanharry
Glamorgan CF72 9LH
Tel and Fax 01443 226216
Email Davies@Glebe.demon.co.uk
Employment medico-legal specialists. Consultancy advice on occupational health and safety practice for employers, doctors, lawyers and disability interest groups. Good practice guidance, tribunal reviews commentary, research and case commissions.

Deaf Association, the British
1–3 Worship Street
London EC2A 2AB
Voice and Minicom 020 7588 3520

Deafblind UK
100 Bridge Street
Peterborough
Cambridgeshire PE1 1DY
24-hour helpline 0800 132320
Tel 01733 358100

Deaf People, Friends for Young
FYD, East Court Mansion
College Lane
East Grinstead
West Sussex RH19 3LT
Tel 01342 323 444
Fax 01342 410 232
Minicom 01342 312 639
*Activities include deaf awareness
training for employers and training for
young deaf people.*

Deaf People, Council for
Advancement of Communication
with
Pelaw House
School of Education
University of Durham
Durham DH1 1TA
Voice & Minicom 0191 374 3607
Fax 0191 374 7864
*Produces a national directory of qualified
sign language interpreters and
lipspeakers, classified by region,
experience and expertise.*

Deaf People, Royal Association in
Aid of,
Walsingham Road
Colchester
Essex CO2 7BP
Tel 01206 509509
Minicom 01206 577090

Deaf People, Royal National
Institute for (RNID)
19–23 Featherstone Street
London EC1Y 8SL
Helpline 0870 605 0123
Tinnitus helpline 0845 709 0210
Voice 020 7296 8000
Text 020 7296 8001
*Campaigns for a better quality of life for
people with hearing impairments,
provides services and information about
employment and undertakes research.*

Diabetic Association, British
10 Queen Anne Street
London W1M 0BD
Tel 020 7323 1531
Information and advice on diabetes.

DIAL UK
Park Lodge
St Catherine's Hospital
Tickhill Road
Balby
Doncaster DN4 8QN
Tel 01302 310123
*Supports UK-wide disability information
and advice services.*

Disability Consultancy
c/o RNIB
Redhill College
Philanthropic Road
Redhill
Surrey RH1 4DG
Voice and minicom 01737 761490
*Disability Discrimination Act workplace
compliance assessments and training.*

Disability Information Trust
Mary Marlborough Centre
Nuffield Orthopaedic Centre
Headington
Oxford OX3 7LD
Tel 01865 227592
*Tests and assesses equipment and self-
help devices and publishes practical
guides.*

Disability Resource Team
Office 2
Pelmark House
11 Amwell End, Ware
Hertfordshire SG12 0LX
Voice and minicom 01920 466005
*Training, consultancy and transcription
services.*

Disability Rights Commission
DRC Helpline
Freepost MID 02164
Stratford upon Avon
CV37 9BR
Tel 08457 622 633
Text 08457 622 644
Fax 08457 778 878

Disabled Access to Technology
Association
Broomfield House
Bolling Road
Bradford BD4 7BG
Tel 01274 370019
Provides training in computing.

Disabled Living Foundation
380–384 Harrow Road
London W9 2HU
Helpline 0870 603 9177
Textphone 0870 603 9176
Tel 020 7289 6111
*Information and advice about daily
living equipment for disabled people.*

Disabled Professionals, Association
of
Chair: Sue Maynard Campbell, BCM
ADP
London WC1N 3XX
Tel 01924 283253
Minicom 01924 270335
Fax 01924 283 253
www.adp.org.uk

Disfigurement Guidance Centre –
Laserfair
PO Box 7
Cupar
Fife KY15 4PF
Tel 01337 870281
*Information, help and publications; SAE
essential for reply.*

Downs Syndrome Association
155 Mitcham Road
London SW17 9PG
Tel 020 8682 4001

Dyslexia Association, British
98 London Road
Reading
Berkshire RG1 5AU
Helpline 01189 668271
Tel 0118 9662677

Dyslexia Institute
133 Gresham Road
Staines
Middlesex TW18 2AJ
Tel 01784 463851
*Nationwide service offering educational
assessment, teaching, training and
advice.*

Dyslexia Organisation, Adult
336 Brixton Road
London SW9 7AA
Office tel 0207 727 7646
Email dyslexia.hq@dial.pipex.com
*Offers advice about psychological and
teacher assessments, tuition, a helpline, a
research group, a newsletter and various
pamphlets and videos.*

Dystonia Society
46/47 Britton Street
London EC1M 5UJ
Tel 020 7490 5671
*Support for those affected by dystonia,
research and welfare.*

Eating Disorders Association
1st Floor
Wensum House
103 Prince of Wales Road
Norwich NR1 1DW
Helpline 01603 621414
Youth helpline 01603 765050
Fax 01603 664915
www.edauk.com

Eczema Society, National
163 Eversholt Street
London NW1 1BU
Tel 020 7388 4097

Employers' Forum on Disability
Nutmeg House
60 Gainsford Street
London SE1 2NY
Tel/minicom 020 7403 3020
Fax 020 7403 0404
Range of publications of briefing papers
and other publications available on best
practice for employing disabled people
and serving disabled customers.

Environments, Centre for Accessible
Nutmeg House
60 Gainsford Street
London SE1 2NY
Voice and minicom 020 7357 8182

Employment Appeal Tribunal
(London)
Audit House
58 Victoria Embankment
London EC4Y 0DS
Tel 020 7273 1040
www.employmentappeals.gov.uk

Employment Appeal Tribunal
(Scotland)
52 Melville Street
Edinburgh EH3 7HS
Tel 0131 225 3963

Epilepsy Association, British
New Anstey House
Gate Way Drive
Yeadon
Leeds LS19 7XY
Helpline 0808 8005050
Tel 0113 210 8800

Epilepsy, National Society for
Chesham Lane
Chalfont St Peter
Buckinghamshire SL9 0RJ
Helpline 01494 601400
Tel 01494 601300
Assessment, rehabilitation, long-term
care, advice and local groups.

Equal Opportunities Commission
Overseas House
Quay Street
Manchester M3 3HN
Voice and minicom 0161 833 9244

Europe, Advice on Individual
Rights in
74 Eurolink Business Centre
49 Effra Road
London SW2 1BZ
Tel 020 7924 0927

Group for Solicitors with Disabilities
Law Society
114 Chancery Lane
London WC2A 1PL
Tel 020 7320 5793
Aims to achieve equality for disabled
people: solicitors and their clients.

Haemophilia Society
3rd Floor
Chesterfield House
385 Euston Road
London NW1 3AU
Helpline 0800 0186068
Tel 020 7380 0600

Headway – the Brain Injury
Association
4 King Edward Court
King Edward Street
Nottingham NG1 1EW
Tel 0115 924 0800
Help, information and support to people
with head injuries, their families and
carers.

Health and Safety Executive
Rose Court
2 Southwark Bridge
London SE1
Tel 020 7717 6000
Statutory body responsible for ensuring
health and safety in the workplace.

Heart Foundation, British
14 Fitzhardinge Street
London W3 7JL
Tel 020 7935 0185

IBS Network
Northern General Hospital
Sheffield S5 7AU
Tel 0114 261 1531
Self-help organisation for people with
Irritable Bowel Syndrome.

Ileostomy and Internal Pouch
Support Group
PO Box 132
Scunthorpe DN15 9YW
Tel 01724 720 150
Helps people return to active lives
following surgery for removal of the colon.
Local groups UK-wide.

Independent Living Alternatives
Trafalgar House
Grenville Place
London NW7 3SA
Tel 020 8906 9265
Support and advice on employing
personal assistants.

Independent Living Fund
PO Box 183
Nottingham NG8 3RD
Tel 0115 942 8191
A government-funded trust to help
severely disabled people aged 16–65
employ personal or domestic care on top of
social services provision.

Independent Living, National
Centre for
250 Kennington Lane
London SE11 5RD
Tel 020 7587 1663
Provides information, consultancy and
training on personal assistance and
direct payments.

Insurers, Association of British
51 Gresham Street
London EC2V 7HQ
Tel 020 7600 3333
Fax 020 7696 8996

Kidney Patient Association, British
Bordon
Hampshire GU35 9JZ
Tel 01421 472021

Kidney Research Fund, National
Kings Chambers
Priestgate
Peterborough PE1 1FG
Tel 01733 704650

Law Centres Federation
Duchess House
13–19 Warren Street
London W1P 5DP
Tel 020 7387 8570
also at:
3rd Floor
Elisabeth House
16 St Peters Square
Manchester M2 3DF
Tel 0161 236 5333
Information on local law centres.

Law Society
114 Chancery Lane
London WC2A 1PL
Tel 020 7320 5793

Learning Disabilities, British
Institute of
Wolverhampton Road
Kidderminster DY10 3PP
Tel 01562 850251

Learning Disabilities, Foundation for
People with
20–21 Cornwall Terrace
London NW1 4QL
Tel 020 7535 7400

Leonard Cheshire
30 Millbank
London SW1P 4QD
Tel 020 7802 8200

Leukaemia Research Fund
43 Great Ormond Street
London WC1N 3JJ
Booklets on leukaemia and related blood cancers.

Liberty (The National Council for Civil Liberties)
21 Tabard Street
London SE1 4LA
Legal advice line 020 7378 8659
Tel 020 7403 3888

Limbless Association
The Rehabilitation Centre
Roehampton Lane
London SW15 5PR
Tel 020 8590 1124

Limbless Ex-Service Men's Association, British
Frankland Moore House
185–187 High Road
Chadwell Heath
Romford
Essex RM6 6NA
Tel 020 8788 1777

London Lighthouse
111–117 Lancaster Road
London W11 1QT
Tel 020 7792 1200
Minicom 020 7792 2979
Support centre for people affected by HIV and AIDS.

Low Pay Unit
27–29 Amwell Street
London EC1R 1TL
Tel 020 7713 7616
Employment rights helpline 020 7713 7583

Lupus UK
St James House
Eastern Road
Romford
Essex RM1 3NH
Tel 01708 731251

Macmillan Cancer Relief
Anchor House
15–19 Britten Street
London SW3 3TZ
Tel 020 7351 7811
Information line 0845 601 6161

Manic Depression Fellowship
8–10 High Street
Kingston upon Thames
Surrey KT1 1EY
Tel 020 8974 6550
Fax 020 8974 6600
Provides advice and information on employment issues.

Maternity Alliance
45 Beech Street
London EC2P 2LX
Advice 020 7588 8582
Tel 020 7588 8583

Medical Accidents, Action for Victims of
44 High Street
Croydon
Surrey CR0 1YB
Tel 020 8686 8333
Advisory service for victims of medical negligence.

Medical Foundation for Care of Victims of Torture
96–98 Grafton Road
London NW5 3EJ
Tel 020 7813 7777
Medical treatment and practical help in the UK for survivors of torture.

Mencap (Royal Society for Mentally
Handicapped Children and Adults)
123 Golden Lane
London EC1Y 0RT
Tel 020 7454 0454

Meningitis Trust, The National
Fern House
Bath Road
Stroud
Gloucestershire GL5 3TJ
24-hour helpline 0845 600 0800
Tel 01453 768000

Mental Health Act Commission
Maid Marian House
56 Houndsgate
Nottingham
NG1 6BG
Tel 0115 943 7100
Statutory body to protect the rights of
people with mental health problems.

Mental Health Foundation
21–21 Cornwall Terrace
London NW1 4QL
Tel 020 7535 7400

Migraine Action Association
178a High Road
Byfleet
West Byfleet
Surrey KT14 7ED
Tel 01932 352 468
Research, newsletter, leaflets and free
information service.

Migraine Trust
45 Great Ormond Street
London WC1N 3HZ
Tel 020 7831 4818
Full sufferer service, literature, newsletter,
helpline, clinics and educational service.

MIND (The National Association of
Mental Health)
Granta House
15–19 Broadway
London E15 4BQ
Tel 020 8519 2122
London info line 020 8522 1728
Outside London 0845 766 0163

Mobility Centre, Banstead
Damson Way
Fountain Drive
Carshalton
Surrey SM5 4NR
Tel 020 8770 1151
Free information service, assessments for
car drivers, passengers and wheelchair
users. Driving tuition and residential
accommodation.

Mobility for Disabled People, Joint
Committee on
11 Rothesay Court
Le May Avenue
London SE12 0BA
Liaising and campaigning body on
mobility, access and transport.

Mobility Information Service,
National Mobility Centre
Unit 2
Atcham Estate
Shrewsbury SY4 4UG
Tel 01743 761889
Information on mobility. Driving
assessment for disabled drivers.

Motability
Goodman House
Station Approach
Harlow
Essex CM20 2ET
Tel 01279 635666

Motor Neurone Disease Association
PO Box 246
Northampton NN1 2PR
Helpline 08457 626262
Tel 01604 250505

Multiple Sclerosis Resource Centre
7 Peartree Business Centre
Peartree Road
Stanway
Colchester
Essex CV03 5JN
Helpline 0800 783 0581
Tel 01206 505444

Multiple Sclerosis Society of Great
Britain and Northern Ireland
25 Effie Road
London SW6 1EE
Helpline 0808 800 8000
Tel 020 7610 7171

Muscular Dystrophy Campaign
7–11 Prescott Place
London SW4 6BS
Tel 020 7720 8055

Myalgic Encephalomyelitis (ME),
Action for
PO Box 1302
Wells
Somerset BA5 1YE
Tel 01749 670799

Myalgic Encephalomyelitis (ME
Association)
4 Corringham Road
Stanford-le-Hope
Essex SS17 0AH
Helpline 01375 361013
Tel 01375 642466

Myasthenia Gravis Association
Central Office
Keynes House
Chester Park
Alfreton Road
Derby DE21 4AS
Tel 01332 2901219

Narcolepsy Association (UK)
Craven House
1st Floor
121 Kingsway
London WC2B 6PA
Tel 020 7721 8904

National Schizophrenia Fellowship
Advice Service:
Tel 0208 974 6814
email advice@nsf.org.uk
www.nsf.org.uk

Occupational and Environmental
Diseases Association
Mitre House
66 Abbey Road
Bush Hill Park
Enfield EN1 2QH
Tel 020 8360 8490

Occupational Medicine, Society of
6 St Andrew's Place
Regents Park
London NW1 4LB
Tel 020 7486 2641
*Guidelines for Occupational Physicians
on the DDA 1995 (price £1.50).*

Osteoporosis Society, National
PO Box 10
Radstock
Bath
Somerset BA3 3YB
Helpline 01761 472721
Tel 01761 471771

Outset Ltd
Telemax House
15 New Bedford Road
Luton LU1 1SA
Tel 0870 200 0001
*Promotes employment and training for all
people with disabilities.*

Parkinson's Disease Society of the
UK
215 Vauxhall Bridge Road
London SW1V 1EJ
Tel 020 7931 8080

Partially Sighted Society
PO Box 322
Doncaster DN1 2XA
Tel 01302 323132
London office 020 7371 0289

Pensions Advisory Service
11 Belgrave Road
London SW1V 1RB
Tel 020 7233 8080
Free help to people with personal,
occupational and State pensions queries.

Polio Fellowship, British
Unit A
Eagle Office Centre
The Runway
South Ruislip
Middlesex HA4 6SE
Tel 020 8842 4999
Freephone 0800 018 0586

Physiotherapy, Chartered Society of
14 Bedford Row
London WC1R 4ED
Tel 020 7306 6666
Fax 020 7306 6611
www.csphysio.org.uk

Premenstrual Syndrome, National
Association for
7 Swift's Court
High Street
Seal
Kent TN15 0EG
Helpline 01732 760012
Tel 01732 760011

Primary Immunodeficiency
Association
Alliance House
12 Caxton Street
London SW1H 0QS
Tel 020 7976 7640
Information on treatment and care of the
primary immunodeficiencies and advice
on benefits.

Psoriasis Association
7 Milton Street
Northampton NN2 7JG
Tel 01604 711129

Public Law Project
Room E608
Birkbeck College
University of London
Malet Street
London WC1E 7HX
Tel 020 7467 9807 (advisers only)

Racial Equality, Commission for
Elliott House
10–12 Allington Street
London SW1E 5EH
Tel 020 7828 7022

REMAP
JJ Wright
National Organiser
Hazeldene
Ightham
Sevenoaks
Kent TN15 9AD
Tel 01732 883818
Makes or adapts aids for disabled people
when not commercially available at no
charge to the disabled person.

Remploy Ltd
415 Edgware Road
Cricklewood
London NW2 6LR
Tel 020 8235 0500

Restricted Growth Association
Mrs Honor Rawlings
PO Box 8
Countesthorpe
Leicester LE8 5ZS
Tel 0116 247 8913

Retinitis Pigmentosa, British
PO Box 350
Buckingham MK18 5EL
Helpline 01280 860195
Tel 01280 860195

Rheumatism, British League Against
41 Eagle Street
London WC1R 4AR
Tel 020 7669 6510

Repetitive Strain Injury Association
380–384 Harrow Road
London W9 2HU
Tel 020 7266 2000
Freephone helpline 0800 018 5012
Email rsia@dial.pipex.com
Website www.demon.co.uk
Advice and information on RSI.

Royal National Association for
Disability and Rehabilitation
12 City Forum
250 City Road
London EC1V 8AF
Tel 020 7828 7022
Minicom 020 7250 4119

SANE
1st Floor
Cityside House
40 Adler Street
London E1 1EE
Saneline 0845 767 8000
Tel 020 7375 1002
*Provides information and support for
anyone affected by mental illness.*

Saville and Holdsworth
3AC Court
Thames Ditton
Surrey KT7 0SR
Tel 020 8339 2222
*Provide guidelines for testing people with
disabilities as part of the recruitment
process – Guidelines for Testing People
with Disabilities.*

Schizophrenia Association, UK
Bryn Hyfryd
The Crescent
Bangor
Gwynedd LL57 2AG
Tel 01248 354048

Schizophrenia Fellowship, National
28 Castle Street
Kingston upon Thames
Surrey KT1 1SS
Advice line 020 8974 6814
Tel 01248 454048

Shaw Trust
Shaw House
Epsom Square
White Horse Business Park
Trowbridge
Wiltshire BA14 0XJ
Tel 01225 716350
*Supported placements, rehabilitation,
vocational training and work
preparation.*

Sickle Cell Society
54 Station Road
London NW10 4UA
Tel 020 8961 7795

Skin Foundation, British
19 Fitzroy Square
London W1P 5HQ
Tel 020 7383 0266

Speakability
1 Royal Street
London SE1 7LL
Tel 020 7261 9572
*Information, advice and support for
those with language impairment
following stroke, head injury or
neurological illness.*

Spinal Injuries Association
76 St James's Lane
London N10 3DF
Freephone 0800 980 0501
Tel 020 8444 2121

Stammering Association, British
15 Old Ford Road
London E2 9PJ
Helpline 0845 603 2001
Tel 020 8983 1003

Stroke Association
Stroke House
Whitecross Street
London EC1Y 8JJ
Information service 0845 303 3100
Tel 020 7566 0300

Terence Higgins Trust
52–54 Gray's Inn Road
London WC1X 8JU
Helpline 020 7242 1010
Legal 020 7405 2381
Tel 020 7831 0330

Tinnitus Association, British
4th Floor
White Building
Fitzalan Square
Sheffield S1 2AZ
Freephone 0800 018 0527
Tel 0114 279 6600

Typetalk
John Wood House
Glacier Building
Harrington Road
Brunswick Business Park
Liverpool L3 4DF
Tel 0800 731 1888
Text 0800 500888
Telephone relay service for the deaf, deafblind and speech impaired. Also test users rebate scheme (TURS).

Appendix 2

DDA CASES LISTED BY DISABILITY

This is not a comprehensive list of all DDA cases and nor was disability disputed in all of these cases. The cases are listed merely as an indication of the types of disabilities that have been the subject of cases before the tribunals.

References have been given wherever possible. Where no reference is given, copies of the decision may be obtainable from the Central Office of Tribunals.[1]

NO DIAGNOSIS

HJ Heinz Co Ltd v Kenrick [2000] IRLR 144, EAT.
Howden v Capital Copiers (Edinburgh) Ltd (1997) IDS Brief 598/14.

AGORAPHOBIA

Jeary v MIE Ltd, Case No 1700685/98.

ARMS, HANDS, MANUAL DEXTERITY

Mulligan v Commissioner for Inland Revenue, EAT No 691/99.
Fozard v Greater Manchester Police Authority, Case No 2401143/97, EOR DCLD No 33 Autumn 1997.

ARTHRITIS

Quinn v Schwarzkopf [2001] IRLR 67, EAT.
Ishiguro v Financial Times Ltd, Case No 2301852/98, EOR DCLD No 40 Summer 1999.
Hopkins v ERF Manchester Ltd, Case No 2400863/97, EOR DCLD No 32 Summer 1997.

---

1   The Employment Tribunals, Field Support Unit, 100 Southgate Street, Bury St Edmunds, Suffolk IP33 2AQ.

ASTHMA

Cox v The Post Office, Case No 1301162/97.
Hardy v Gower Furniture Ltd, Case No 1802093/97.
Henderson v Scottish Widows Fund (2001) IDS Brief 682/16, Scotland.
Jones v Cadsart Limited, Case No 2101363/96.
Kerrigan v Rover Group Ltd, Case No 1401406/97, EOR DCLD No 40 Summer 1999.

BACK PROBLEMS

Clark v Novacold Ltd [1998] IRLR 420, EAT, [1999] IRLR 318, CA.
Hardy v Gower Furniture Ltd, Case No 1802093/97, EOR DCLD No 33 Autumn 1997.
Mansfield v Saunders, November 1997, Case No 1401315/97.
Mingo v Kent County Council, July 1998, Case No 1101673/97, EOR DCLD No 37 Autumn 1998.
Rowley v Walkers Nonsuch Limited, April 1997, Case No 1700168/97, EOR DCLD No 33 Autumn 1997.
Sandy v Hampshire Constabulary, July 1997.
Short v Scottish and Southern Energy plc, August 1999, Case No 2701447/98.
Stone v Smith Industries Aerospace, Case No 1400808/97. Whiplash injury.
Wilding v British Telecom plc, January 1999, Case No 2202759/98, EOR DCLD No 42 Winter 1999.

BULIMIA NERVOSA

Harley v Commissioner for the Metropolis, EAT No 518/00.

CANCER

Harvey Clements v Jane Saunders Manning Ltd, Case No 2302081/98.
Hay v Highdorn Co Ltd, Case No 2201755/98.
McLauchlan v Stolt Comex Seaway Ltd, Case No S/200809/99, EOR DCLD No 41 Autumn 1999.
Sander v the Chief Education Officer, Somerset County Council, April 2000, Case No 1402980/99. Breast cancer.

CEREBRAL PALSY

Bridges v Sita (GB) Ltd, Case No 2301175/99, EOR DCLD No 43 Spring 2000.
Kenny v Hampshire Constabulary [1999] IRLR 76, EAT.

CHRONIC FATIGUE SYNDROME (see also MYALGIC ENCEPHALOMYELITIS

HJ Heinz Co Ltd v Kenrick [2000] IRLR 144, EAT.
O'Neill v Symm and Company Ltd [1998] IRLR 233, EAT.
Terry v Sheldon School, March 1998, Case No 1401832/97.

COLITIS

Allen v Till Note Ltd, March/April 1998, Case No 1800017/98.
O'Neill v HSBC Bank plc (ulcerative colitis), Case No 2202292/2000.

DEPRESSION AND STRESS

'A' v 'B', April 1999, Case No 2600067/99.
Bush v Rolls Royce, July 1999, Case Nos 1401054/98 and 1401495/98. Harassment because of depression and recommendation for disability awareness training.
Butler v Eastleigh Housing Association Ltd, December 1997, Case No 3101121/97.
Cassidy v The Benefits Agency, Case No 1900624/97.
Crampton v Bonar Cartons Ltd, May 1998, Case No 1800556/98.
Delamaine v Abbey National plc.
Farrell v The Hammersmith Hospital NHS Trust and Others, Case No 2200918/97.
Greenwood v British Airways plc [1999] IRLR 600, EAT. Tribunal should consider adverse effects of the applicant's condition up to and including the employment tribunal hearing.
Henton v Knauf UK GMBU, November 1997, Case No 2102795/97. Post-traumatic stress disorder accepted as a disability.
Hill v Lister-Petter Ltd, May 1998, Case No 1400187/98.
Jones v The Selcare Trust, June 1998, Case No 24004641/97.
Kapadia v Lambeth London Borough Council [2000] IRLR 14, EAT.
Lang v Redland Roofing Systems Ltd, Case No S/400788/97, Scotland.
Leonard v Southern Derbyshire Chamber of Commerce [2001] IRLR 19. Clinical depression. Use of the Guidance considered by the EAT.
Naylor v Newsquest (Wiltshire) Ltd, February 1998, Case No 1402404/97.
Shiel v The Cats Protection League, December 1997.
Toffel v London Underground Ltd, January 1998, Case No 2204880/97.
Tolladay v HSBC Ltd, Case No 1401186/99, EOR DCLD No 46 Winter 2000.
Ward v Signs by Morrell Ltd, March 1998, Case No 2106342/97.

Williams v Autoquip (Factors) Ltd, April 1998, Case No 1701770/97.

DIABETES

Arboshe v East London Bus and Coach Co Ltd, EAT No 877/98.
Cooray v North Herts NHS Trust, May 1999, Case Nos 1200304/98 and 1200289/98.[1]
Matty v Tesco Stores Ltd, October 1997. Insulin controlled diabetes.
Poulton v H Walton, Case No 1805515/97. Diet controlled diabetes.
Woodhead v Halifax plc, November 1998 and January 1999, Case No 1802483/98, EOR DCLD No 42 Winter 1999.

DYSLEXIA

Cook v Thorne House Autistic Community [1999] Disc LR 100, EAT.
Harling v CL Plastics Ltd, January 2000, Case No 1804928/99. Harassment.
Henderson v Scottish Widows Fund, Case No S/400692/97, Scotland.
Reedman v Fresh Connection Ltd, 14 October 1997, Case No 2600538/97.

EMPHYSEMA

Forder v Southern Water, 18 May 1998, Case No 3101262/97.

EPILEPSY

Alexander v Driving Standards Agency, August 1998, Case No 2601058/98. Not substantial so not a disability.
British Gas Services Ltd v McCaull [2001] IRLR 60, EAT.
Butterfield v Rapidmark Ltd, EAT No 131/98.
Calvert v Jewelglen Ltd, October 1997, Case No 2403989/97.
Holmes v Whittingham and Porter Ltd, October 1997, Case No 1802799/97.
Jordan v JH Haskins and Sons Ltd, May 1998.
Reilly v EXI Ltd, Case No S/400489/97, Scotland.
Ridout v TC Group, October 1997, Case No 2900464/97, [1998] IRLR 628, EAT.
Smith v Carpets International UK plc, September 1997, Case No 1800507/97.

---

1   See also 'Visual impairment'.

HEARING IMPAIRMENTS

Hughes v The London Borough of Hillingdon, November 1999, Case No 6001328/98.
London Underground Ltd v Bragg, June 1999, EAT No 847/98.
Murphy v Sheffield Hallam University, November 1998, Case No 2800489/98, EOR DCLD No 40 Summer 1999.
Roberts v ASD, April 1998.
Williams v Channel 5 Engineering Services Ltd, October 1997, Case No 2302136/97.

HEART CONDITION

Hardy v Gower Furniture Ltd, Case No 1802093/97.
Quinlan v B&Q plc, EAT No 1386/97.

HERNIA

Fenwick v Brighton and Hove Bus and Coach Company, Case No 3100534/99.

HIV

Akkerman v City Centre Restaurants (UK) Limited, Case No 2201530.

IRRITABLE BOWEL SYNDROME

Tiquin v Abbey National plc, Case No 2400947/98, EOR DCLD No 43 Spring 2000.

IMMUNE DISORDERS (see also HIV)

Murphy v SEC Ltd, Case No 2202607/97, EOR DCLD No 39 Spring 1999. Hypogammaglobulinaemia.

KIDNEY DISEASE

Jones v Selcare Trust, June 1998, Case No 24004641/97.

LEARNING DISABILITIES

Poppy v Bournemouth and Christchurch Hospital NHS Trust.
Green v Harmony Healthcare plc and The Shaw Trust, Case No 2700232/97.

LEGS AND FEET

Fletcher v Chivers Hartley, December 1998, Case No 1500367/98, EOR DCLD No 41 Autumn 1999.
Foord v Johnston and Sons, Case No S/200300/97, Scotland.
Reedman v Fresh Connection Ltd, September 1997, Case No 2600538/97.
Tarling v Wisdom Toothbrushes (1997) IDS Brief 597/15.

MENTAL HEALTH (see also DEPRESSION AND STRESS)

Alvares v London Borough of Hounslow, 29 July 1998, Case No 2300651/97, EOR DCLD No 37 Autumn 1998. Auditory hallucinations and fantasies of mass murder.
Bush v Rolls Royce, July 1999, Case Nos 1401054/98 and 1401495/98. Harassment because of depression and recommendation for disability awareness training.
Goodwin v Patent Office [1999] IRLR 4, EAT. Schizophrenia.
Lang v Redland Roofing Systems, Case No S/400788/97, Scotland, EOR DCLD No 35 Spring 1998.

MIGRAINE HEADACHES

Hood v London Clubs Management Ltd, February 2000, Case No 603188/99.
Foster v Hampshire Fire and Rescue Service, Case No 3101562/97.

MYALGIC ENCEPHALOMYELITIS (ME) (see also CHRONIC FATIGUE SYNDROME)

HJ Heinz Co Ltd v Kenrick [2000] IRLR 144, EAT.
O'Neill v Symm and Company Ltd [1998] IRLR 233, EAT.
Terry v Sheldon School, March 1998, Case No 1401832/97.

MULTIPLE SCLEROSIS

Buxton v Equinox Design, Case No 1802596/97, [1999] IRLR 158, EAT.
Livermore v First Service Ltd, Case No 2303059/98.

Rathbone v Dudley College of Technology, February 1999, Case No 1301325/98, EOR DCLD No 40 Summer 1999.
Samuels v Wesleyan Assurance Society, July 1997, Case No 2100703/97, EOR DCLD No 33 Autumn 1997.

REPETITIVE STRAIN INJURY (see also UPPER LIMB DISORDERS)

Palmer v Caradon Mira Ltd, August 1998.
Vicary v British Telecommunications plc [1999] IRLR 680, EAT.

RHEUMATOID ARTHRITIS

Hopkins v ERF Manchester Limited, Case No 2400863/97.
Robinson v Ashfield District Council, March 1998.

SCHIZOPHRENIA

Goodwin v Patent Office [1999] IRLR 4, EAT.
Sheen v The Writers Guild of Great Britain, June 1998, Case No 36669/96.

SKIN CONDITIONS

Robinson v The Post Office [2000] IRLR 804, EAT.

STOMACH PAIN

Howden v Capital Copiers (Edinburgh) Ltd (1997) IDS Brief 598/14, Scotland.

STRESS

See Depression and Stress above.

UPPER LIMB DISORDERS

Ishiguro v Financial Times Ltd, February 1999, Case No 2301852/98, EOR DCLD No 40 Summer 1999. Tribunal held that neither stress nor ULD were disabilities.

Vicary v British Telecommunications plc [1999] IRLR 680, EAT.

VISUAL IMPAIRMENTS

Abbot v The Governors of St Mary's Catholic Primary School, Case No 3204241/97/S.
Cooray v North Herts NHS Trust, May 1999, Case Nos 1200289/98 and 12300304/98. Vitreous detachment of the eye and cataract linked to diabetes.
Durbin v Security Plus Ltd, Case No 2601078/97. Squint/double vision.
Gailey v Haes Systems Ltd, 26 November 1999, Case No 6002720/99, EOR DCLD No 43 Spring 2000.
Glynn v London Transport, Case No 3200909/98, EOR DCLD No 43 Spring 2000.
Kirker v British Sugar Plc, Case No 2601249/97, [1998] IRLR 624.
Shah v Commissioners of HM Customs & Excise, Case No 2302040/98.
Thorpe v The Royal Hospitals NHS Trust, March 1998, Case No 3202104/97. Applicant with sight in only one eye not disabled.
Winning v Belfast City Airport Ltd, Case No 01987/RP.

Appendix 3

THE ACCESS TO WORK SCHEME[1]

INTRODUCTION

The Access to Work (ATW) scheme is a government scheme designed to provide practical help to overcome the barriers that disabled people experience in the workplace. Through this scheme the government will either pay for or make a substantial grant towards the costs of additional support needed as a result of disability.

SUPPORT AVAILABLE

The types of support available under the ATW scheme are as follows.
- **Adaptations to premises and equipment** This involves modifying the employer's premises or equipment to make it accessible for a person with a disability.
- **Special aids to employment** Provision of aids and equipment to a disabled person, to enable them to carry out the full job description and put them on a par with their non-disabled colleagues.
- **Support workers** Help with the costs of employing personal support for a person with a disability at a job interview, on their journey to and from work or in the workplace. The support worker element of ATW is not available to people in supported employment or on the Blind Home Workers Scheme. A personal reader element is also available.
- **Travel to work** Support when a disabled person incurs extra costs in travelling to and from work because of their disability. Beneficiaries are expected to contribute the usual costs of travelling to work by public transport.

---

1   Based on a factsheet by the RNIB.
     RNIB, Education and Employment Information Service
     224 Great Portland Street
     London W1N 6AA
     Tel 020 7391 2112 or 020 7391 2057
     Fax 020 7383 4921
     Email sraisanen@rnib.org.uk
            arehahn@rnib.org.uk

–   **Communication support at interview**   Help with the cost of employing an
      interpreter or communicator to accompany a hearing-impaired person,
      where there might be communication difficulties at a job interview with a
      prospective employer.
–   **Miscellaneous**   This will pay for those 'one-off' items of support that do
      not fall within other categories.

FUNDING AVAILABLE

Funding varies as follows depending on a person's employment status.

–   **Unemployed people (unemployed people moving into new employment)**
      100% of identified costs of all elements.
–   **People changing jobs**   100% of identified costs of all elements.
–   **Employed people**   Employers are required to make a one-off payment of
      the first £300 of ATW support. Above this sum the government will pay
      80% of agreed costs up to £10,000 and the employer is expected to pay the
      remaining 20%. The government will then pay 100% of agreed costs
      above £10,000.
–   **Self-employed people**   The government will pay 100% of agreed costs.
–   **Travel to work**   100% of identified costs irrespective of employment
      status.
–   **Communicator support at interview**   100% of identified costs irrespec-
      tive of employment status.

In some cases, ATW support may incur a business benefit, for example if other
members of staff use the specialist equipment as part of their own work. In
these instances, the business benefit costs will be estimated and deducted from
the ATW costs. The government will pay 80% of the remaining amount.

WHERE TO GO FOR SUPPORT

The ATW scheme is administered by the government's disability services teams
or disability advisory service in Northern Ireland, who are based at job centres.
Within these teams are disability specialists called disability employment
advisers. There may also be technical officers who have specialist knowledge of
equipment and adaptations, which can be obtained under the ATW scheme.

HOW TO APPLY FOR SUPPORT

Contacting the disability employment adviser

Applications for support are usually prompted by an initial request for help to
the local disability services team.[1] If the employee is not familiar with the

_____

1   Address and telephone number available from the local job centre.

scheme, it may be helpful for them and the employer to have a meeting with the disability employment adviser to discuss the programme and consider eligibility, funding arrangements (including employer charge) and the support options available.

The application form

The employee will then be asked to complete an application form (ATW1), which gives details of the employment and states why the support is needed. This enables the disability employment adviser to make an initial assessment of eligibility and nature of disability, identify who in the company they need to contact and prepare for discussion about the support that is required.

Appraisal of needs

Once initial approval has been granted, the disability employment adviser will make an appointment to visit the workplace to undertake a full appraisal of the employee's needs. The adviser will assess details of the job and the effects of the employee's disability on doing that job. If support is easily identifiable, the adviser will progress with arrangements to get support into place. If the type of help is not immediately obvious, particularly regarding adaptations or specialist equipment, a more detailed technical assessment may be recommended. This can be done by the technical officer or through an external organisation such as the RNIB.

Action plan

Following the assessment and regardless of whether support is readily identifiable or further investigation is required, the employee and employer receive a written action plan from the adviser. This will ensure that both have time to consider the solution and are clear about what action the adviser will take next.

Exploring the options

The disability employment adviser will need to explore likely support systems and outline the costs of the options available. This may involve a technical assessment and work trials on different types of equipment until the best option is found.

It is essential that adequate specialist installation and training are provided to enable users to become conversant with new equipment. This training usually takes only a few days, but it can be vital.

Approval of provision

Once the support has been identified and associated cost obtained, the disability employment adviser will discuss them with the employee and the employer and agree any cost sharing (where appropriate). After this, the adviser will provide the authority to commit expenditure.

It is then the responsibility of the employer to purchase the agreed equipment, and to claim the agreed amount back from the disability services team on submission of the relevant invoices. Equipment provided in this way becomes the property of the employer, who will be responsible for insurance and maintenance.

Receipt of equipment or support

On receipt of the equipment or support, it is important to ensure that the employee feels familiar with and confident in the use of whatever support is put in place. In some cases separate training will have been requested as part of the ATW application.

Follow-up action

Once support has been put in place, a follow-up visit or interview is arranged by the adviser. This is designed to ensure that the support systems originally identified are still right for the employee's needs and identifies difficulties for which further support is required. Follow-up visits are then arranged periodically over the term for which support has been made available.

IMPORTANT INFORMATION TO NOTE

If the employee is turned down or unhappy with support

If the employee's application is rejected or if there is dissatisfaction with the support being received under the ATW scheme, the employee can ask for the decision to be reviewed. This involves sending a written request to the manager of the disability services team outlining the reasons, requesting a review and setting out any further information to support the case. In all cases, the results of the review, and the reason for the decision, must be given in writing. If the employee is unhappy with the manager's decision, it can be taken to the next level, which is that of the regional director. A request for a review can be discussed with an outside agency such as the RNIB.[1]

If unreasonable delays are experienced

In the majority of cases, the ATW support is put in place in a relatively short space of time. However, sometimes the process can be quite complex and take much longer, especially if support systems are not immediately obvious. An employee who experiences difficulties because of long delays must contact the

---

1   Education and Employment Information Service on 020 7391 2112 or 020 7391 2057.

disability services team. The team may be able to provide interim systems, such as the use of support worker or loan equipment.

Appendix 4

ALTERNATIVE FORMATS, INTERPRETERS AND TRANSCRIPTION SERVICES

PROVIDERS OF TRANSCRIPTION TO BRAILLE, MOON, LARGE PRINT AND AUDIO CASSETTE

Access to Print
Central Library
Princes Way
Bradford
BD1 1NN
01274 754 681 voice
01274 395 108 fax
Provides Braille, large print and cassette.

adept
The Old Forge
7a Waterloo Road
Linslade
Bedfordshire
LU7 7NR
01525 337190 voice
01525 333390 fax
Provides an audio tape, Braille and large print transcription service.

AIRS (Access to Information and
Reading Services)
Gateshead Central Library
Prince Consort Road
Gateshead
NE8 4LN
0191 477 3478 voice
0191 478 2060 text
0191 477 7852 fax
email info@airsghd.demon.co.uk
Provides Braille, large print, cassette and sign language video alternative formats.

Braille Bureau
County Hall
West Bridgford
Nottingham
NG2 7QP
0115 982 3823 x3157 voice
0115 981 7153 fax
Provides Braille, large print and cassette.

Braille Transcription Service
23 Masefield Ave
Upper Stratton
Swindon
Wiltshire
SN2 6HT
Judith Furse 01793 644346 voice
Braillist and proof-reader providing transcription service, print to Braille or Braille to print.

Braudio Transcriptions
8 Morpeth Terrace
North Shields
Northumberland
NR29 7AN
0191 253 6324 voice (between 2pm and 10pm)
Audio cassette transcriptions.

Cadwell Recording Service for the Blind
17 Trusthams
Broadwindsor
Beaminster
Dorset
Mrs Cadwell 01308 868 500 voice
Provides audio cassette transcription.

Disability Resource Team
2nd Floor
6 Park Road
Teddington
Middlesex
TW11 0AA
Tel/minicom 020 8943 0022
Fax 020 8943 5162
Provides tape, braille and large print transcription service.

Dog Rose
26 Bell Lane
Ludlow
Shropshire
SY8 1LZ
01584 874848 voice
01584 874567 fax
Provides facilities for the understanding of all environments for people who are blind or visually impaired. Specialises in the design of tactile material, acoustic sound guides, scale models with accompanying interactive sound commentaries, large print and Braille guides.

Lilac Recording Service
Lilac Cottage
Moorhouses
New Bolingbroke
Near Boston
Lincs
PE22 7JL
Bill Cox 01526 342 918
Provides audio transcription services.

MagRay Document Services
178 Castle Rd
Northolt
Middlesex
UB5 4SG
020 8864 7208
020 8933 5740 fax
email magray@argonet.co.uk
website www.argonet.co.uk/business/rayd
Braille transcription and embossing service. Print to Braille or Braille to print.

Monument Tape Services
20 Laburnam Road
Wellington
Somerset
TA21 8EL
01823 662 104 voice
Transcription to audio cassette.

Off The Page
188 Wellfield Road
London
SW16 2BU
020 8769 9682 voice
020 8769 9682 fax
Provides audio taped recordings, Braille and large print transcription. Readers include speakers of European and ethnic minority languages.

Partially Sighted Society
PO Box 322
Doncaster
DN1 2XA
01302 323 132 voice
The Partially Sighted Society provides information in large print. It has 20 regional branches.

Pia Ltd
102 Bute Street
Cardiff Bay
South Glamorgan
CF1 6AD
029 2030 1000 voice
email publishing@intouch.co.uk
*Braille and large print production
services including tactile diagrams.*

Playback Service for the Blind
Resource Centre for the Blind
276 St Vincent Street
Glasgow
G2 5RP
0141 334 2983 voice
Provides audio transcription.

Rakaso Systems Ltd
PO Box 931
London
N12 9XF
020 8446 5555 voice
020 8446 8620 fax
*Provides Braille, large print and can also
do audio cassette transcriptions if
required.*

**Repro House in association with
Leads**
Repro House
5 Ashfield Grove
Whitely Bay
Tyne and Wear
NE26 1RT
0191 253 3712 voice
0191 297 1053 fax
*Provides transcription to Braille, large
print, audio cassette and computer disk.*

RNIB (Royal National Institute for
the Blind)
24 Great Portland Street
London
W1N 6AA
020 7388 1266 voice
020 7388 2034 fax
*Provides transcription to a range of
alternative formats, including Braille,
cassette and moon. Has regional offices.*

**Shropshire Disability Information
Forum**
Disability Resource Centre
Lancaster Road
Harlescott
Shrewsbury
Shropshire
SY1 3NJ
Darren Limbert 01743 444599
01743 440000 Transcription Service
*Visually Impaired Communication
Service (VICS), a transcription service for
large print and Braille and audio
cassette.*

Talking Eyes
Birmingham Focus
Dawn Finch
48 Woodwile Road
Harbone
Birmingham
B17 9AT
0121 428 5046 voice
*Talking Eyes provide transcription to
Braille, cassette and moon.*

Techno-Vision Braille Services Ltd
76 Bunting Road Industrial Estate
Northampton
NN2 6EE
01604 792 777 voice
01604 792 726 fax
email info@techno-vision.co.uk
Provides transcription to Braille.

V.I.P.E.R.
Huddersfield Library
The Reading Service
Princes Alexandra Walk
Huddersfield
HD1 2SU
01484 221 955 voice
Provides transcription services to Braille, audio cassette, computer disk and tactile maps.

Vis-Ability
Helen Bollington
Central Library, Walker Place
Rotherham
South Yorks
S65 1JH
01709 373 658 voice
Transcription to Braille.

VOCALEYES
25 Short Street
London
SE1 8LJ
0870 902 0002 Info and Bookings
020 7450 1990 voice
020 7450 1991 fax
email vocaleyes@mcmail.com
A charity set up to service the needs of theatres and theatre companies wishing to present audio description to their visually impaired audiences.

Voluntary Braille Transcribers Group
8 Segbourne Road
Rubery
Birmingham
West Midlands
B45 9SX
Wynne Batchelor 0121 453 4268
20 members who hold the RNIB Braille proficiency certificate. Will take on commissions from companies.

PROVIDERS OF SIGN LANGUAGE INTERPRETERS AND VIDEO SUBTITLES

BDA (British Deaf Association)
1–3 Worship Street
London
EC2A 2AB
020 7588 3520 voice
020 7588 3529 text
020 7588 3527 fax
Provides consultation on and production of BSL videos, primarily in the London area.

Confederation of Tape Information Services (COTIS)
Project Office
67 High Street
Tarporley
Cheshire
CW6 0DP
01829 733351 Secretary
Self-help grouping of tape recording services, cassette libraries etc large and small, to share knowledge and expertise. Registered charity, have produced guidelines and tapes to improve production of tape recordings.

Council for the Advancement of Communication with Deaf People
Pelaw House
School for Education
University of Durham
Durham
DH1 1TA
0191 383 1155 voice
0191 383 7195 text
0191 383 7194 fax
email durham@cacdp.demon.co.uk
A directory of sign language interpreters.

RNID (Royal National Institute for Deaf People)
19–23 Featherstone Street
London
EC14 8SL
020 7296 8000 voice
020 7296 8001 text
020 7296 8199 fax
Sign language interpreters, deaf-blind interpreters, lip speakers, note takers and speech to text services are available.

Scottish Association of Sign Language Interpreters
31 York Place
Edinburgh
EH1 3HP
0131 557 6370 voice and text
The register of sign language interpreters in Scotland.

Screen Subtitling Systems
The Old Rectory
Church Lane
Claydon
Ipswich
Suffolk
IP6 0ED
01473 831700 voice
01473 830078 fax
email sales@screen.subtitling.com
website www.screen.subtitling.com
Providers of subtitling.

Sign Language Information Centre
Criffel Riggs
Drumburn
Kirkbean
Dumfries
DG2 8DL
01387 880 222 voice and text
01387 880 333 fax
Providers of sign language interpreters.

Sign Language Video People
42 Leicester Road
Nuneaton
Warwickshire
CV11 6AD
Producers of signed videos.

Softel
7 Horseshoe Park
Horseshoe Road
Pangbourne
Reading
Berkshire
RG8 7JN
0118 984 2151 voice
0118 237 7950 fax
email sales@softel.co.uk
website www.softel.co.uk
Producers of subtitled videos.

Subtitling International UK Ltd
Cambridge House
100 Cambridge Grove
London
W6 0LE
020 8237 7960 voice
020 8237 7950 fax
email sales@subtitling.international-uk.com
Providers of subtitling.

Trosol Subtitles
Unit 1
Cwrty
Parc Ty Glas
Llanisten
Cardiff
CF4 SDU
01286 673090 voice
01286 673093 fax
email data@trosol.co.uk
Providers of subtitling.

Voice and Script International
132 Cleveland Street
London
W1P 6AB
020 7692 7700 voice
020 7692 7711 fax
email aradco@compuserve.com
website www.v-s-l.com
Providers of subtitling in all languages.

PROVIDERS OF TRANSCRIPTION SERVICES FOR THOSE WITH LEARNING DISABILITIES

CHANGE
69–85 Old Street
London
EC1V 9HY
020 7490 2668 voice
020 7490 3483 text
020 7490 3581 fax
email contact@changeuk.demon.co.uk
Change provides information to companies on how they can go about making their work more accessible to people with learning difficulties and sensory impairment. This includes advising on specific documents as well as a CD-rom which includes a database of line drawings suitable for producing such information.

Makaton Vocabulary Development Project
31 Firwood Drive
Camberley
Surrey
GU12 3QD
01276 61390 voice
91276 681368 fax
email mvdp@makaton.org
website www.makaton.org
Makaton is a language using symbols. This organisation can give further advice.

Widgit Software Ltd
102 Radford Road
Leamington Spa
CV31 1LF
01926 885 303 voice
01926 885 293 fax
email literacy@widgit.com
website www.widgit.com
Their software, Writing with Symbols 2000, can be used to create a document with both words and symbols to aid people with learning difficulties.

SUPPLIERS OF BRAILLE EQUIPMENT

Blazie Engineering Ltd

1 Watling Gate
297–303 Edgware Road
London
NW9 6NB
020 8205 4646 voice
020 8205 1192 fax
website www.blazie.co.uk
*Offer a wide range of equipment
including embossers, Braille notetakers,
software and magnifiers.*

Choice Technology and Training

7 The Rookery
Orton Wistow
Peterborough
PE2 6YT
01733 234 441 voice
*Suppliers of equipment to produce Braille
and large print.*

Concept Systems

204–206 Queen's Road
Beeston
Nottingham
NG9 2DB
0115 925 5988 voice
*Offer a range of equipment including soft
Braille displays and CCTV magnifiers.*

Dolphin Systems for People with Disabilities

Unit 96C
Blackpool Trading Estate West
Worcester
WR3 8TU
01905 754 577 voice
*Suppliers of Braille embossers and paper,
as well as screen reading software for the
visually impaired.*

Technovision Systems Ltd

Unit 12
76 Bunting Road
Industrial Estate
Northampton
NN2 6EE
01604 792 777 voice
Suppliers of Braille equipment.

Appendix 5

THE DISABILITY COMMUNICATION GUIDE[1] – COMMUNICATING WITH DISABLED COLLEAGUES AND CUSTOMERS

THE EMPLOYERS' FORUM ON DISABILITY

The Employers' Forum on Disability is the employers' organisation focused on the issue of disability in the workplace. Funded and managed by over 350 members, the Forum represents organisations employing nearly 20% of the UK workforce. The Forum has come to be recognised as the authoritative employers' voice. Membership encompasses all industry sectors including retail, financial, manufacturing, media, government departments and education. We work closely with government and other stakeholders, sharing best practice to make it easier to employ disabled people and serve disabled customers.

WHO SHOULD READ THIS?

This guide is aimed at human resources managers, line managers and anyone who works with or provides for people. We expect that most readers will relate this advice to their everyday working life. The guide suggests how:

- to assist people with specific impairments
- to help develop a greater understanding of the views and preferences of disabled people in general
- to recognise and avoid the attitudes and behaviours, which could create barriers and misunderstandings.

---

1   The Disability Communication Guide is reproduced with the kind permission of the Employers' Forum on Disability (www.employers-forum.co.uk). The Forum is the authoritative employers' voice on disability as it affects business. Through networking events, publications, briefings, website and help-line, the Forum makes it easier to employ and retain disabled people and to serve disabled customers. Forum members represent organisations employing over 20 per cent of the UK workforce.

COMMUNICATING WITH DISABLED PEOPLE AT WORK

The changing climate

The position of disabled people in society is changing. With improved technology and a more sophisticated understanding of disability, a greater number of disabled people can enjoy a full life – they can follow careers that are appropriate to their talents, and use services and buildings which are gradually becoming accessible to everyone.

As you think about the best way to work with and to serve people with disabilities, communication is probably the first thing that comes to mind. Using language sensitively and having good communication skills makes it easier to treat everyone as you yourself would expect to be treated. You will understand that certain language and behaviour can cause offence. There can be misunderstandings, perhaps because you think of disability in terms of dated stereotypes or simply because you may have had very little personal contact with disabled people. This lack of understanding can create unnecessary barriers and can even result in discrimination.

Watch, ask and listen

Perhaps you are preparing to interview a disabled person for the first time, or you want to improve your communication with disabled customers. Although the important thing is always to ask, and to take your lead from the person, this guide will give you some basics to build on through your own contact with disabled people. Remember to keep in touch with what individuals prefer.

Communication skills can go a very long way. Watch carefully, really listen to people, and only then offer help and adjustments. This is vital to treating someone with respect and consideration – whether or not they seem to be disabled. Be alert to the needs of others. This should also make life easier for those coping with children or heavy bags, delivery people, those with English as a second language and older people – indeed for everyone.

Does it apply to us?

The Disability Discrimination Act (1995) (DDA) may protect certain people with a wide range of impairments – for example, dyslexia, epilepsy, severe facial disfigurement, angina, ME or mental health problems. The parts of the Act that relate to employment apply to every organisation with 15 or more employees. More measures affecting all service providers, however small, were introduced in October 1999 to protect disabled customers. Further legislation affecting premises will come into force in 2004. **The customer-related responsibilities apply to all organisations, however small.**[1]

---

1   The Act is described in more detail in other publications which you can order from the Employers' Forum on Disability.

Disability affects one in four people

Disability is not always immediately obvious. There may be no visible signs, such as a white stick or crutches. Fewer than 5% of disabled people, around 400,000, use a wheelchair all the time.

- there are 8.7 million disabled people in the UK
- over 5 million are of working age
- one in every four consumers is disabled, or close to someone who is.

Some basics

- removing barriers is not just about spending money on structural alterations
- 'access' should be applied in its broadest sense, to all communications and opportunities
- the Act protects individuals who have, or have ever had, any mental or physical impairment which lasted, or is expected to last, at least 12 months, and which has a substantial adverse effect on their day-to-day activities
- disability is not sickness: the general health of most disabled people is as good as that of anyone else.

WHEN MEETING A DISABLED PERSON

- only offer help if it seems appropriate; always wait until your offer is accepted before you do anything; listen to what the person says
- only use the disabled person's first name if you are also using other people's first names
- treat a disabled person with the same respect you would treat anyone else
- do not treat disabled adults as children
- do not lean on someone's wheelchair: it is their personal space
- communicate directly with the disabled person, not to their companion or interpreter
- only make the same physical contact as you would make with anyone else; do not help someone to get up or sit down, without first offering to help and listening to their reply
- do not use extravagant gestures or language which draws attention to the person's disability.

Meeting people who have personal assistants

Some disabled people have a personal assistant to help them at work, in meetings or in social activities.

- when you are planning the meeting you will need to provide for personal assistants, in terms of seating, catering and so on; some assistants, such as interpreters and palantypists (speed-text typists who type speech on a

laptop or a large screen), may need better lighting, different seating, a small table, a glass of water, short rest breaks – so keeping to time is vital
- some disabled people prefer not to introduce their assistant when they are working; take your lead from the person with a disability.

In any case, remember to communicate directly with the disabled person.

LANGUAGE

Certain words and phrases may give offence. Although there are no hard and fast rules, it is helpful to understand the background.

Some people prefer to be called 'disabled people', which they believe gives the message that they are disabled by society's barriers. Others prefer to be called 'people with disabilities', which they believe gives the message that they are people first, who also have a disability. Preferences change with time. Ask people what they prefer. The Forum respects both points of view and uses both terms.

- do not be embarrassed about using common expressions which could relate to someone's impairment, for example, 'see you later' or 'I'll be running along then'
- many people object to the word 'handicapped', which has been used by many charities over the years, as they believe it reinforces the message that disabled people are dependent on charity
- people do not want to be given a medical label, which can be very misleading: no two people are the same. Labels say little about the individual, they just reinforce stereotypes of disabled people as being 'sick' and dependent on the medical profession
- you should say 'someone with cerebral palsy' and never 'a spastic'; and 'someone with epilepsy' and not 'an epileptic'
- the phrase 'mental handicap' has been replaced by 'people with learning disabilities'; people with learning disabilities are increasingly speaking for themselves and this is their preference
- you should not use collective nouns such as 'the disabled', 'the blind', 'the deaf', 'the disfigured'; these terms imply people are part of a uniform group which is separate from the rest of society
- you should never use insulting labels like 'cripple', 'retarded', 'blind as a bat' or 'mentally defective' even as a joke, whether or not a disabled person is present.

Do not use language which suggests that disabled people are always frail or dependent on others, or which could make disabled people objects of pity. Also, you should remember that the opposite of 'disabled' is not 'able-bodied'. This suggests that disability is only physical. 'Non-disabled' means neither physically nor mentally disabled.

Do not say	say
– victim of .../ crippled by .../ suffering from .../ afflicted by .../ 'an invalid'	– person who has .../ person with ...
– wheelchair-bound/ confined to a wheelchair (a wheelchair is a 'liberating device')	– wheelchair-user/ person who uses a wheelchair
– deaf and dumb	– deaf without speech

MEETING PEOPLE

Meeting people with impaired vision

– introduce yourself and other people clearly; say where people are in the room
– a guide dog is a working dog and should not be treated as a pet
– if the person seems to need help, ask 'may I offer you an arm?'; that way, you can guide, rather than seeming to propel the person
– when you are offering a handshake say, 'shall we shake hands?'
– when you are offering a seat, guide the person's hand to the back or the arm of the seat, and say that is what you are going to do
– offer minutes of meetings, or any other written communications in the person's preferred format (on floppy disc, in large print, on audio cassette or in Braille)
– where someone might normally take notes, ask if they would like to tape the meeting or conversation
– tell the person if you are going to move away, so that they are not left talking into empty space.

Meeting people who are deaf

There are different degrees and types of deafness, and different ways for deaf people or those who are hard-of-hearing to communicate.

– ask the person to tell you how they prefer to communicate, and to help you to find and book interpreters or other support in advance
– for interviews and meetings, use a qualified sign language interpreter, not someone who just knows a little sign language (qualified interpreters are either CACDP (Council for the Advancement of Communication with Deaf People) registered interpreters or registered trainee interpreters)
– if there is a sign language interpeter, speak to the individual, not to the interpreter

– you might also need lip-speakers (trained to speak in a way which lip-readers will find easy to understand), or palantype operators (speed-text communicators, using laptops or a larger screen) to help you to communicate
– in meetings or gatherings, speak one at a time
– written notes might help you to present complicated information
– make sure a deaf person is looking at you before you start speaking; a gentle touch on the shoulder or arm will capture their attention
– keep background noise as low as possible
– do not shout
– check regularly that you have been understood
– tell people when you are changing the subject and give people notes before a meeting – stick to the agenda.

Lip-reading

Some deaf and hard-of-hearing people rely heavily on this demanding skill.

– look directly at the person you are speaking to; stop talking if you have to turn away
– speak clearly in normal speech rhythm and a little more slowly
– do not use exaggerated gestures
– make sure you are visible in a good light
– do not block your mouth with your hands, cigarettes or food.

Meeting people who are deafblind

Deafblindness is a combination of hearing and sight impairments, but deafblind people are not always completely deaf and blind. In fact, most deafblind people do have some residual hearing or sight or both. So the advice provided in the sections on people with impaired vision or hearing may also apply. In addition:

– let the person know you are there: approach from the front and touch the person lightly on the arm or shoulder to attract their attention
– many deafblind people need to be guided; different people like to be guided in different ways: some deafblind people experience poor balance
– do not grab or propel or pull a person – let them know you are offering to escort them by guiding their hand to your elbow.

Communication methods used by deafblind people can include the following:

– lip-reading
– writing notes
– sign language, which a specially skilled interpreter might adapt for the person
– block alphabet: this is where you use your forefinger to write words on the palm of the deafblind person's hand – use the whole palm and write in clear capital letters
– deafblind manual alphabet.

Meeting people who use a wheelchair or crutches

If you are talking for more than a few moments to someone in a wheelchair, try to position yourself so that you are at the same level, or at least ask the person if they would like you to sit down

– if there is a high desk or counter, move to the front
– do not tidy away someone's crutches when they sit down
– if you know it is not easy to move around your building in a wheelchair, offer to help; heavy doors or deep-pile carpets are just some of the hazards to watch for – do not assume that ramps solve everything – they may be too steep or too slippery.

Meeting people with speech difficulties

– pay attention to a person with speech difficulties; be patient and be encouraging – do not butt in and finish sentences
– slowness or impaired speech has nothing to do with someone's intelligence
– if you need information, break down your questions to deal with individual points
– do not pretend to understand if you have not.

Meeting people with mental health problems

People with a past history of mental health problems can experience discrimination. Most people make a full recovery. However, someone experiencing the emotional distress and confusion associated with mental health problems may find everyday activities very hard.

– be patient and non-judgemental, give the person time to make decisions.

Meeting people with learning disabilities

Many people born with learning disabilities, people in the early stages of dementia or who acquire a brain injury, live full and independent lives in the community, making their own choices, with varying levels of support. These notes might apply to any of these individuals.

SOME TIPS

– start by assuming the person will understand you; be prepared to explain things more than once in different ways
– break down complicated information to give one piece at a time: preview and review it
– keep distractions (background noise and bustling environment) to a minimum
– consider putting information in writing, include your name and phone number; perhaps offer to tape a conversation so that the person can consider it later and keep a record.

Meeting people with facial disfigurement

Some people are born with a disfigurement and others acquire it through an accident or illness. Disfigurement is 'only skin-deep'. Like any disability, it does not mean the person is any different and certainly does not affect his or her intelligence. Most of the difficulties, indeed discrimination, people with facial disfigurement experience, stem from other people's behaviour.

–   if you are surprised by someone's appearance, or feel uncomfortable, try not to show it.
–   make eye contact, as you would with anyone else; try not to stare
–   listen carefully, and do not let the person's appearance distract you
–   never ask, 'what happened to you?': restrain your curiosity.

INTERVIEWING DISABLED PEOPLE

When you are preparing to interview a disabled person, you may need to adjust your usual arrangements. Do not assume that you know what will be needed. Ask the individual.

You might need to do the following:

–   change to a more accessible interview room, re-arrange the seating or lighting
–   arrange for someone to help you communicate with the person (see 'Meeting Disabled People')
–   allow the person to bring someone with them for support
–   be prepared to make adjustments, but do not make assumptions about what a person can or cannot do; disabled people often develop their own creative solutions to work-based problems; most do not need technical or personal help
–   focus on the main tasks and requirements of the job and the person's skills; do not be distracted by issues which are not related to work such as their gender, age, disability or ethnic origin
–   restrict questions about the effect of the person's disability on their ability to do the job: only ask about the person's life outside work, if you would normally ask such questions of all other candidates
–   if necessary seek advice from people with related disability expertise. In the first instance contact your local Jobcentre for a Disability Employment Adviser.

PLANNING A MEETING OR EVENT

When you are planning a meeting or event, you should remember the following:

- 'access' refers to facilities as well as buildings – it covers entrances, floor surfaces, lifts, speaker platforms, lecterns, catering and toilets, and would cover providing extra time, interpreters and communications support, notes in Braille or on audio cassette, large print programmes and auxiliary aids such as portable hearing loops
- if you think there may be access problems, either tell people in advance and discuss options, or find a better venue
- advertise that the venue is fully accessible or disabled people may not risk coming
- make sure that reception staff know you are expecting disabled people: make sure that they have read this guide and tell them about any particular requests
- ensure there is room for people with visual or mobility impairments to move about easily, both at the meeting and when taking refreshments; make sure help is available – it is difficult to sign with a glass of champagne in your hand!
- reduce or remove all together any background noise
- offer clipboards to wheelchair users
- make sure parking arrangements are adequate; provide directions and if necessary valet parking
- clearly sign the most suitable toilet facilities, and make sure all staff know where these are.

Invitations

On papers that go out before the meeting, ask people to let you know what adjustments they need. Instead of referring to 'special needs', ask if people have 'particular requirements'. Use a phrase such as 'please let us know what we can do to make our reception fully accessible to you' or 'do you need us to change anything to make sure that you can play a full part in this meeting?'

Endnote

Finally, if you are in doubt, rely on your own common sense and understanding. If you are not sure what to do, feel confident about asking the disabled person.

MORE ESSENTIAL INFORMATION

The Employers' Forum on Disability have developed a uniquely accessible Web site which gives more information on the Forum's activities including: other publications, events, research and membership benefits.

The Web site also acts as a resource for all employees of member companies, providing more detailed information on the DDA and disability issues.

For more information visit our Web site at www.employers-forum.co.uk.

INDEX

References are to paragraph numbers, case studies (CS) and Appendices.